BEYOND THE POWER OF NOW
A Guide to, and Beyond, Eckhart Tolle's Teachings

By L. Ron Gardner

CONTENTS

Introduction

The Nature of This Book

Eckhart Tolle's *The Power of Now* has been a colossal success since its first publication. And after Tolle appeared on Oprah and informed the world about the power of the "Now," his popularity soared to heights towering above all other New Age gurus. Millions of people now follow Tolle, and for these devotees, his message—"that there is a way out of suffering and into peace"—has been a liberating one that has changed their lives.

Although Eckhart Tolle's teachings on enlightenment have been widely praised, acclaim for them has not been universal. Critics of Tolle include religious fundamentalists and scientific materialists, but the most noteworthy of his critics are serious students of spiritual truth—mystics and esotericists who are unimpressed by Tolle's slick but superficial repackaging of the "perennial philosophy." These critics typically use terms such as "warmed-over Buddhism" or "dumbed-down Krishnamurti" to describe Tolle's teachings, and more than one Tolle basher has referred to *The Power of Now* as "insipid."

Where do I stand on Eckhart Tolle? Although I agree *in principle*, but *not in detail*, with his two core spiritual practices of "conscious presence" and "surrender," I disagree with most of his points of view and answers to questions in *The Power of Now*. Unlike Deepak Chopra, who says of *The Power of Now*: "Every sentence rings with truth and power," I say: Most every page is filled with the warmed-over, dumbed-down spirituality that his spiritual critics properly accuse him of preaching.

At this point, you might be asking, "Who are you to criticize Eckhart Tolle's teachings? After all, if Tolle's an enlightened being, as he claims, and I'm just a no-name schmuck in the peanut gallery, why should the seeds I toss at his Oprah-approved spiritual Dharma put even a micro-dent in his star or a hint of a blemish on his überpopular NOW Age message?

My response to these questions is threefold. First off, I wouldn't wager a plugged nickel on Tolle's being *fully* enlightened, in the mode of, say, a Buddha. The man no doubt is an advanced mystic, able to abide in the silence and stillness beyond the mind, but there is nothing profound about him or his teachings, nothing that would indicate he is rested in *Sahaj Samadhi*, the natural, effortless, Heart (or Self)-radiant state of a true Seer, such as the late Ramana Maharshi (1879–1950). And I'm not the only one who questions Tolle's level of spiritual enlightenment. Among the skeptical is my friend Gary Schmad, a filmmaker who spent over an hour interviewing Tolle for his spiritual documentary *Chasing the Light*. According to Gary, Tolle seemed nervous during the interview, parts of which are in the movie. Although Gary liked Tolle and his message, he couldn't understand why an enlightened being would suffer from nerves.

Second, I am an accomplished mystic myself. I regularly abide in a state of blissful at-one-ment with the Spirit. Over the past forty years, I have practiced Transcendental Meditation, Self-Realization Fellowship meditation, Buddhist *Vipassana* meditation, Zen meditation, Tibetan Buddhist meditation (*Mahamudra* and *Dzogchen*), J. Krishnamurti's "choiceless awareness," Ramana Maharshi's Self-enquiry, Adi Da's "radical understanding," Kashmir Shaivist *Shaktipat,* and hermetic Christian Holy Communion.

And third, I have devoted my life to studying all the great spiritual traditions, East and West. And my knowledge in the spiritual field, in conjunction with my experience as a mystic, provides me with the ability to expertly deconstruct Tolle's *exoteric* teachings while simultaneously presenting the *esoteric* Dharma (or Teaching) that characterizes the greatest spiritual traditions.

Although I disagree with the majority of Tolle's teachings, the gist of my criticism centers on three topics: 1) Tolle's attack on the human mind, 2) his understanding of the power of Now, and 3) his "new earth" prophecy. The next three paragraphs will, in order, briefly describe my points of view relative to Tolle's on these topics.

Eckhart Tolle's attack on man's mind, his conceptual faculty, is akin to renowned philosopher Immanuel Kant's (1724–1804)—but much more vicious and hateful. Tolle believes that the human mind is essentially a powerless abomination. According to Tolle, the human mind is not creative at all, is not capable of forgiving, is not capable of recognizing beauty and truth, and does not possess the capacity to freely choose. In contrast to Tolle, I argue the opposite. Throughout this book, I counter Tolle's anti-mind attack, exposing it as destructive and irrational.

The Power of Now is about the coolest title imaginable—but it doesn't belong on the cover of Eckhart Tolle's book. The sad truth is that his book has virtually nothing to say about the *power* of Now. His book only describes the power of Now as "the power of your presence." Beyond this terse and cryptic description, Tolle is mum. Which raises the question: What, exactly, is this power of Now? Is it the same thing as Hindu *Shakti* or the Buddhist *Sambhogakaya* or the Christian Holy Spirit? Tolle doesn't say. It is nothing short of amazing that Tolle can continually refer to the Bible and Jesus and never once mention the Holy Spirit and how it relates to the power of Now. In contrast to Tolle, I make it clear that the *true* power of Now *is* the Holy Spirit, which *is* the same divine Light-energy as Hindu *Shakti* and the Buddhist *Sambhogakaya*. Throughout this book, I explain and extoll the *true* power of Now and castigate Tolle for failing to identify and describe it.

To some, Eckhart Tolle is a New (or Now) Age visionary, describing a "new earth" that can materialize if mankind, en masse, awakens to the power of Now. But to others, like me, he is simply a histrionic ranter full of empty rhetoric. Tolle's apocalyptic eschatology, which centers around the destruction of civilization *unless* mankind awakens to the Now, identifies "madness" or "insanity" as the culprit threatening the world's existence. But Tolle never specifies what exactly this "madness" or "insanity" is. Is it Communism? Capitalism? Corporate fascism? Radical Islam? Tolle doesn't say. And he never describes the socioeconomic system that will reign supreme upon the dawning of the New (or Now) Age that he envisions. Will this Now-age Shangri-la emphasize statism or individualism, socialism or capitalism? Tolle, floating in thick London-type fog, neglects to inform us regarding these important matters. Throughout my book, I continually point out, from different angles, the folly of Tolle's New (or Now) Age chimera.

Beyond his beliefs about the human mind, the power of Now, and a "new earth," I take Tolle to task on virtually every subject he addresses. Most significantly, I rebut his arguments that: 1) emotions can be trusted more than thought; 2) time is a mind-created illusion; 3) psychological time is insanity; 4) the present moment is the Now; 5) the "inner" body is the direct link to the Now; 6) your cells stop aging when you live in the Now; 7) women are spiritually more evolved than men; and 8) animals such as ducks and cats are Zen masters. Eckhart Tolle's teachings are replete with erroneous ideas, and I point out the major flaws in his principal arguments.

The Truth Is Trinitarian

Eckhart Tolle, as I see him, is a trite, error-ridden pop guru who peddles the shell of mysticism while ignoring the nut. His Dharma is unsystematized and undeveloped, consisting of fragments extracted from various traditions and gurus. He takes these fragments and gussies them up within a psychologized New Age framework, and this slick repackaging of the "perennial philosophy" accounts for much of his popularity. But when it comes to addressing critical spiritual subjects—such as right diet, conservation of sexual energy, *kundalini* awakening, and the necessity of a regular meditation practice—Tolle is inexcusably silent. Most glaringly, he fails to consider the role of *Shakti*, the Holy Spirit, the true power of Now, in the enlightenment process. And because he never considers the role of the Holy Spirit—one third of the Trinity—in enlightenment, I classify Tolle as a two-dimensional, rather than a three-dimensional, mystic.

As a two-dimensional, or "flat," mystic, Tolle pushes a fragmented, or incomplete, version of Raja Yoga (the classical Hindu system of yoga) as his essential Dharma. Thus, Tolle's fundamental teaching, like Raja Yoga, is *not* based on directly connecting to Spirit; instead, it is based on disidentification from the time-bound mind, which functions only in a past-future (but never a present-moment) framework. Tolle himself confirms this when he states, "...the single most vital step on your journey toward enlightenment is this: learn to disidentify from your mind."

Because Tolle views disidentification from the mind as the key to spiritual awakening, he also views the mind as the "greatest obstacle to enlightenment." Consequently, Tolle, like many two-dimensional mystics, has nothing but contempt for man's conceptual faculty, blaming it for most every problem on the planet, and failing to praise or acknowledge its myriad achievements. Because Tolle's Dharma focuses on the *isolation* of consciousness from arising thought-forms (rather than on the *uniting* of consciousness with universal Spirit), his yoga of disidentification from the mind is fundamentally exclusive and reductive, rather than wholistic, in nature. His yoga, in and by itself, does not result in spiritual en-Light-enment because it is not based on connecting to Spirit, divine Light-energy.

By contrast, the yoga I recommend—Divine (or Holy) Communion—is based on directly connecting to the Holy Spirit and allowing its Power, or Light-energy, to en-Light-en you by spontaneously outshining your thought-forms. Because the yoga of Holy Communion fully incorporates both branches (or vines) of the Absolute—consciousness and spirit—it is intrinsically Divine. And because this Divinity is realized through the incarnate soul (or potential Christ (or Self)-consciousness), it is trinitarian, or three-dimensional, in nature. Thus, in contradistinction to Tolle's Dharma, which is two-dimensional (or flat), the Dharma I recommend is three-dimensional (or full); in others words, truly Holy (or Wholistic) and all-inclusive (or non-reductive) in nature.

Although my mission is to expose the flaws in Tolle's Dharma, in all fairness to him it must be said that his message represents a big step up from most of the New Age drivel currently flooding the spiritual marketplace. Thus, even though his Dharma is flat—lacking verticality (height and depth)—it cannot be denied that his message is one that has truly liberated or changed the lives of countless people. Praise where praise is due.

But it must also be said that Tolle's Dharma is limited and full of errors, and that there is a Way beyond the two-dimensional mysticism he preaches. My goal in this book is twofold: first, to expose the limitation and faults of his Dharma; second, to point people to the Dharma beyond it: three-dimensional, or trinitarian, mysticism, which is exemplified by the spiritual traditions of Hindu Kashmir Shaivism, Tibetan Buddhist Dzogchen, Daism, and Christian Hermeticism. This book emphasizes Christian terminology—such as Holy Communion, the Holy Spirit, and baptism—because most Western readers are familiar with these terms. But the same concepts, in different terms, can be found in all great trinitarian Dharmas. Because I think it's important for serious students of Truth to study these Dharmas, as well as select two-dimensional ones and other texts, I have provided a comprehensive recommended Spiritual Reading List at the back of the book.

In order to make this book suitable as a study guide to *The Power of Now*, I have simply rephrased or paraphrased most of the chapter titles, subchapter titles, and questions in Tolle's book. This makes it easy for students of Eckhart Tolle to compare my answers to questions and my points of view on topics he discusses to his own.

Eckhart Tolle awakened the world to the *concept* of the power of Now. In this book, my aim is to awaken people to the power of Now itself— the Holy Spirit, or *Shakti*, or *Sambhogakaya*. For without awakening to this Power, this Light-energy, full en-Light-enment (or perfect Self-realization) is not possible. It is my hope that this book will serve to awaken people to the *true* power of Now.

CHAPTER ONE

Enlightenment and the Mind

The Primal Obstruction to Enlightenment

What is enlightenment?

Eckhart Tolle, author of the *New York Times* bestseller *The Power of Now,* describes enlightenment as "your natural state of felt oneness with Being." Tolle's description of enlightenment is certainly correct, but not quite complete. Full enlightenment is not merely connectedness with (the supreme) Being, it is also conductivity of the Light-energy, or Power, that stems from this Being.

The supreme Being is a *divine* Being, meaning that it has two *vines*: static transcendental Presence and dynamic spiritual Power. The vine of transcendental Presence is the timeless Now, and the vine of spiritual Power is the dynamic power of Now. When you are able to truly connect to the presence of the Now, then, spontaneously, the power of Now *en-Light-ens* you with its radiant energy.

In mystical Christian terms, Holy Communion is a synonym for oneness with the divine Being (or Now), and the Holy Spirit is a synonym for the Light-energy (or power of Now) that the disciple receives in communion. In other words, the enlightenment process not only involves connectedness (or *fusion*) with Being, but also the reception of Being's power, the down-flow (or *infusion*) of spiritual energy into and through one's bodymind.

Contrary to popular New Age opinion, spiritual enlightenment is not, fundamentally, a psychological phenomenon; it is, first and foremost, an energetic reality. Spiritual Light is the radiance of the energy emanating from the divine Being (or Source), the eternal Now. When you consciously connect to this Source, then, spontaneously, the radiant energy (or power of Now) stemming from this connection en-Light-ens (or outshines) your primal darkness (or spiritual ignorance). This influx of divine Light-energy—which is true spiritual Grace—supersedes and exceeds your disconnected and unhappy mind forms, replacing them with the literal Blessing (or bliss-inducing) Power flowing from the divine Source.

An individual's spiritual ignorance (or darkness) is primal and, as such, cannot be removed through psychological strategies that result in a "better you." An individual's spiritual ignorance is caused by only one thing: the *ignoring* of a direct connection to the divine Source and its Light. Therefore, the only cure for spiritual ignorance is a direct connection to the divine Source-Light itself.

The Buddha's term for enlightenment is *Nirvana,* and the literal definition of *Nirvana* is "the end of becoming." "Becoming" (*samsara*) means going, successively, from one conditioned (or limited and contracted) state to another. Since *Nirvana* is the end of becoming, it is also a synonym for permanent oneness with *Being,* which is a concise synonym for the immutable and illimitable Reality, or divine Source-Light, that underlies and transcends all change, all becoming.

Advanced spiritual practitioners regularly experience powerful connections to the divine Source-Light, and can be characterized as *conditionally* enlightened. But only the rarest beings, such as Jesus, Buddha, and the late Indian sage Ramana Maharshi are able to effortlessly and permanently abide in and *as* the divine Source-Light itself. Such beings can be characterized as *unconditionally* enlightened, or Self-realized. The degree to which you can maintain a direct connection to the divine Source and radiate its Light is the degree to which you are spiritually en-Light-ened.

Can you elaborate on the meaning of the term Being?

The term *Being* is a pithy but non-descriptive synonym for the divine Reality or Source. As earlier stated, the term *divine* signifies a two-vine (or two-branch) Reality—a Divinity that is at once static transcendental Presence (or Awareness) and dynamic spiritual Power (or Light-energy). The fact that the divine Being is not merely static Presence but also dynamic Light-energy, or divinizing Spirit-power, is what makes en-Light-enment possible for individuals who commune with It.

You can feel the presence and power of Being when your connection to the divine Source, the eternal Now, is full enough and intense enough to awaken the descent of divine Light-energy into and through your bodymind. When the infusion of divine Light-energy outshines your bodymind, you spontaneously experience your true Self (or Buddha-nature) as pure, radiant, blissful Being.

Eckhart Tolle is correct when he states that Being can be felt but not understood mentally. This is the case because Being is not a separate "object" that can be grasped by the mind. Being, as such, cannot be "known" in the conventional dualistic sense; it can only be radically intuited, or felt-realized—and this can only happen when you spiritually (or yogically) coincide with It. In Indian yoga, the experience of oneness with the Divine is often described as the "feeling of Being." The great Indian yoga formula—*Sat* (Being) = *Cit* (Consciousness)-*Ananda* (Bliss-Power)—informs us that this experience of Being is the feeling-realization of our true, divine nature as Self-aware, Self-radiant Bliss.

If Being *is the same "Thing" as God, why not just use the word* God *when you talk about* Ultimate Reality?

Because the word *God* has so many different meanings and connotations associated with it, it is not a good synonym for Ultimate Reality. Different religions have different concepts of God, and these differences have led to bloody wars and conflicts throughout history. Human beings like to superimpose human traits on the Deity, and as a result, in some religions we end up with an angry, jealous, and vengeful God—a terrible Father in the sky who represents the worst human traits. Religions tend to create God in the image of man, and this has perverted the meaning of the word *God*.

The word *Being*, on the other hand, is an excellent synonym for Ultimate Reality, the Absolute. *Being* implies an unqualified or illimitable Existent or existence. And unless a qualifying adjective is added to *Being*, it remains a term that defies limiting adjuncts. Furthermore, when a spiritual practitioner achieves identity with the Absolute, his realization can most succinctly be described as the "feeling of Being," the feeling of transcendentally existing beyond all limited states and conditions. Finally, whereas the word *God* has dualistic implications, the word *Being* doesn't. The word *God* implies a great Object or Other to be worshipped, whereas the term *Being* alludes to the possibility of a nondual Self-realization that transcends all subject-object dichotomies.

What is the primary obstruction to the experience of Being?

According to Eckhart Tolle, identification with the mind is the greatest obstacle to enlightenment, the experience of Reality, or Being. Tolle's point of view is a prevalent one in many Eastern spiritual traditions, but it is not one that I share.

As a Zen practitioner, I spent years attempting to empty my mind and disidentify from my thoughts. As thoughts would arise, I would simply watch them and attempt to "void" them by neither accepting nor rejecting them. I experienced many profound states of "no-mind" via this approach, and by constantly letting go of concepts as they arose, I dramatically stimulated the movement of energy through my body. My neck would twist and my head would jerk as the *kundalini* (uncoiled "serpent power") forcefully ripped through me. But this type of meditation practice did not enable me to awaken to my Buddha-nature, and it did not lead me to peace. Instead, I was constantly in conflict with myself, as I continually struggled to disidentify from arising thoughts.

What I eventually discovered—thanks to the teachings of J. Krishnamurti (1895–1986) and Adi Da (1939–2008) and the traditions of Tibetan Dzogchen and Christian mysticism—is that the greatest obstacle to enlightenment, to the experience of Being, is the moment-to-moment avoidance of relationship. Krishnamurti says, "To be related is to *be*." In other words, when relationship is direct and unqualified (and thereby blessed by Light from above), then it spontaneously morphs into the experience, or feeling, of Being. Terms such as *oneness*, *unity*, and *communion* can be considered synonyms for relationship. The Christian term *Holy Communion*, from a mystical perspective, means to be wholly or fully present and at one with both life (relative existence) and the Divine (the Absolute Existent). In fact, the word *atonement* can be broken down to *at-one-ment*. From a mystical perspective, therefore, the primal sin, the fundamental obstacle to enlightenment, is the moment-to-moment avoidance of relationship, or at-one-ment, with life and the Divine.

It is certainly imperative to transcend identification with the mind, but this happens naturally when you first establish yourself in oneness. When you are fully present and at one with life and the Divine, the mind naturally becomes more still. And when your practice of oneness, or *fusion* contemplation, morphs into *infused* contemplation, the influx, or descent, of Light-energy from the divine Source literally outshines your mind, temporarily severing your identification with it. Instead of perceiving yourself as a mere bodymind, you now experience yourself as a radiant spiritual being.

From a mystical Christian perspective, when the disciple's practice of Holy Communion is full and intense, the Holy Spirit spontaneously pours down on him. The Holy Spirit, or Holy Ghost, is the radiant power of the divine Being. In the Sermon on the Mount, Jesus says, "If thine eye [consciousness] be single, thy whole body will be filled with Light." What Jesus means is: if you are consciously at one with the Deity, you will be en-Light-ened. Jesus doesn't tell you to strategically disidentify from your mind to achieve enlightenment; he tells you to single-pointedly focus your full attention on the divine Being if you want to be filled with mind-transcending Light. Instead of seeking to disidentify from your mind, "Seek ye first the Kingdom of Heaven [the divine domain of eternal Being], and all else will be added unto you."

Eckhart Tolle considers the mind to be the chief impediment to enlightenment, and he views the mind as an instrument that has run amok, taking you over and making your life miserable. Tolle states, "[Your mind] uses you... The instrument has taken you over." Tolle here doesn't explain the "mechanics," or working structure, of the mind and how it seems to "take you over." Nor does he broach the subject of psychological reprogramming of the mind. These are important matters to consider, but Tolle fails to address them.

In my opinion, any serious consideration of the mind's working structure must begin with the interplay between the mind's conscious and subconscious components. When we aren't consciously, volitionally thinking, our mind goes on automatic pilot, so to speak, and all kinds of thoughts and feelings—some pleasant and inspiring, some unpleasant and depressing—arise from our subconscious. Because our thoughts and feelings arise spontaneously, it can seem as if the mind is "using" us, filling our head with unwanted "mental garbage" and painful memories. But in reality, what arises from our subconscious is nothing other than what we have knowingly or unknowingly programmed into it, based on our life experiences, perception of reality, and value judgments. (It should be noted that if we believe in astrology, karma, and reincarnation, we might see our thought-form patterns as having roots in a previous incarnation.) Because human beings are blessed with free will, we all have the capacity to consciously reprogram our subconscious and free ourselves (to some extent) from the feeling of being "taken over" by our mind (even if its programming does have roots in a previous incarnation). It's certainly not easy to reprogram our mind, or "mental computer," but it's something that each of us, to one degree or another, is capable of doing.

◊ ◊ ◊

I can choose to use my mind to accomplish many things. I don't believe that my mind has taken me over.

Unless you're fully enlightened or you've completely and perfectly programmed your mind—which is impossible—your mind has no doubt taken you over to some extent. Can you, as Tolle asks, "be free of your mind whenever you want?" And have you found the "off" button to it?

You mean utterly stop thinking whenever I want? I can stop only for a few moments. Then the thoughts start again.

Then you're a slave to your mind. It possesses you rather than you possessing it. But before we consider the solution to your mental enslavement, it's important to understand why it's so difficult to turn the mind off.

According to philosopher-novelist Ayn Rand (1905–1982), man is the *rational* animal, and unlike other animals, his chief means of survival is his mind, not his body or instincts. Consequently, the reason your mind doesn't have an "off" button is the same reason your breathing cycle doesn't: you're biologically programmed to depend on its near-constant activity. The mind's incessant activity is a survival mechanism, which is why the mind is so hard to turn off for any length of time.

Now, let's consider Tolle's "solution" to the "problem" of the mind. According to Tolle, "The beginning of freedom [from your mind] is the realization that you aren't the possessing entity—the thinker." To break identification with the thinker, Tolle recommends that you "watch the thinker." Watching the thinker, says Tolle, activates a "higher level of consciousness" that enables you to realize "that thought is only a tiny aspect of a vast realm of intelligence beyond thought."

Let's scrutinize what Tolle says. First, he says that you're not the thinker and that you can break identity with the thinker by watching the thinker. If you're not the thinker, then who is? How can there be thoughts without a thinker? There can't be. Even if your true spiritual identity is the pure, transcendental consciousness that witnesses your thoughts, you, as the bodymind complex, can, at will, think specific thoughts. Yes, the "thinker" can't be found when you look for him, but this is so because your consciousness can only operate in one mode at a time. When the mode is switched from conception to perception, in the form of watching, conceptual "you" is temporarily obviated or made to vanish. Tolle's viewpoint, a classical Eastern spiritual one, is not one that I share. From my viewpoint, yes, your true identity as spiritual consciousness transcends the mind, but this does not mean that you, as the psycho-physical entity, aren't the thinker.

Second, Tolle states that watching the thinker activates a "higher level of consciousness." What does Tolle mean by a "higher level of consciousness?" Thoughts are mental concretes, or structures, that contract consciousness into successive limited states of existence. ("As a man thinks, so he becomes," says the Buddha.) As contracted forms (or formations) of consciousness, thoughts, or concepts, attenuate the natural intensity of consciousness, thereby lowering its vibrational frequency. Pure consciousness vibrates as pure Light-energy, but thoughts contract (and sully) this pure Light-energy by lowering its absolute frequency, thereby making it, to one degree or another, vibrationally dense (or "dark"). Hence, when thinking—consciousness contraction—is supplanted by pure, or thought-free, consciousness, then consciousness is naturally more intense, seems to expand, and vibrates at a faster frequency. Thus, a "higher level of consciousness" is said to be attained.

Even though watching the thinker can activate or lead to a higher level of consciousness, it does not do so automatically. If a meditator is unable to generate enough conscious force in his "witness," or "mindfulness," practice to achieve a thought-free state for protracted periods of time, he won't experience the radiant intensity of pure consciousness. I spent years involved with people in Buddhist groups, and even though many of these people practiced forms of witnessing, or mindfulness, few of them awakened to the force-flow of divine Light-energy, the radiant power of Now.

"Watching the thinker" is not a form of meditation that I practice or highly recommend. Because it involves focusing or concentrating attention on a specific function—mentation, in this case—it narrows, or contracts, the field of natural awareness into an exclusive and reductive state. Furthermore, it is a purely "head," or "gnostic," practice that excludes the naturally expansive feeling-dimension of consciousness. Certainly, if you have not done so already, give the "watching the thinker" method a try—but then compare it to the practice that I recommend: direct and immediate relationship, or Holy Communion. In this practice, instead of strategically, exclusively watching the thinker, you simply assume the "position," or "stance," of being whole-bodily present and connected to existence as a whole. Once you assume, or can assume, this position of merely or fully being present, notice these things: 1) The feeling of being directly, immediately, and unqualifiedly related is the fullest and most intense expression of consciousness possible. 2) The feeling of being unqualifiedly related spontaneously morphs into the feeling of *being-ness*. 3) Your root, or primal ego-centric, tendency is to retract from this position of direct, immediate communion, or connected *at-one-ment*. 4) In any moment, you can *atone* for your "sinful" retraction simply by re-assuming the position of connected at-one-ment. 5) The "function" of merely being present and at-one spontaneously transcends and includes the "sub-function" of "watching the thinker," thus enabling you to naturally, rather than strategically, transcend identification with the mind.

When your practice of direct and immediate relationship, or Holy Communion, is sufficiently full and intense, then, spontaneously, you are *baptized (initiated* by the Holy Spirit), and divine spiritual Power, or Light-energy, is poured into you. The Holy Spirit—what Hindus call *Shakti* and Mahayana Buddhists the *Sambhogakaya*—is nothing other than the power of Now, the awakened force and flow of divine Light-energy.

The way of conscious at-one-ment, or Holy Communion, and its relationship to the Holy Spirit, or power of Now, will be further elaborated upon throughout the remainder of this book. If you haven't already done so, experiment with being whole-bodily present, in direct and immediate relationship to existence as a whole. This will provide you with a frame of reference for our further, more in-depth consideration of the subject.

Freedom from the Mind

What, exactly, is meant by "watching the thinker"?

"Watching the thinker" means to mindfully witness your mental activity without judging it. Whatever thought-forms arise in your consciousness, you neither accept nor reject them. Instead, you simply remain choicelessly aware, allowing thoughts to arise and fall of their own accord.

You'll quickly notice that non-judgmental witnessing of your mind tends to dissolve your thoughts, enabling you to awaken to a state of stillness, or emptiness.

When you discover who, or what, perceives this stillness, or void, then you've awakened to your true *I Am* nature—pure transcendental awareness. But it must be emphasized that merely recognizing your Self (or Buddha)-nature is a far cry from being able to abide in and *as* It.

Eckhart Tolle describes how listening to a thought breaks your identification with it and is "the beginning of the end of involuntary and compulsive thinking." If only it were that easy! I spent years in the company of various spiritual practitioners, and not a single one, to my knowledge, managed to permanently put an end to involuntary and compulsive thinking. Short of Buddhahood, or *Nirvana*, even the most advanced meditators struggle with the same involuntary and compulsive thought patterns as everyone else. Read a couple of books about the Buddha's life. Until the moment he entered *Nirvana*, he was still beset with vexing thoughts.

Yes, listening to a thought temporarily breaks your identification with it, but thoughts continue to arise, one after another, and the moment-to-moment practice of listening to or watching them becomes quite arduous. Such watching or listening is a willful act, and because efforts are always spasmodic, so are the results. Here is a typical example: You begin meditating, and thoughts about the large sum of money you just blew in a bad investment arise. You non-judgmentally witness the thoughts, they vanish, and you experience a gap of "no-mind." But you can bet whatever money you have left that these same thoughts will soon arise again... and again.

My point is this: When the mind is viewed as the enemy that enslaves you, and your battle plan is to "defeat," or break identification with, it by relentlessly witnessing its activity from moment to moment, then you're starting a war with yourself that is next to impossible to win. I fought that war for years and lost. And in the forty years that I've been involved in the spiritual field, I've yet to meet anyone who has won it.

Tolle claims that "gaps of 'no-mind'" lead to "stillness and peace" and the "natural state of felt oneness with Being." If "no-mind" leads to enlightenment, then why doesn't deep sleep spiritually awaken everyone? Drugs and hypnosis can also render the mind temporarily still and peaceful. Do they lead to enlightenment? "No-mind" is a cool but overrated spiritual concept, and if you understand what true spiritual life is about, you'll pass on the pop Zen that Tolle pushes.

Tolle tells you to "go more deeply into the realm of no-mind." But if there is no-mind, there is nothing to go more deeply into. Your consciousness perceives a lack of mental objects (thoughts) and labels this new object "no-mind," or "the void." The void, or empty space, is nothing but a backdrop to focus your attention on. Mahayana Buddhism, which includes Zen, is the only religious tradition that apotheosizes the void, sometimes (and mistakenly) equating it with *Nirvana* or Ultimate Reality.

Empty space (the void) is a wonderful meditation object—I use it myself—but it is simply a doorway to the luminous presence and power of Being that is behind and beyond it. Until emptiness "dances," or comes alive as the *Sambhogakaya* (or Holy Spirit) in your practice, genuine spiritual enlightenment is not a possibility for you.

Tolle mentions being "fully present," but fails to explain how that translates into spiritual en-Light-enment. I will explain for him. When you are fully present and at one with the divine Source, then "God," the divine Being, sheds his Grace, or Blessing Power, on you. This Blessing Power, which is palpable Light-energy, crashes down on you, incinerating your thoughts. When this radiant Blessing Power (which Indian yogis term *Shaktipat*) pours down upon you, it literally outshines your mind, rendering it impotent as an obstruction to the divine Light. When *Shaktipat*, the descending current of Light-energy, penetrates to your spiritual (or "Sacred") Heart-center (just to the right of the center of your chest), you intuit your true Self-nature as one with the divine Being. And when the Heart-knot is finally severed by *Shaktipat*, the down-poured Holy Spirit, then you permanently awaken as a Christ-like Self—the divine Being personified.

You can take the laborious path to enlightenment and burden yourself with the onerous task of ceaselessly watching your mind and disidentifying from your thoughts. Or, you can simply connect to the divine Source and allow its Grace, the power of Now, to outshine your mind and en-Light-en you. The choice is yours.

Tolle next presents an alternative method to "watching the thinker." He tells you to "direct the focus of your attention into the Now." "For example," he says, "every time you walk up and down the stairs in your house or place of work, pay close attention to every step, every movement, even your breathing."

Whether you watch the thinker or focus your attention on your movement or breathing, this type of practice falls under the category of Buddhist Vipassana (or insight) meditation. Vipassana is simply the practice of moment-to-moment mindfulness relative to your bodymind and its interaction with life. Vipassana meditation has its roots in Theravada (or Hinayana) Buddhism.

I spent years practicing Vipassana, as well as Zen and Tibetan Buddhist meditation. Based on my personal experience, it's easy for me to understand why practitioners of Zen and Tibetan Buddhism consider Vipassana a rudimentary, or lower-level, spiritual practice. Vipassana is, in a word, *drudgery*. It's a practice devoted to the mundane and divorced from the Divine. Instead of directly and immediately plugging into the eternal Now and receiving and enjoying its Grace, or Blessing Power, your attention is tethered to the ephemeral "now."

Compare Vipassana to Dzogchen, the highest form of Tibetan Buddhist meditation. In Dzogchen, the essential practice is to be directly and immediately present to (or plugged into) the supreme Source (*Dharmakaya-Sambhogakaya*), which is analogous to Hindu *Siva-Shakti*. When you are truly one with the *Dharmakaya*, the divine Presence, you spontaneously receive and enjoy the *Sambhogakaya*, the divine Power, or Light-energy, emanating from It. If you are interested in the practice of Dzogchen, get a copy of the outstanding contemplation manual *The Cycle of Day and Night*, by Namkhai Norbu.

Eckhart Tolle repeats his "mantra" in this short section when he says, "So the single most vital step on your journey toward enlightenment is this: learn to disidentify from your mind." My mantra is: "Seek ye first the divine Source, or eternal Now, and its radiant Power shall outshine your mind, en-Light-ening you."

Enlightenment: Transcending Your Mind

Isn't thinking man's essential tool of survival?

Indeed, it is. Man is biologically programmed to continually think in order to ensure his survival and well-being. "Biological man" perceives himself as a separate entity, whose existence, to one degree or another, is always threatened. So his mind, as a survival mechanism, works almost nonstop in an attempt to secure his current and future well-being.

When "biological man" becomes "spiritual man" by connecting to the divine Source, he feels full and sustained rather than empty and threatened. His mind relaxes in the Divine's presence, and he allows the Divine's power to outshine his arising thoughts, which results in his en-Light-enment. "Spiritual man" realizes that his thoughts are merely ephemeral, non-binding modifications of the radiant, transcendental consciousness of Being. So it doesn't matter to him whether he rests thought-free (in the continuum of radiance), or if thoughts arise. And because his thoughts arise in the context of Holy Communion, they are generally wholesome and positive rather than dysfunctional and negative.

Once "spiritual man" becomes "biological man" by committing the "original sin" of separating from the Divine, his mind begins to run amok, and he is besieged with repetitive, useless, and harmful thoughts. If "biological man" wishes to exorcise his inner "demons," salvation is always—directly and immediately—available in the presence of the Spirit, which freely pours its mind-transcending power upon anyone who "repents" and turns to It.

Why are we addicted to thinking?

We are addicted to thinking because thinking is the means to becoming, to changing our state. When you separate, or retract, from Being, you contract into a limited, or exclusive and reductive, mental state. Because thinking is a limited state of being, it is not ultimately satisfying, so you seek another state. And because the new state is also limited and ultimately unsatisfying, you seek yet another state. This goes on ad infinitum—and in Buddhism, this endless becoming, which continues from lifetime to lifetime, is termed *samsara,* the Wheel of Birth and Death.

Tolle links the mind to the ego, defining the *ego* as a "false self, created by unconscious identification with the mind." Tolle says, "We may call this phantom self the ego. It consists of mind activity and can only be kept going through constant thinking." In other words, Tolle (in line with most "causal" schools of mysticism), believes that mind and ego are essentially the same Truth-obstructing phenomenon. The "causal" view of the mind-ego relation can be summarized thus: Instead of simply *being* the true (illimitable) Self (pure *I Am-ness* or Consciousness), you *become* a false (limited) self by grasping hold of mental images and imagining: *I am this or that.*

In contrast to Tolle, I do not embrace the "causal" school's view of the ego. Instead, I endorse the "radical" school's view, developed and championed by the late Adi Da. Here is my summary version of it: The root *ego* is *not* the "false self created by unconscious identification with the mind." The root, or primal, ego is the separate-self sensation, or self-contraction, generated by the very act of separating, or retracting, from Being. The act of separating from Being is prior to the unconscious activity that creates a false-self-image via identification. Therefore, if the ego is to be undone at its root, it is the primal act of *ontological* separation rather than the secondary act of *mental* identification that must be eradicated.

Relative to the enlightenment process, a third view of the ego merits consideration: Ayn Rand's. In contrast to the "causal" and "radical" definitions of the ego, which reflect a transpersonal point of view, Rand's definition of the ego—*rational self-interest*—reflects a personal one. And unlike the "causal" and "radical" points of view, which condemn man's ego, Rand's point of view liberates man's ego, freeing it from the grip of *altruism*, the pernicious moral code that pronounces *self-sacrifice* as man's highest calling.

Prior to beginning the spiritual journey, an individual is only concerned with the present in relation to the past and future. Once the spiritual journey is begun, he focuses his attention on living in the timeless Present. The same *egoic* motive—rational self-interest—fuels his pre-spiritual life and his subsequent spiritual life. It could be said that a person with a truly healthy (or highly developed) ego would naturally turn to esoteric spiritual life, because such a choice represents the epitome of rational, enlightened self-interest.

The mind is a wonderful faculty. Why would I want to stop its activity? Without it, man would be just another animal.

The mind, as Tolle points out, is not consciousness itself. Consciousness, the essence of Being, is a universal constant that exists prior to and beyond thought. The mind is a function or application of consciousness that enables you to mentally understand the universe you live in. When you think, you are using the uniquely human faculty of mind, which, via the process of concept formation, is able to create mental "concretes" that accurately measure and reflect the world you perceive through your senses. Thinking enables you to measure (or *ratio*-nally compare, contrast, and comprehend) the sensible universe—that which has been "measured out" as a manifestion of the Unmanifested—and, via concepts, form intelligent and creative conclusions about the things you perceive. Thinking, in other words, is a nonpareil tool for *measuring* conditional reality, the manifested. But Ultimate Reality, the Unmanifested, is immeasurable and, in fact, is often referred to as *the Immeasurable.* Therefore, if you want to access the Immeasurable, you have to do so with a tool other than thinking. And because you can only use one tool at a time, mentation must be set aside when you devote yourself to meditation, the process of contemplating, or communing with, the Immeasurable.

So the mind is a marvelous tool for understanding measurable phenomena, but an improper one for contemplating the Immeasurable. But is the human mind creative? Not according to Tolle, who claims that "[the mind] is not at all creative."

If creativity is defined as the power to bring something into existence out of nothing, then man's mind is not creative. But if it is defined as the ability to combine or integrate things that exist into unique arrangements or innovative products, then man's mind is very creative.

If "no-mind," rather than mind, is the secret to creativity, as Tolle claims, then why don't Zen Buddhists lead the world in creativity and new inventions? In the book *Wild Ivy,* the Zen master Hakuin (1686–1768) and other Zen monks develop energy disorders as a result of their meditation practice. But all their years of mind-emptying meditation fail to provide them with a *satori*-inspired solution to their problem, and the Zen tradition itself has no answer for their disease. In order to cure themselves, the Zen master and the monks are forced to resort to the Taoist tradition, which, unlike the Zen tradition, emphasizes a holistic rather than a quasi-nihilistic approach toward life.

If great scientific discoveries are mainly dependent on "no-mind" rather than mind, then why have most been made by men with stratospheric IQs and extensive education? Creative breakthroughs do often come at times of mental quietude. But this isn't because the mind has stopped working; it's because the subconscious mind has been working on the problem all along, and when the conscious mind temporarily relaxes its efforts, the answers spring forth from the subconscious. To those unfamiliar with modern psychology—including Einstein and the hundred leading physicists who, in 1900, participated in mathematician Jacques Hadamard's survey (See: *Psychology of Invention in the Mathematical Field,* by Jacques Hadamard)—it might indeed seem that great insights arise from a mystical "place" beyond conscious thought. But that "place" isn't the "realm of no-mind;" it's the "realm of the individual's subconscious mind," which confers creative insights only in response to the individual's *previous* conscious efforts.

Emotion: The Mind as Feeling-Energy

How about emotions? They cause me more trouble than my mind.

Human consciousness operates through two essential modes: thinking and feeling. Thinking (or knowing) is the "male," or mental, mode, and feeling (consciously sensing) is the "female," or affective, mode. All thinking is done via concepts, and all feeling is experienced via emotions.

Thinking causes trouble when it errs, and feeling experiences the pain of that trouble. If you make a mental mistake, a miscalculation, and buy a stock that crashes, you might feel angry at yourself for your mistake and depressed about the money you lost. The mental mistake that led to the anger and depression caused the trouble, but because you're suffering emotionally in reaction to your mental error, you likely will view your emotions as more troublesome than your thinking.

Emotions are energetically charged feeling-reactions to life occurrences. They are conditioned responses to life that reflect an individual's value judgments. Emotions arise from the subconscious and determine what the individual is feeling, what his state of being is in a given moment. For example, an investor spontaneously experiences joy upon learning that his stocks skyrocketed that day because he values money and the financial security that it represents.

Emotional reactions are experienced on a visceral level, so you can feel how they affect your body. For example, when you get angry, you can feel your body clench and your heart beat faster and harder, which, of course, elevates your blood pressure. When you experience joy, your body actually feels lighter, while depression makes it feel noticeably heavier.

Just as human consciousness operates through the two essential modes of knowing (or thinking) and feeling (or consciously sensing), so does divine consciousness. Divine consciousness, or spiritual enlightenment, is the state of both *knowing* and *feeling* that your true nature is pure Being.

Sometimes thinking and feeling, mind and emotions, are in conflict with each other.

Eckhart Tolle states that, "If there is an apparent conflict between them, the thought will be the lie, the emotion will be the truth." This is hardly the case. For example, say you're on a strict natural-food diet, and you walk into a bakery with a friend. Your emotional reaction to the smell of the goodies is, *Give in to the temptation! A few cookies are not a sin.* But your rational, thinking mind tells you that breaking your diet will have negative consequences that aren't worth the momentary pleasure you'll get from titillating your taste buds.

The late Paul Bragg, a famous health food guru, had this to say about the body-mind, or feeling-thinking, relationship: "Flesh is dumb... It took me years to get the emotions out of my eating." In other words, emotions don't represent truth; they represent past conditioning that can obstruct rational behavior.

What Tolle fails to recognize is that emotions are not tools of cognition. Emotions are conditioned responses to stimuli and should be governed by reason. Feelings should not be suppressed or ignored, nor should they be mindlessly obeyed or indulged. Instead, they should be acknowledged and then considered in the light of reason.

Yes, as Tolle states, emotions do have a strong physical component. But no, they do not necessarily give you a truthful reflection of your mind. All that emotions reflect is your past. They are conditioned responses— in the form of automatic feeling-reactions—to internal and external stimuli.

The watcher can, of course, observe his emotions. But contrary to what Tolle says—"If you practice this, all that is *unconscious* in you will be brought into the light of consciousness"—emotions are not unconscious; they're *subconscious*, meaning that their roots are traceable to particular experiences and value judgments. When I use the term "unconscious," I mean a lack of conscious presence or knowledge, not a repository of deeply buried emotional dross that is disconnected from and unavailable to the mind. Whatever buried emotions are brought into the light of consciousness are subconscious in nature, not unconscious. To illustrate this point, consider that most people are already aware of how they'll react to certain stimuli before they're confronted with them. Consequently, they often avoid certain situations or topics of discussion because they know what feelings they'll trigger. For example, if someone asks my friend about his beloved cat that recently died, he and I both know that he'll get very sad.

Is observing emotions as important as observing thoughts?

You don't need to deliberately observe your thoughts or emotions to awaken to your Buddha-nature. Thoughts and emotions are like clouds in the sky that appear and disappear of their own accord. Your Buddha-nature is like the sky—ever-present regardless of the absence or presence of clouds. If you are simply, directly, whole-bodily present, you'll naturally, rather than strategically, be cognizant of your thoughts and emotions as they appear and disappear in the "sky" of your awareness. You can be present to your "inner energy field," as Tolle recommends, or you can be present to the outer totality. Experiment with both modes of practice.

As J. Krishnamurti says, "To be [unqualifiedly] related is to *be*." Therefore, the direct "doorway into Being" is not through the deliberate observation of your emotions and your "inner energy field"; it is through the practice of unqualified relationship, the practice of being directly, immediately, whole-bodily present to, through, and beyond the "clouds," the arising pattern in the moment.

Eckhart Tolle devotes a good deal of space in *The Power of Now* to discussing the origin of emotional pain and the relation between emotions and the mind. Tolle's viewpoint on the subject can be summarized in three statements: 1) "All emotions are modifications of one primordial, undifferentiated emotion"—*pain*—that originates in your estrangement from your Self-nature. 2) Because the mind is an "intrinsic part of this 'problem,'" it can never find a solution to this pain. 3) The mind is part of the "problem" because its relationship to emotion often is that of a "vicious circle," wherein thinking and emotion reinforce each other.

In the first statement, Tolle claims that all emotions stem from one fundamental, underlying emotion: pain. Tolle defines emotions as "disturbances" and differentiates these "negative" emotions from "positive" emotions such as love, joy, and peace, which he does not classify as emotions. The reason he classifies "negative" emotions as the only true emotions is because they originate in the mind and therefore (because the mind is dualistic) are subject to the "law of opposites" (which, as Tolle puts it, "means you cannot have good without bad"). "Positive" emotions, on the other hand, Tolle asserts, are rooted in nondual Being, and as such have no opposite.

Tolle's claim that all "negative" emotions are modifications of the existential pain of separation from your true identity is not one that all prominent spiritual gurus second. Adi Da, for example, claims that all emotions—including fear, sorrow, and anger, the three principal negative emotions—are modifications, or contractions, not of pain, but of Love, which he defines as "unobstructed feeling-attention," or the "feeling of Being." Psychiatrist-guru David R. Hawkins agrees with Adi Da, insisting that all emotions, whether "good" or "bad," are "gradations on the same continuum, not on two opposing ones." According to Dr. Hawkins, there is only Love, and various emotions, positive and negative, indicate Love's relative presence or absence. Hawkins uses the *seeming* opposites of light and darkness to illustrate this point. He writes, "You cannot shine darkness into an area... Thus, there is only *one variable*: the presence or absence of light."

Tolle's viewpoint that "pain" is the fundamental emotional condition of beings estranged from their Self-nature is a common one in Eastern philosophy. Although I personally embrace this point of view, I find Tolle's version of it problematic. In fact, Tolle starts out on the wrong foot when, in the second statement, he says, because the mind is an "intrinsic part of the problem," it can never find a solution to this pain. The fact is, Tolle's mind did find a solution—by directing him to, and on, the spiritual path. If the mind were as pathetic as Tolle makes it out to be, it would never seek to transcend itself in the Spirit.

In the third statement, Tolle describes the mind-emotion relationship as often being that of a "vicious circle," wherein thinking and emotion reinforce each other. According to Tolle, "The thought pattern creates a magnified reflection of itself in the form of an emotion, and the vibrational frequency of the emotion keeps feeding the original thought pattern. By dwelling mentally on the situation, event, or person that is the perceived cause of the emotion, the thought feeds energy to the emotion, which in turn energizes the thought pattern, and so on." What Tolle fails to point out is the fundamental reason for the "vicious circle" between thought and emotion: that is, the mind's failure to "husband" emotion. When the conscious mind adopts rational and life-positive premises—appropriate values and standards—it simultaneously "programs" the subconscious mind with them. Emotions are automatic, subconscious responses to stimuli that reflect an individual's value judgments. If the conscious mind has programmed the subconscious with the right premises, then mind-emotion conflicts and vicious circles don't tend to occur.

The human mind is hardly impotent when it comes to dealing with emotional problems, and no one illustrates this better than Ayn Rand. Whereas Tolle takes a negative view of the mind as an "intrinsic part of the problem," Rand takes a positive view of the mind as the essential part of the "solution." Rand's view on the mind-emotion dynamic is an important one to consider for both atheists and spiritual seekers.

According to Rand, emotions are like computer printouts from a man's mind, informing him what he is feeling relative to particular things in his internal or external environment. What he feels relative to a particular thing stems from his value judgments, held implicitly or explicitly. If his value judgments are rational ones—meaning that they further his well-being and don't contradict the facts of reality—then his emotions will tend to be positive, enjoyable ones. On the other hand, if his conscious mind has "programmed" his subconscious with irrational, self-destructive premises that contradict the facts of reality, then he will suffer the consequences and experience emotional pain and conflict. In other words, as the computer information acronym GIGO informs us, "Garbage in, garbage out."

An emotion is an effect, not a cause. And if the effect is to be positive, the cause, the premises one holds, must be positive, meaning rational and life-affirming. Rand holds that there are two basic emotions: joy or suffering. If the former is to be the dominant emotion in a man's life, then he must consciously "program" his subconscious with the right premises. The mind and emotions can work in perfect harmony—but only when the mind is the conscious guide and emotions its automatic effect. If the roles are reversed and emotions are taken as the cause and the mind as their effect, then reason is abdicated, as the mind is reduced to the function of rationalizing or justifying one's feelings. As Rand warns, if a man subordinates his mind to his emotions—"*then* he is acting immorally, he is condemning himself to misery, failure, defeat, and he will achieve nothing but destruction—his own and that of others."

If we examine Tolle's mind-emotion "vicious circle" from a Randian (or Objectivist) perspective, the reason for the disorder is obvious: the man suffering from it has failed to subordinate his emotions to his mind. And the reason he has failed to do so is that he has not based his life on rational premises. Instead, by allowing his emotions, his whims and subjective feelings, to "reflect" his mind, he has, in effect, allowed the inmates to take over the *prison*.

In the last sentence, I purposely used the word *prison* to point out the limitation of the Randian (or Objectivist) perspective. Even though Rand establishes order in the "prison," a synonym for the human condition in esoteric teachings, she fails to recognize that the human condition, even when *rationally* ordered, is still a prison. A man's mind can rule his emotions—but it cannot, directly, free itself. The mind's nature, via the process of concept-formation, is to continually grasp, and this grasping activity contracts, or encloses, consciousness into one limited state after another. The mind functions under the illusion of absolute freedom because it can freely change its thinking, and hence its emotional state, in any moment. But this ability to change states is analogous to a man in prison who can freely change cells. He may upgrade from the "outhouse" cell to the "penthouse" cell, but in either case he is still in prison.

George Gurdjieff (1877–1949), a renowned Western mystic, said: "If you are to get out of prison the first thing you must realize is you are in prison." If, like a Randian Objectivist, you think that you're free (to "program" your emotional state) and don't acknowledge the underlying existential pain of your exile from the divine Source, then you won't concede that the fundamental human condition is one of "imprisonment," of separation and suffering. If, like Tolle and me, you see separation from Being as a primordial "pain" that can be excised only through spiritual enlightenment, then you'll seek oneness with the Divine as the solution to your root emotional "problem" of psychic imprisonment.

Though Tolle and I share the view that separation from Being is the cause of man's primordial pain, we differ markedly in our assessments of the human mind. Whereas Tolle makes it a point to denigrate man's mind, I make it a point to defend it. I have presented Rand's perspective relative to Tolle's mind-emotion vicious circle to illustrate the important point that, even though the mind cannot, by itself, escape from the prison of primordial separation and self-enclosure, the mind does indeed have the ability to break Tolle's mind-emotion vicious circle.

Can you elaborate on positive emotions such as love and joy and explain how they relate to enlightenment?

The Holy Spirit, the power of Now, *is* Love and Bliss. The degree to which you can tap into and channel the Holy Spirit, the Spirit-power of Being, is the degree to which you will experience love and bliss.

The degree to which you experience love and bliss can be expressed via a hierarchical scale. In Christian mysticism, for example, the following hierarchy is employed to describe levels of spiritual bliss:

Beatitude
Bliss
Joy
Pleasure

Beatitude represents the highest level of bliss because it is nondual in nature. When you are awake as a Christ or a Buddha, you no longer experience bliss as separate from your own nature. Instead, you are literally *being* It, and this feeling of *being* Bliss *is* Beatitude. As an awakened being, you spontaneously radiate your Blissful Energy as Blessing Power that serves to en-Light-en others.

Bliss is the experience of receiving Grace, the Blessing Power of the Holy Spirit. When, via the practice of Holy Communion, you achieve "locked-in" at-one-ment (*samadhi*) with the divine Being, the Holy Spirit pours down from above, infilling you with its blissful, en-Light-ening energy.

Joy is a happy state that ensues when individuals achieve or experience something meaningful to them. Because it involves the mind and the concept of time, it is peculiar to human beings. Joy is an emotional state that spontaneously intensifies the soul's *élan vital*.

Pleasure is the most superficial form of bliss and is experienced by animals as well as humans. It always involves the senses and has no redeeming spiritual value. It is simple enjoyment devoid of meaningfulness.

What is *love*? Spiritually speaking, it's the pure, radiant, Blessing Energy that stems from Being. And this Blessing Energy *is* the Holy Spirit, the power of Being. True spiritual life is simply a matter of directly tapping into the divine Being and *allowing* its Spirit-power, or Love-energy, to radiate through you.

It is beyond the capacity of human beings to selflessly radiate love. So you shouldn't feel depressed because you perceive yourself as incapable of selfless love. A true guru is not someone with a rare ability to love; a true guru is someone who has tapped into the Holy Spirit and allows *Its* Love to radiate though him and outshine all his lesser, "human," emotions. The Holy Spirit, or power of Now, *is* universal, *transcendental Love*, and the degree to which you can lock into the Now and allow *Its* Power to flow through you is the degree to which you are capable of selfless love.

Human beings are very capable of selfish love—of willfully channeling degrees of love on objects of their devotion—but as Tolle points out, such "love" can easily turn into "hate" when an object of devotion fails to meet one's standards. For example, a wife might love her husband dearly, but if she finds out he's been cheating on her by having sex with the neighbor, then her love can turn into hate in a heartbeat. Selfish love can be measured by the degree of one's devotion to an object; selfless love can be measured by the degree one can radiate the power of Now.

Peace, in and of itself, is hardly a deep state of Being—unless you believe a cow grazing in the grass is expressing its Buddha-nature. You can shoot an angry man full of tranquilizers and transform his state into a "peaceful" one, but not a spiritual one. I've been around plenty of so-called "peaceful" people who didn't radiate an iota of spiritual energy. The "peace that passeth understanding" is not that of a grazing cow, a drugged zombie, or a mindless simpleton; it is that of an individual rested in the Holy Spirit, the thought (and conflict)-transcending power of Now.

The Buddha says that "Nirvana is the destruction of craving." How is it possible to end all craving?

First, it is important to differentiate between natural desires and unwholesome craving. In Zen, the popular saying, "When I'm hungry I eat, when I'm tired I sleep" illustrates this point. A Zen master satisfies his biological drives sans conflict and is free of the cravings that beset unenlightened individuals.

Craving is the bodymind's attempt to heal the primal dis-ease of separation from Being. A Buddha is free of unwholesome craving because he is wholly at-one with the *Nirvanic,* or divine, Source.

Tolle is correct when he says not to seek to become free of craving. Craving is a symptom of the dis-ease of separation. Instead of dealing with the symptom of the dis-ease, root out the dis-ease itself by becoming present to, and at one with, the divine Source. Because the Light-energy, or *Sambhogakaya,* stems from the divine Source, en-Light-enment naturally accompanies a full and intense connection to the Source. Therefore, instead of seeking to "achieve" enlightenment, simply connect to the divine Source and allow its Light-energy, the *Sambhogakaya,* or Holy Spirit, to en-Light-en you.

The term *Buddha* is derived from the root *budh*, which means "to *know*." A Buddha is a being who, as free (or awakened) consciousness, *knows* that he is permanently one with Ultimate Reality, the *Nirvanic* Source. An "Awakened One" is simultaneously an "En-Light-ened One," because the Light, or radiant Energy, of his awakened (or permanently connected) consciousness outshines his mind, rendering it transparent and non-binding.

CHAPTER TWO

Consciousness and Pain

Pain in the Present Moment

Pain and sorrow are a reality. How should we deal with them?

There are three main *conscious* ways to deal with sorrow and *emotional* pain: 1) a Randian-type psycho-epistemological approach (summarized in Chapter One), wherein you reprogram your subconscious by cultivating rational, life-positive premises; 2) a classical yogic/Buddhist approach, wherein you disidentify from your mind and your suffering; and 3) a radical spiritual approach, wherein you transcend your pain by directly tapping into the healing power of the Now.

Tolle, in the first chapter of his book, emphasizes the classical yogic/Buddhist approach of disidentifying from the mind as the means to obviate pain. In his second chapter, he begins to describe the radical spiritual approach of non-avoidance of the Now as the means to stop the creation of pain. When Tolle identifies the creation of pain as the avoidance or denial of the Now, he is simply restating the *Eucharist* (the act of Holy Communion) in psychological terms. Connecting to the Now is tantamount to communing with the supreme Being, and channeling the power of Now is equivalent to receiving the Holy Spirit.

Although Tolle deifies the Now as the *Nirvana* beyond pain, shockingly, he never describes the power of Now in detail nor explains how it relates to the enlightenment process. *The Power of Now* is certainly a catchy title, but, unfortunately, it has little to do with the material in Tolle's book.

Tolle not only fails to describe the power of Now in detail, but he also fails to provide a graphic, holistic description of the act of avoiding the

Now. The denial or avoidance of the Now is not merely a matter of mind, as Tolle contends; it is a matter of the entire psycho-physical organism, the whole person. The avoidance of the Now is an act of whole-bodily recoil or retraction from the "position" of direct connectedness to the divine Being. The ordinary spiritual seeker has already retracted from whole-bodily oneness with Being into abstraction and becoming, so he mistakenly views the mind as the "problem." But the fundamental spiritual problem is *not* the mind. Rather, the fundamental spiritual problem *is* the avoidance of organismic intercourse with the Deity.

Eckhhart Tolle is a refined European gentleman, an ex-Cambridge scholar. And much of what he says is derived from the teachings of the late renowned mystic J. Krishnamurti, a European-educated Indian. Predictably, then, Tolle's words are rather flat and formal, lacking the descriptive fullness that does the mystical experience justice. In the highest mystical experience, the entire bodily-being is not merely present to the moment; it's also felt to be pressing against, even embracing, the radiant force field of the divine Being, which is ever prior to and beyond the moment. The divine Being floods the mystic-devotee with Its down-pouring *Shakti* (or Spirit-power), and when this *Shakti*, the Holy Spirit, penetrates the devotee's Sacred (or Mystic) Heart-center (just to the right of the center of the chest), the devotee experiences mystical oneness with the Deity. In the rarest mystics— those blessed with extremely intense *Shaktipat* (down-pouring *Shakti*, or Grace)—the forceful down-flow of the Holy Spirit, in a "timeless moment," severs the "knot of karma" in their Mystic Heart-center, thereby enabling them to unite forever with the divine Being.

Eckhart Tolle states that, "Time and mind are in fact inseparable." Tolle's statement is pure mystical poppycock. It is time and change, not time and mind, that are in fact inseparable. Mind is merely the faculty that measures time—rate of change relative to a standard—and that rate of change relative to that standard exists whether the mind recognizes it or not. For example, the Earth rotates 365 times in the course of its one-year orbit around the Sun. Whether the mind recognizes this cycle or not, it still exists. Just because the mind is rendered silent in mystical *samadhi* hardly negates the reality of time. Contrary to what Tolle says, even animals measure time in their own way. When birds migrate or a squirrel stores nuts for the winter, they are, implicitly, acknowledging the reality of time.

Tolle tells us to stop "creating" time. He says, "Realize deeply that the present moment is all you ever have. Make the Now the primary focus of your life." First, human beings do not create time; they simply recognize it as a reality. Second, the idea that the present moment is all we ever have sounds like a mantra Tolle extracted directly from a '70s LSD-inspired hippie manual. Anyone with his brain intact knows that before the "present moment" there were endless past moments, and that after the present moment there will be endless future moments. Anyone who drops past and future moments from the context of his life is going to end up in serious trouble. If you don't believe it, consider this: in 2008, renowned New Age guru Wayne Dyer was soliciting donations on public television for Baba Ram Dass, the now-needy author of the cult spiritual classic *Be Here Now*, who was hoping to retire in Maui.

A serious problem with Tolle is his tendency to conflate the present moment with the Now. The present moment, what conditionally *is,* is *not* the timeless Now. The present moment is the passing, or temporal, "now," not the changeless, or eternal, Now. The present moment can be, but isn't necessarily, a doorway to the Now. Being present to the moment opens the door to the Now—but unless you step across the threshold to the "other side," you'll simply be present to arising phenomena and oblivious to the noumenal Reality beyond it.

Many successful people live part of their lives in the present moment, but that doesn't grant them automatic access to the Now. For example, living in the manifest "now" is common for great artists and athletes, who possess the ability to single-pointedly focus their attention on immediate conditional phenomena. Many of these artists and athletes possess monstrous egos, so Tolle's claim that resistance to the present moment reflects the egoic mind hardly accords with the observable evidence.

The present moment is not always pleasant.

Eckhart Tolle says, "It is as it is," and "by watching the mechanics of the mind, you step out of its resistance patterns, and you can then *allow the present moment to be*." Put more descriptively, if you simply are present to your psychic content and allow it to be exactly as it is, without accepting or rejecting it, then it tends to dissolve, and the Now, which is prior to and beyond your mind, begins to make its presence felt.

Tolle says to accept the present moment "as if you had chosen it" and to "always work with it, not against it." Put more descriptively, the way to "accept" the present moment is simply to allow it to arise and fall of its own accord, and the way to "work with it" is simply to be whole-bodily present to, through, and beyond it.

Past and Present Pain: Transcending the Pain-Body

The "pain-body," according to Tolle, is a "negative energy field that occupies your body and mind." It is an invisible entity that, in his words, "consists of trapped life-energy that has split off from your total energy field and has become autonomous through the unnatural process of mind identification."

As far as I can determine, the term "pain-body" is unique to Eckhart Tolle. I Googled the term, and the only references I found pertained to Tolle and *The Power of Now*. But the concept of a pain-body-type entity is not unique, and the spiritual traditions of Daism and Hindu Kashmir Shaivism have an even better term to describe this entity: *self-contraction*.

I have already used the term *self-contraction* in this book, and I'll now elaborate on it further. In the ordinary (unenlightened) man, separation from Being, or the Now, has already occurred. He has *retracted* from

Being, or the Now, into incessant mental *abstraction* (conceptualization) and becoming (successive enclosed, limited states of Being). This retraction not only contracts a man's consciousness into enclosed and limited formations, it simultaneously—literally and viscerally— contracts his naturally happy, expansive feeling (or emotional) nature into a constricted psycho-energetic one, which could be termed a "pain-body."

In Buddhism, there is a great metaphor for the self-contraction. This metaphor, which Adi Da, the founder of Daism, calls the "hand/fist metaphor," provides a graphic example of the "mechanism" of consciousness that generates the self-contraction, or pain-body. Think of an open hand in the midst of infinite empty space. Now visualize the open hand closing into a fist. As soon as the open hand begins to close into a fist, the space inside the hand becomes compressed and closed off from the field of infinite empty space. The hand curling upon itself and forming a fist is analogous to the bodymind retracting from the Now by constantly grasping hold of concepts. Mental grasping "curls" consciousness into a closed-off, or separate, state—a contraction. And this contraction is the pain-body.

The self-contraction, or pain-body, can seem to be dormant or almost unnoticeable at times—but this is only because you've succeeded in distracting yourself or making yourself unconscious. If you busy yourself with endless tasks and diversions, you can temporarily become oblivious to the pain of separation. And if you watch enough TV, drink enough alcohol, or take enough drugs, you can also temporarily become comfortably numb to the pain. But when your ability to distract or numb yourself fails and you revert to your ordinary, default state of separate consciousness, your pain-body is always there to "greet" you.

Why are some pain bodies more pernicious than others? The tighter the "fist" of consciousness clenches, the more intense the self-contraction becomes. Conventionally happy people grasp less and worry less, but the only way to be unconditionally happy is to utterly eradicate the pain-body—and that can only happen when Grace, the power of Now, permanently opens the clenched fist of consciousness.

Tolle says that merely by observing or witnessing the pain-body, you can dissolve it. He claims that "sustained conscious attention" will enable you to "sever the link between the pain-body and your thought processes." Is he correct? Yes and no. As I've stated before, the practice of witnessing, or mindfulness, does enable you to *temporarily* dissolve mind-forms and emotions. But such a practice alone *cannot* fully or permanently eradicate the self-contraction, or pain-body. Why not? Because such practices involve will or effort, and these generate their own forms of contraction. Rightfully applied, will or effort can put you into the right, or *righteous*, position of direct and immediate relationship to the Divine, but only Grace, in the form of the Holy Spirit, can set you free. Only when the Holy Spirit pours into the Sacred Heart-center with enough power to "crack it open," will the self-contraction, or pain-body, be *permanently* dissolved. Until then, the pain-body, in one form or another, will continue to plague you.

In my opinion, an ideal way to better understand the pain-body and how to transcend it is to examine it in the context of two of the world's foremost wholistic spiritual traditions: Tibetan Vajrayana Buddhism and Christian mysticism. These two traditions share an important common denominator: They are "Trinitarian," meaning they believe that Ultimate Reality can best be explained in terms of three "dimensions," "bodies," or "persons." When the pain-body is considered in the context of these three bodies, not only does its "structure" become apparent, but the way through and beyond this structure also becomes clear.

Although various sects of Mahayana Buddhism, including Zen, subscribe to the doctrine of three bodies—the *Trikaya*—it is only in the highest *tantra* teachings of Vajrayana Buddhism that the realization or union of these three bodies is emphasized and properly understood. In Mahayana and Vajrayana Buddhism, the three bodies are the *Dharmakaya* (the Truth, or Essence, Body), the *Sambhogakaya* (the Bliss, or Light, Body), and the *Nirmanakaya* (the Emanation, or Transformation, Body).

In the practice of *Ati yoga* (a.k.a. *Dzogchen),* the highest tantra teaching of Vajrayana Buddhism, the goal is to realize the three bodies, or dimensions, of existence, as a single, indivisible unity. With this in mind, the *initiated* yogi simply remains present to the *Dharmakaya* (the Great Void, or formless, all-pervading divine Presence) and allows the *Sambhogkaya* (the continuum of blissful Light-energy emitted from the *Dharmakaya)* to irradiate his *Nirmanakaya* (his "emanated" psycho-physical vehicle).

Now, let's consider the pain-body relative to the three bodies of the *Trikaya.* The *Dharmakaya* has nothing to with the pain-body because it is pure, formless Presence—the divine Now. And the *Sambhogakaya* has nothing to with the pain-body because its nature is blissful Light-energy—the power of Now. The pain-body must therefore pertain to the *Nirmanakaya,* the psycho-physical body. The truth is, not only does the pain-body pertain to the *Nirmanakaya,* but the pain-body *is* the *Nirmanakaya* (the physically embodied yogi)—in the state of separation from the Now (the *Dharmakaya,* or Essence Body) and its Blessing Power (the *Sambhogakaya,* or Light-energy Body).

The fundamental, existential condition of separation from the pure Presence of the *Dharmakaya* and the Blessing (and Bliss-bestowing) Power of the *Sambhogakaya* is, in a word, *pain.* Although we, as separated and contracted entities, experience trickles of Grace, in the form of consoling pleasure and joy, our underlying naked condition is one of existential pain. The only way beyond this deep-seated angst— experienced in various forms of fear, sorrow, and anger—is through the unification of the three bodies of the *Trikaya.* In any moment that we can connect to the *Dharmakaya* (the presence of Now) and allow the *Sambhogakaya* (the power of Now) to infill us (the emanated *Nirmanakaya)* with saving Grace, the pain-body is instantly vanished, or outshined, in the mass, or body, of Light-energy poured down from above. When the *Sambhogakaya* (spiritual Light-energy) and the *Dharmakaya* (universal Consciousness) permanently unite in the opened Heart-center of the *Nirmanakaya,* Buddhahood is attained and the pain-body is forever vanquished.

In Christian mysticism, the three "bodies," or "persons," are the Father, the Holy Spirit, and the Son. Like the *Dharmakaya*, the Father is pure, formless, all-pervading Awareness—the Now. Like the *Sambhogakaya*, the Holy Spirit is pure, radiant Blessing Energy—the power of Now. And like the *Nirmanakaya*, the Son is the embodied disciple, who, upon full en-Light-enment, becomes Christ-like.

Prior to full enlightenment, or divine union, the disciple suffers whenever he is in the "fallen state" of separation from the Father and the Holy Spirit. The primal pain of separation begets the pain-body, and the mature disciple, realizing that his pain-body stems from his fallen, separate state, seeks to reunite with the Father and the Holy Spirit. In order to do so, and thus regain his primal state of wholeness (holiness), the disciple religiously practices the discipline, or concentrated act, of Holy Communion. He whole-bodily connects to and communes with the timeless, spaceless Presence that is the Holy Father, and he receives the Father's Blessing—the Holy Spirit, which "cleanses" him of his "sins," including the primal, or cardinal, one of separation.

When the Holy Spirit descends into, and through, the disciple, it infills him with radiant Light-energy that "heals" him by making him whole (or holy). In other words, the healing power of the Holy Spirit, the "Great Physician," not only relieves the blessed disciple of his primal pain of separation (in the form of the pain-body), it also enables him to experience his spiritual identity as a Christ-like Son who is one with his Holy Father. And when the Holy Spirit, in a "Grace-full" moment, pierces the *Gordian knot* in the disciple's Sacred Heart-center, separation and its attendant pain-body are vanquished forevermore, as the awakened disciple realizes the three persons, or hypostases, of the Godhead as eternally One.

What happens to the pain-body when consciousness breaks identification with it?

First of all, individuals don't necessarily identify with their pain-bodies. The pain-body is often experienced as an alien or demonic "body" that individuals want to rid themselves of but don't know how. If you suffer from a physical ailment, such as a cold or fever, you don't identify with it; you want to get rid of it. The same can be said of most psychic ailments. The problem isn't necessarily identification with the psychic ailment; rather, the problem usually is: 1) knowing how to get rid of the ailment, and 2) being skillful and disciplined enough to do so.

The essence of Tolle's argument relative to dissolving the pain-body is: "Unconsciousness creates it [the pain-body]; consciousness transmutes it into itself." "Unconsciousness," according to Tolle, is the "absence of the watcher," and consciousness is the presence of the watcher. Can the mere presence of the watcher transmute the pain-body into consciousness? Only temporarily, spasmodically, and partially. Tolle advises his readers to be the "ever-alert guardian of your inner space," which implies constant diligence and ceaseless discipline. The truth is, no one can maintain constant vigilance over his inner space. Such an act involves will and effort, and as the great Indian sage Ramana Maharshi put it, "Efforts are spasmodic, and so are the results."

Yes, when consciousness mindfully watches, or focuses attention on, modifications of itself in the form of the pain-body, the pain-body can seem to dissolve—but only for brief periods unless the practitioner has been "initiated" by the Holy Spirit. For until the Holy Spirit invades the practitioner's bodymind, it is not possible for him to sustain the dissolution of mind-forms and the concomitant pain-body for protracted periods of time. But once he receives the Holy Spirit, the power of Now, his attention can then rest in the down-pouring Current from above, which not only dissolves the pain-body, but also leads the practitioner into blissful states of mystical absorption.

Eckhart Tolle, for the first time in his book, defines the power of Now. He says that it is "the power of your conscious presence." But he fails to elaborate on this terse description, leaving it to readers to wonder whether this power is personal or divine in nature. And if it is divine, what is its relationship to Hindu *Shakti*, the Buddhist *Sambhogakaya*, and the Christian Holy Spirit? Sad to say, Tolle fails to answer these important questions.

Ego Development and the Pain-Body

Eckhart Tolle tells us that "ego identification with the pain-body" due to "absence of the watcher" is the fundamental cause of human suffering. But what he doesn't tell us is how important it is for an individual to undergo ego development before he can even get to the point of wanting to disidentify from his pain-body.

Only an individual with a developed ego, with self-esteem, will seek to understand the root cause of his suffering, and then strive to eradicate it. A person with a developed, or mature, ego truly values his life and will do everything possible to maximize his happiness and minimize his suffering. Such an individual is a likely candidate to investigate the field of esoteric spirituality, in the hopes of finding a remedy for his pain and a means to increase his joy.

Whereas an individual with a developed, or mature, ego will seek self-growth in every important area of his life, an individual with an immature, or undeveloped, ego will simply stagnate or self-destruct due to a lack of positive self-concern. People who are plagued with deficient, unhealthy egos often wallow in self-made misery, staunchly identifying with their pain-bodies and stubbornly resisting solutions to alleviate their suffering.

My late mother, unfortunately, was a person who suffered from a deficient, unhealthy ego. All she ever did, or wanted to do, was complain about her pain. But when my sister and I would give her positive suggestions to help her feel better—quit smoking and junk food; start exercising, and get some fresh air and sunshine—she would ignore our advice and continue her self-destructive habits.

People like my mother are almost hopeless. But, again, their problem is not ego, but lack of ego, lack of self-esteem. Anyone who is sane and rational cares about their own well-being, and anyone who cares about their own well-being will seek to eliminate pain and misery from their life. They will adopt a healthful lifestyle and seek to understand and eradicate the causes of psychological distress in their life. Such people do not identify with their pain-body. They perceive their pain-body as an alien entity that they want to rid themselves of, but they lack the wherewithal to do so. So they read spiritual books like *The Power of Now* to help them understand the root cause of their pain and the way to eliminate or transcend it. But if they didn't possess mature egos and rational self-concern, they would never get to the point of serious spiritual seeking. Hence, it could be said that it is ego-deficiency, rather than ego-identification with the pain-body, that is at the root of human suffering.

In order to extirpate the pain-body, Eckhart Tolle, again, recommends that you "stay present as the witness," which he says will initiate the pain-body's transmutation in the "fire" of consciousness. But what Tolle's doesn't tell you regarding the fire of consciousness is this: The real fire of consciousness is the *Baptist Fire*, the Holy Spirit. And only when your spiritual practice progresses from rudimentary witnessing to locked-in communion with the Deity, the Holy One, can you "pull down" the Fire from Above, the true power of Now.

Fear and Separation

Fear seems to be the most basic, underlying emotion. Why does it rule our lives, and what can be done to get rid of it?

As long as you perceive yourself as a separate entity whose existence could be snuffed out at any moment, it's perfectly natural to experience fear. And because everything in this world is impermanent, you're threatened by the loss of not only your own existence, but of every being or thing you hold dear.

Eckhart Tolle rightly states that fear "comes in many forms: unease, worry, anxiety, nervousness, tension, dread, phobia, and so on." But the "structure" of every form of fear is the same: there is you, an apparently separate entity, and there some object (an entity or an event) that in some way threatens your well-being. Hence, until you can transcend the self-other (subject-object) duality, fear will continue to be a reality in your life.

Because fear is the most pervasive emotion, it is usually what turns people to religion. Although it is true that through fanatical religious belief—exemplified by terrorists who willingly, even gleefully, sacrifice their lives for a cause—fear can temporarily be transcended, no rational person would ever opt for such cultic brainwashing. Consequently, unless being transformed into a brainwashed zombie is your cup of tea, you'll want to find a more enlightened way to deal with your fear.

Since your fear is a product of your separation from the divine Source, the most rational and enlightened way to deal with it is to eliminate your separation. And the only way to do that is through *yoga*, the taproot of all religions. Yoga, according to *Merriam Webster's Third Unabridged Dictionary*, is the "union of the individual self with the universal Spirit." Yoga, in essence, is the mystical practice of removing the interval between man and Spirit. Therefore, the more you practice true yoga—fully and intensely connecting to the divine Source, absolute Spirit—the more you'll find your fear fading. And when divine union is finally attained, separation and fear are vanquished forevermore.

The Ego's Avoidance of Wholeness

From the radical spiritual point of view, the ego is the separate-self sense created by the self-retraction from the Whole, meaning the universal Spirit and the universe. The self-retraction from the Whole—the moment-to-moment act of avoiding relationship to the present moment and the divine Being behind it—generates a contraction in the universal field of consciousness, and this self-contraction results in a separate-self sense, the ego.

The ego, as Tolle rightly states, is a "derived sense of self." In other words, the ego-centric, or self-centric, act of retracting from the divine Being, or Self, creates a separate and contracted, or exclusive and reductive, Being, or Self—the ego-self. Thus, from a spiritual perspective, the ego-self can be viewed as a derivative of the divine Being, or Self.

Because the ego-self, as a contracted and apparently separate entity, feels estranged from the Whole, it experiences various existential dis-eases of separation, such as fear, emptiness, isolation, and incompleteness. And because every dis-ease has its craving, the ego-self unconsciously attempts to heal its dis-ease of separation, its lack of wholeness (or oneness with the Whole), by seeking fulfillment through various external things, such as work, possessions, relationships, social status, and so forth.

Tolle is correct in his damning assessment of the un-whole (or unholy) human condition, but the Vipassana-type practice of mindful witnessing that he recommends does not provide a wholistic solution to the problem. This type of practice is partial and reductive for at least three reasons:

1. It is a "head" practice that does not involve the *whole* person, the entire bodymind, the incarnate *soul*. The act of communion, in contrast, is a whole-bodily "gesture," or *mudra*, that directly and immediately integrates the whole person into, and potentially beyond, the present moment.

2. The meditative act of mindful witnessing is *not* a full, wholistic expression of consciousness, and as such, does not feel complete or right. The meditative act of whole-bodily communion, or relationship, in contrast, is *the* full, wholistic expression of consciousness, and it does feel complete and right. Communion, or relationship, is consciousness + oneness (consciousness directly, immediately, and organismically plugged into, and potentially through, the present moment). As such, it is the fullest and most intense form of meditation possible. Moreover, communion, or relationship, as the definitive *function* of consciousness relative to life, spontaneously includes and transcends the *sub-function* of mindful witnessing.

3. Mere watching or witnessing alone is an un-whole (or unholy) "spiritual" practice because it doesn't directly involve the Spirit—the Holy Spirit. It is *Siva* without *Shakti*. In other words, it is an exclusive-reductive "male" practice that ignores the "female" role of Grace-reception, or *Shaktipat*, in the enlightenment process. The mystical practice of Holy Communion, in contrast, is about wholeness in every way: the whole person wholly connecting to the Whole and receiving the whole influx of Blessing Power from above.

Tolle ends his subchapter on the ego's search for wholeness by describing the negative activity of the egoic mind and the way beyond it. Your egoic mind, according to Tolle, identifies with external things that are not you, and it is your attachment to and craving for these things that creates your suffering. Because death is the stripping away of all these things, Tolle enjoins you to die to them before you physically die. Tolle says, "The secret to life is to 'die' before you die—and find that there is no death."

The way of ego death that Tolle recommends—*disidentification* from everything external to your true spiritual identity—is, by itself, a one-dimensional, rather than a wholistic, spiritual practice. Moreover, Tolle doesn't provide specifics regarding the implementation of his recommended practice.

What Tolle doesn't tell you about the practice of *disidentification* is this: It is part of a wholistic spiritual process, but to emphasize it exclusively, outside the full context of this process, results in an incomplete state of en-Light-enment. The process of spiritual enlightenment is analogous to generating electrical light. Before the light can shine, the lamp (bodymind) must be plugged in (oneness), turned on (awareness), and the current allowed to flow (disidentification). Just as the current, or energy, that flows through the lamp's circuit must be unimpeded for the light to shine, likewise the spiritual current, or energy, must be unobstructed if the yogi is to radiate as the Light of the Self. By disidentifying from his thought-forms (which contract or obstruct the spiritual current, the Holy Spirit), the yogi is able to "die" to his relative self and awaken to his absolute Self. And the way the truly wholistic yogi disidentifies from his thought-forms is simply by allowing the spiritual current, the Holy Spirit, to outshine them, vanishing them as they arise.

CHAPTER THREE

Living in the Now

The Mental Search for Self

I feel that there is so much for me to learn about my mind before I'm ready for spiritual enlightenment or full consciousness.

You're wrong. Spiritual enlightenment is not a psychological growth process whereby you learn more and more about yourself until cumulative self-knowledge morphs into illumination. Spiritual en-Light-enment is an *energetic* process whereby you channel progressively greater intensities of Spirit-power, or Light-energy, until you awaken. When the Spirit-power is sufficiently violent, it severs your Heart-knot, and you spontaneously recognize yourself as *Siva*—inseparably united with *Shakti* in an eternal Dance.

Tolle, correctly, recommends being *present* as a way to transcend unconsciousness and identification with the finite self, but he fails to elaborate on how being fully present, or conscious, actually translates into spiritual enlightenment. He says not to seek your self in the mind, but he doesn't explain how the practice of *presence* enables you to "locate" your "true self rooted in Being." "The devil is in the details," the saying goes, and if your reading doesn't extend beyond Tolle's simplistic platitudes, you will encounter him when the descent of the Divine's power makes your spiritual life more complex. If you're a serious spiritual seeker, you will do yourself a favor by studying the greatest tantric traditions: Vajrayana Buddhism, Hindu Kashmir Shaivism, and Daism. They'll provide what Tolle doesn't—practical knowledge about the Divine's power, the true power of Now.

The Reality of Time

Disidentification from the mind seems like an impossible task. How do you end it?

The key is the Holy Spirit. The way to disidentify from your mind is to *let go* and *allow* the Power, or Light-energy, of the Holy Spirit to vanish your thoughts by outshining them. But before this "outshining" can happen, you must first be *baptized* by the Holy Spirit. And this baptism, or *initiation* by Spirit-force, spontaneously occurs when your practice of Holy Communion (*presence* + *oneness*) is sufficiently "locked-in" and unobstructed.

Tolle says the key to disidentification from the mind is "ending the delusion of time." As I explained in Chapter Two, time is a reality, not a delusion, and anyone who chooses to function under the illusion that time is unreal runs the risk of ruining his life.

As a means to transcend time, Tolle enjoins us to "honor and acknowledge the present moment and *allow it to be*." What if a crazed criminal were about to kill your child, would you simply "honor" and allow it? I don't know about you, but if I had a gun on me, I'd pull it out and shoot the bastard. Tolle's idea of "allowing" relative to the present moment is not only irrational and irresponsible, but in some cases it is even immoral.

Time is very precious. Without it we couldn't function in the world and our lives would have no meaning.

Time is the measure of change and becoming. As long as there is change and becoming, meaning manifest existence, there is time. To deny the reality of time is to deny the reality of the manifest. If time is an illusion, as Tolle claims, then the world, by implication, is also unreal. If you believe the world is unreal, then time isn't precious at all. If, on the other hand, you accept the reality you perceive via your senses and mind, then time, necessarily, becomes very important.

Tolle states that the Now is "the most precious thing" because it is "the *only* thing.... It's all there is." Tolle then tells us that the Now is the "only point that can take [an individual] beyond the limited confines of the mind... the only point of access into the timeless and formless realm of Being." Tolle's statements raise a few questions: If the Now is the *only* thing, then why does Tolle describe it as a "point of access" into Being rather than *as* all-inclusive Being itself? Why does he create a division between the Now and Being, with the implication being that the Now is a separate point of access that leads to transcendent Being? If the timeless Now is a "point" of access, what, exactly, is this point? We know it can't be the present moment, the ephemeral now, which, as Tolle says, is simply passing phenomena rooted in "illusory time." What, then, is this "point of access"? Tolle fails to tell us.

Nothing Happens Outside the Now

Since the present has no meaning without the past and future, aren't the past and future just as real and important?

Don't confuse the "present moment" with the timeless Now. In reality, because change is ceaseless, there can be no such thing as a "timeless" present moment. The instant you take a snapshot of the so-called present moment, it has already changed. There is nothing wrong with referring to a series of immediate events as the present moment, just as long as you remember that the present moment pertains to a time frame and not to the timeless now.

As long as you perceive yourself to be a separate entity existing in space and time, past and future will be real and important to you. As a cognitive entity, your life would have no meaning without the past and the future as reference points. And without a "past" and a "future," you couldn't even conceive of a "present moment."

Are the past and the future real? As real as phenomena! Phenomena are things changing, and things can only change if time is a reality. Thus, if you deny the reality of time, you also deny the reality of phenomenal existence.

According to Tolle, "Nothing ever happened in the past; it happened in the Now. Nothing will ever happen in the future; it will happen in the Now." Even if, as Tolle contends, the timeless Now, the all-pervading Being or Presence underlying phenomenal existence, is the context within which all change occurs, this does not mean that life doesn't also simultaneously happen in time. Consider the analogy of a man in an indoor pool. He is at once swimming in a building (analogous to timelessness) and in a pool (analogous to time). But if we apply Tolle's exclusive and reductive perspective to this situation, we would only acknowledge the reality of the building (timelessness), while denying that of the pool (time).

Tolle says that past and future "obviously have no reality of their own," that their reality is "'borrowed' from the Now." Contrary to what Tolle says, it isn't the least bit "obvious" that past and future are merely the "borrowed" reality that he claims they are. If it were obvious, there would be universal agreement, rather than universal disagreement, with his assessment of time.

Tolle summarizes his only-the-Now-exists argument by stating that it "cannot be understood by the mind." He is wrong. All understanding is via the mind, via mental concepts. Whether an experience is a mystical one or an emotional one, it can only be understood via the process of thought. Mystical experience—direct, immediate contact with the Absolute—results in *gnosis* (higher knowledge), but even this gnosis is only understanding by the mind.

Openings to the Spiritual Dimension

Dangerous, life-threatening situations can produce a shift in consciousness in a man. But does this shift into a state of intense alertness and stillness provide an opening to the spiritual dimension? Yes, if a man knows how to take advantage of the heightened intensity resulting from the situation.

An ordinary man's usual mental state is that of *con-fusion*, resulting from the lack of *fusion*. This *confusion*, which is caused by *diffuse* thoughts competing with each other, is temporarily obviated in life situations that demand a man's full attention. In such situations, a man's mind becomes still because it is undividedly focused on the present moment. This engrossment in the moment often results in a state of exhilaration, the feeling of intensified aliveness. And, consciously or unconsciously, it is this state of exhilaration, this feeling of intensified aliveness, which a man seeks when he devotes himself to a dangerous, life-threatening sport or activity.

The intensified aliveness available in dangerous situations does not have a spiritual dimension. If it did, Green Berets, Mafia hit men, and professional martial artists would all be Buddhas. There is only one true spiritual dimension—the *Sambhogakaya,* or Holy Spirit—and the sheer intensity of life-threatening situations provides nothing more than an opening to this realm of Spirit-power.

An opening to the realm of Spirit is nothing special; it is simply a favorable opportunity to access the spiritual dimension, the Holy Spirit, or power of Now. The power of Now is ever-present, so it is always available to access. But certain conditions facilitate this Holy connection, and such conditions are sometimes referred to as "openings."

Openings to the spiritual dimension abound, so you don't need to take up extreme skiing or join forces with super-agent Jack Bauer in order to access the power of Now. In fact, you can create your own opening to the Divine any time you choose. All you have to do is to be consciously present and ask God to bless you with His Power. By opening (or being empty, or "absent") in the context of being present (to God, or Being), you allow yourself to receive the Benediction, the descent of Divine power, the true power of Now.

◇ ◇ ◇

Eckhart Tolle states that "Since ancient times, spiritual masters of all traditions have pointed to the Now as the key to the spiritual dimension." And yet, says Tolle, "It seems to have remained a secret... not taught in churches and temples."

Tolle is correct when he says that mystical truth has remained a secret not taught in churches and temples, but he doesn't tell us why. Mystical truth has remained a secret because most mystics, like Tolle himself, are incapable of explaining the spiritual process in a clear-cut, systematic way. Mystics like Tolle blur, rather than define, their terms, and the mystical experience is thus reduced to an "ineffable" or "unspeakable" epiphany that can't be spoken of coherently. And for this reason, churches and temples don't teach it.

Tolle seems allergic to defining and delineating his terms. For example, he never tells us what the "spiritual dimension" is or how—or if—it differs from "Being," the "Now," and the "power of Now." Tolle bemoans the fact that churches don't "seem to realize that [Jesus' teachings] are meant to be lived and so bring about a profound inner transformation." "Profound inner transformation?" What might that be? Such a nebulous description could just as easily pertain to puberty as it does to enlightenment.

Is it true, as Tolle asserts, that the "whole essence of Zen consists in walking along the razor's edge of Now?" No, it isn't. The Japanese term *Zen* is derived from the Chinese term *Ch'an*, which, in turn, is derived from the Indian Sanskrit term *Dyhana*. *Dyhana* means meditation; therefore, the essence of Zen Buddhism is simply any practice of meditation that helps lead you to Buddhahood.

If you seriously study Zen, which I did for years, you won't find any clear, concise instructions on how to directly and immediately access the Now. In fact, the Now, or eternal Presence, is scarcely mentioned in Zen literature. Most Zen "instruction" books emphasize directives enjoining you to cease clinging and empty your mind, or *koans* (paradoxical conundrums or questions) designed to confound your discursive thought processing. In either case, the goal is the same: to stop your mind from thinking, much like the spiritual practice Tolle himself recommends.

Even though Zen, as a Mahayana Buddhist sect, pays lip service to the *Trikaya* (the *Dharmakaya, Sambhogakaya,* and *Nirmanakaya,* the three dimensions, or bodies, of the Absolute), virtually no Zen practitioners I've read or met can tell you what the *Sambhogakaya* is. Zen, in other words, is a reductive, two-dimensional religion that doesn't account for Being as radiant Light-energy (the *Sambhogakaya,* or power of Now). Therefore, if your interest is the power of Now, don't expect to find any useful information on the subject in Zen Buddhism.

In order to bolster his argument that time is unreal, Eckhart Tolle quotes the thirteenth-century mystic and poet Rumi, who declares, "Past and future veil God from our sight; burn up both of them with fire."

The "fire" that Rumi recommends is, of course, the fire of spiritual consciousness. Can this fire burn up the past and future? If you *erroneously* believe that time is only psychological, merely a product of your mind (which can only function in a past-future context), then spiritual consciousness can certainly incinerate the past and future. But if you *correctly* know that time is an existential reality exclusive of your mind, then spiritual consciousness cannot burn up time; it can only, like the light from fire, outshine it.

Tolle also quotes Meister Eckhart, the brilliant thirteenth-century Dominican, who says, "There is no greater obstacle to God than time." The time that Meister Eckhart is talking about is psychological time, *not* existential time. The eternal human soul is never touched by time, yet it lives in time; and to deny the reality of that time is, in effect, to evict yourself from manifest reality.

Connecting to the Power of Now

When I transcend thinking and look at nature, it somehow seems more alive. For example, when I look at a tree, its colors seem brighter and more vibrant. It's almost as if I can feel its essence or inner spirit.

It's not uncommon for people who meditate to experience heightened sense perception. The same thing can be said about people who do drugs, particularly psychedelics. When the mind becomes silent, the energy of consciousness that is ordinarily devoted to conceptualization is transferred to perception, which then becomes more acute. Consequently, a tree's colors appear brighter and sharper, and it's almost as if you can feel the tree's life-energy, its vibrations.

Tolle claims that when you perceive the tree "without the screen of the mind," a "different kind of knowing" is awakened in you: "A knowing that does not destroy the sacredness and mystery of life but contains a deep love and reverence for all that is. A knowing of which the mind knows nothing."

What is this "different kind of knowing" that Tolle exalts? He doesn't say. And he doesn't, and can't, say because there is no such thing as a "different kind of knowing." Only two kinds of knowing are available to human beings: perception and conception. "Psychic" and "spiritual" perception are certainly realities, but they do not represent a "different kind of knowing"; they merely represent different *levels* of knowing. A psychic might be able to "see" what the ordinary person can't, such as auras and karmas, but the structure of her seeing, or perception, is identical to that of the ordinary person: awareness perceiving, or sensing and recognizing, the existence of distinct entities or phenomena. A yogi might perceive his *chakras* vibrating or his *kundalini* rising, but his perception of these spiritual phenomena does not represent a "different kind of knowing"; it simply represents a *deeper,* or *more subtle,* level of knowing.

Does this deeper, subtler level of mind-free "knowing" that Tolle speaks of preserve the "sacredness and mystery of life?" No, it doesn't.

"Sacredness" and "mystery" are merely concepts that have no basis in objective reality. If anything in the universe were truly, inherently sacred, then it wouldn't be subject to decay and death. If a wolf pack spots a "precious" little baby alone in the woods, does it perceive it as sacred? No, it perceives it as lunch! From the viewpoint of the universe, which is an impersonal machine of perpetual creation and destruction, no *thing* is special or sacred.

Eckhart Tolle loves to *selectively* quote Zen masters. If he were truly interested in an objective consideration of "sacredness," he would have included the following famous exchange between Bodhidharma, the Indian monk who introduced Zen (Ch'an) to China, and his disciple.

> Disciple: Why have you brought Zen to China?
>
> Bodhidharma: To introduce the Sacred Doctrine.
>
> Disciple: What is the Sacred Doctrine?
>
> Bodhidharma: That nothing is sacred. That all things are empty and not worth seeking after.

Is life a "mystery"? Only to beings that marvel at it or seek to make sense of it. In and of itself, life is simply existence existing, without answers or questions. It has no intrinsic meaning. Whatever meaning or mystery you choose to attribute to it is nothing but a collection of concepts filling the mind that Tolle, continually, tells you to keep empty.

If you're able to perceive life "without the screen of the mind," as Tolle recommends, will "love and reverence for life" awaken within you? It certainly didn't for the original Buddhists. In his classic text *Buddha and the Gospel of Buddhism*, renowned Buddhist scholar Ananda Coomaraswamy (1877–1947) describes the early Buddhists' attitude toward the world:

> But the early Buddhists, like so many other enthusiasts, used their share of truth for the denial of others: they were so convinced of the sorrows of the world that they

could not sympathize with its joys… [The] early Buddhist literature as a whole is filled with a contempt of the world which inevitably precludes sympathy with its hopes and fears.… The early Buddhist could not possibly grasp the thought that "The soul of sweet delight can never be defiled."

Contrary to what Tolle says, love and reverence for life do not stem from an empty mind. The truth is, love and reverence for what exists can only awaken when one's mind establishes and maintains a philosophic value system that ascribes positive value to life. The great humanists and philanthropists throughout history—men and women who never sought to empty their minds, but yet devoted their lives to making the world a better place—are proof that love and reverence for life do not depend on a "knowing beyond the mind."

According to Tolle, the human mind is incapable of knowing directly. Tolle says, "The mind cannot know the tree. It can only know facts or information *about* the tree.… Being alone knows directly." Tolle's argument that only Being can know an object *directly* is pure mystical hokum. What is this direct "knowing" by Being? Tolle doesn't say. What does this "knowing" know? Again, Tolle is silent. What can Tolle or any sage who is one with Being tell us about a tree that a certified tree expert can't? Nothing that I'm aware of—and I say this as a yogi who has devoted forty years of his life to studying and practicing what the great sages and spiritual traditions preach.

Although I've devoted my life to the practice of spiritual meditation, and although I have experienced, and continue to regularly experience, profound *samadhis*—protracted mystical states of bliss, light, energy, and pure empty-minded awareness—I'm still incapable of "knowing a tree directly." Perhaps your luck with trees will be better than mine.

Tolle, rightly, states that a glimpse of the timeless is not enough. What is needed, he says, is a "permanent shift in consciousness." And to this end, he recommends self-observation, which he says, automatically morphs into mere *presence*. From my experience as a meditation practitioner and teacher, I have not found that the practice of self-observation naturally morphs into mere *presence*. Self-observation, as I have stated, is an exclusive-reductive, concentrative "head" practice. In contrast, *plugged-in presence*, the practice that I unqualifiedly recommend, is an integral, whole-body, "feeling" form of meditation, essentially the same as Tibetan Dzogchen and mystical Holy Communion. If you can practice *plugged-in-presence*, you won't have any interest in Tolle's Vipassana-type self-observation.

Self-observation, Tolle says, introduces a factor "that is not of the mind: the witnessing presence." Does mere self-observation naturally morph into the "witnessing-presence"? Not according to Jesus. In Acts 1:8, Jesus says, "But you shall receive power when the Holy Spirit has come upon you, and you shall be witnesses to Me." In other words, until the Holy Spirit, or power of Now, infuses you with its Light-energy, you cannot become a true or permanent witness to the Divine. Because human efforts are always spasmodic, no "permanent shift in consciousness" is possible without Grace, the Holy Spirit, empowering you with its perpetual Divine life-current.

Tolle says, "Identification with the mind gives it more energy; observation of the mind withdraws energy from it."

What Tolle is trying to say is this: The mind, as a continuum of thought-forms, modifies (or binds and contracts) consciousness from moment to moment, reducing its power. When consciousness, as the "witness," observes the mind, the thought-forms are dissolved, and the mind, now empty of contracting thought-forms, no longer reduces the power, or energy, of consciousness. Because the mind no longer reduces the energy of consciousness, the process of observing the mind *seems* to withdraw energy from it.

According to Tolle, "The energy that is withdrawn from the mind turns into presence."

Contrary to what Tolle says, merely dissolving thought-forms by observing them does not transform the mind into "presence." Moreover, Tolle here fails to explain what presence is. Presence is the state of being consciously present to the moment. When you are consciously present to the moment, you are being present *as* consciousness. When you are present *as* consciousness, you are *being* consciousness; and when you are *being* consciousness (while simultaneously channeling divine Blessing/Blissing Power), you *are* Being-Consciousness-Bliss (or *Sat-Chit-Ananda*).

Clock Time and Psychological Time

Clock time is real time, correlated to the Earth's rotation and solar orbit. Real time began when the universe began. The universe did not expand into space-time; the universe was the beginning of space-time. Space and time are inseparable; you cannot have one without the other. Space is the distance between objects. Without objects, the term *space* is meaningless. All manifested objects, even ones that seem inert, are intensely vibrating and constantly changing. Because motion, or change, is sequential, it can only take place in time. If time is unreal, then so is the universe.

Psychological time is entirely in your head: an hour of steamy sex can seem to last twenty minutes, while twenty minutes in a checkstand line can feel like an hour. And when you meditate, time can seem to disappear altogether.

I can admit the Now exists, but I don't agree that time is an illusion.

The universe, meaning all existing things in space-time, is a reality, not an illusion. The universe exists, and that alone qualifies it as real. Eastern mystics have labeled phenomenal reality an illusion because it veils the transcendental Reality underlying it. But that's like calling the thick coat of dust on a mirror an illusion simply because it blocks or distorts your reflection. The universe itself is not an illusion, but it can be said to possess an illusory quality in the sense that it hides transcendental Reality from the vision of ordinary men.

Time, as the measurable duration from past to present to future, is just as much a reality as the universe. And though time is not an illusion, it is illusory in the sense that it masks the eternal Now, preventing you from perceiving it. The eternal Now exists outside of the universe, outside of space and time. If it existed in space and time, it couldn't be the eternal Now. The eternal Now is an incomprehensible Domain; it is the Heaven of Christ, the Nirvana of Buddha.

The Sanity of Psychological Time

Eckhart Tolle is a virtual one-man crusade against the, ahem, horrors of psychological time. Psychological time to Tolle isn't merely a neurotic disorder; it is, in his words, "insanity... a serious mental illness."

To argue his point that psychological time is a mental disease with grave social consequences, Tolle cites future-driven ideologies that have led to mass enslavement, torture, and death. These ideologies, according to Tolle, include "communism, national socialism or any nationalism, or rigid religious belief systems which operate under the implicit assumption that the highest good lies in the future and that therefore the end justifies the means."

If mankind is to avoid the enslavement, torture, and death that these evil psychological-time intensive ideologies engender, the solution, it might seem, would be to replace them with an ideology that preaches the virtues of living in the Now. And what ideology could be more ideal for this than Zen Buddhism? After all, as Tolle informs us, "The whole essence of Zen consists in walking along the razor's edge of Now."

Luckily, we don't have to resort to speculation about the effect of integrating Zen's Now ideology into a time-intensive sociopolitical system. The case of Japan provides an empirical example that illustrates what can happen when a Now religion like Zen becomes intimately involved with an aggressive, future-oriented state. The following excerpt from Josh Baran's book review of *Zen at War*, by Brian Victoria (full review available at darkzen.com), provides an eye-opening look at the Japanese Zen establishment's complicity with Japan's imperial war machine in the nineteenth and twentieth centuries:

> *Zen at War* is a courageous and exhaustively researched book by Brian Victoria, a western Soto Zen priest and instructor at the University of Auckland. Victoria reveals the inside story of the Japanese Zen establishment's dedicated support of the imperial war machine from the late 1880's through World War Two. He chronicles in detail how prominent Zen leaders perverted the Buddhist teaching to encourage blind obedience, mindless killing, and total devotion to the emperor. The consequences were catastrophic and the impact can still be felt today...
>
> Victoria identifies Sawaki Kodo (1880–1965), one of the great Soto Zen patriarchs of this [20th] century as an evangelical war proponent. Serving in Russia as a soldier, he happily related how he and his comrades had "gorged ourselves on killing people." Later, in 1942, he wrote, "It is just to punish those who disturb the public order. Whether one kills or does not kill, the precept forbidding killing [is preserved]. It is the precept that wields the sword. It is the precept that throws the bomb."
>
> The "precept throws the bomb?" This is an astonishing abuse of Zen language. Kodo also advocated, as did other Zen teachers, that if killing is done without thinking, in a state of no-mind or no-self, then the act is an expression of enlightenment. No thinking = No-mind = No-self = No karma. In this bizarre equation, the victims are always left out, as if they were irrelevant. Killing is just an elegant expression of the koan.

When Colonel Aizawa Saburo was being tried for murdering another general in 1935, he testified, "I was in an absolute sphere, so there was neither affirmation nor negation, neither good nor evil." This approach to Zen is ultimately a perverse narcissism, or even nihilism. Of course, the obvious question that was never asked—if there is no self, why is there any need to kill?

Victoria has brought to light the actual words of those leaders and the written record of this period. *Zen at War* contains dozens of similar passages from leading teachers, proving that this distortion was the rule, not the exception. There were some pacifists, but they were few. Some priests who opposed the war may have quietly retired to distant country temples, but they probably left no record.

The marriage of Zen and the Japanese war machine demonstrates how warped a mind-averse Now ideology can become in the heat of a hellish political climate. Because Zen is a tunnel-vision religion that focuses on the Now while disparaging the mind that dwells on the past and the future, it never developed the strong ethical foundation that characterizes most other schools of Buddhism. Hence, while ideals such as compassion and non-violence are emphasized in non-Zen Buddhist sects, in Zen they are dismissed as superfluous concepts to be expunged from one's mind. The popular Zen saying, "If you meet the Buddha on the road, kill him," perfectly summarizes the Japanese Zen attitude toward anything mind-based, including the moral ideals so essential to making the world a more peaceful place.

And now a final rebuttal to Tolle's argument that future-driven ideologies are responsible for mass enslavement, torture and death: every industrialized nation—regardless of its government's ideology—is geared toward the future. It doesn't matter if the country is overtly Marxist, like Venezuela, or ostensibly capitalist, like the United States, the power elite behind the "throne" are constantly shaping and reshaping government policy with the future in mind. Since every modern government is driven by time, the principal reason that an ideology results in enslavement, torture, and death clearly is *not* a psychological obsession with time; rather, it is the totalitarian nature of the ideology itself. Ideologies that resort to enslavement, torture, and death have one key factor in common: a total disregard for individual rights, including the most important, the right to one's own life. And as the history of Japanese Zen proves, a Now ideology devoid of a strong ethical foundation can demonstrate just as much disregard for human life as a time-driven one.

Negativity, Suffering, and Time

I don't believe it's an illusion that things can get better in the future. No matter how bad things are in the present, the future can be better.

It's certainly possible for the future to be better. Although it's true that the majority of people will, out of habit, maintain the same mindset and level of happiness in the future, some will consciously upgrade their mindset and thus experience increased joy. For example, I know a man who was paralyzed below the waist in a car accident. After the accident, his wife divorced him and his income dropped by 90%. Now, just months after the accident, he tells me that he is happier than ever thanks to a radical new outlook on life.

A new outlook on life can no doubt reduce suffering and increase joy in a man's life. But it cannot enlighten him or enable him to experience the divine bliss of the Spirit, which transcends the mere joy of the mind. Whereas joy is a conditional emotion, based on mental associations, bliss is an unconditional feeling, derived from a direct connection to the Spirit.

Tolle states that "true change" can only occur by accessing the Now, but he doesn't say what this change is. So I will do it for him. True change, or "conversion," occurs when your connection to the Now is full enough and intense enough to awaken the power of Now, the Holy Spirit. The initial awakening of the power of Now is true spiritual baptism, and this baptism by the Spirit means that you are "born from above." Once you've been baptized by the Holy Spirit, you can, at any time, plug into this down-pouring Power from above. This down-pouring Power, the descent of the Divine, floods your entire being with radiant Light-energy that outshines your suffering, negativity, and bondage to time. This alone is "true change."

If you're looking for the bogeyman that makes your life miserable, your search is over. Eckhart Tolle has identified the culprit, and his name is Father Time. According to Inspector Tolle (who probably worked with Scotland Yard on this case), "Time is the cause of your suffering or your problems."

Inspector Tolle, unsurprisingly, is wrong again. Father Time is innocent; the real cause of your suffering or your problems is your mindset, your value judgments. For example, whereas an optimist might view a divorce as an exciting new opportunity, a pessimist might perceive it as just pain and suffering. Some men are untroubled by their hair loss; other men anguish over theirs. A righteous vegetarian would suffer if forced to eat a Big Mac; a typical kid rejoices when he dines at the Golden Arches.

Even *everyone's* most fundamental existential pain—separation from Being or the Now—is not caused by time. It is caused by the habit pattern of retracting from Being into self-contraction, which fuels *becoming,* constant change of state in search of *Nirvana,* permanent oneness with Being. Being is outside of time, and though both your existential pain and mundane problems exist in time, time is simply the medium for, not the cause of, your suffering.

Locating the Bliss-Current Underneath Your Life Situation

I'm extremely unhappy now. The present moment is hellish. I don't know what I'd do without hope, the possibility of an improved future.

An improved future is possible, but it will never be *Nirvana*, which exists beyond time, in the Now. Even if your future state is better, it will be temporary and subject to deterioration. A man may seemingly have "everything"—good health, money, and a loving family—but he is always at risk of losing some or all of it. Ultimately, everything will be taken from us. That is why, as the Buddhas tell us, there is no desirable state or condition. Only Being, the non-state, is *Nirvana;* everything else, including an improved future, is *samsara*, the endless cycle of becoming.

Tolle is correct when he states, "You cannot be both unhappy and fully present in the Now at the same time." The Now is Immanence, and the future is hope. When you are fully, *spiritually*, present in the Now, unhappiness and hope both disappear, dissolved in Immanence, the *Nirvanic* Bliss-current of the supreme Being.

I know that my present life situation is a result of my past actions, but that doesn't make my present situation any better.

Instead of stewing about your life situation, place your attention on your life-energy.

What's the difference between the two?

Obsessing about your life situation further implicates you in *samsara*, the vicious cycle of *becoming*. Focusing your attention on formless life-energy leads you to Divine life-energy, the power of Now.

Your life situation represents the surface of your being—mental activity preoccupied with one problem after another. When you free your attention from your mind-forms and place it on the formless life-energy underneath your mental activity, you can become one with the Power that lives you. The easiest way to connect to formless life-energy is via your breath. Breath is the most tangible expression of formless life-energy, and by directing your full attention to your breathing cycle, you can intensify your life-energy current, feel it, and consciously merge with it.

Buddhist Vipassana meditation applied to breathing is just observation of the breath cycle. While there is nothing wrong with this clinical type of observation, it is not the method of conscious *pranayama* (or breath-related spiritual practice) that I recommend.

What I recommend instead is that you be fully present to your breath cycle, in direct relationship to it. Instead of merely watching your in-breaths and out-breaths, which is a reductive "head-only" practice, be consciously present *as* the whole body relative to your breath cycle. (If you randomly, periodically, for brief moments, place your attention on your hands and the center of the lower half of your forehead, you may find that this momentary "centering" helps you to establish yourself in and as whole-bodily presence.) Once you establish whole-bodily presence, you can assume this wholistic *asana* (or psycho-physical "posture") relative not only to your breath cycle, but to everything.

When you are fully present to life, in direct relationship to existence, you are, in effect, practicing what true Christianity preaches: Holy Communion. Communion with the breath cycle has an alchemical effect: your presence plugged into, or combined with, your breathing intensifies your life-energy current. When the life-energy current is sufficiently intensified, it is felt as a living Force. This Force exerts pressure; it wants to move. If you yield to this pressure while maintaining your "posture," or "stance," of Holy (or whole-bodily) Communion, this living Force will pour down through the frontal half of your head and your body. The descent of this living Force is the awakened power of Now. If you remain consciously present to this Power, you will spontaneously merge with it, and your true, or transcendental, "life-energy" will then reveal itself as radiant Light-energy.

As a means to "finding the life underneath your life situation," Tolle enjoins you to: "Use your senses fully. Be where you are. Look around. Just look, don't interpret. See the light, shapes, colors, textures...

Listen to the sounds, don't judge them…Touch something—anything—and feel and acknowledge its Being… Allow the 'isness' of all things. Move deeply into the Now."

Tolle's recommendation to "use your senses fully" is good advice for achieving psychosomatic relaxation. By shifting your mode of consciousness from conceptual abstraction to perceptual awareness, your mind relaxes its habitual grasping and you experience some moments of peaceful silence. These moments can provide a "jumping-off point" to real spiritual meditation, but in and by themselves they do not qualify as spiritual contemplation. Real spiritual meditation or contemplation must involve conductivity of the Spirit-force. If it doesn't, then it's not real spiritual practice. Tolle glibly uses the terms "Being" and "isness," but until you are *initiated* by the Holy Spirit and experience its *Baptism by Fire,* its radiant intensity invading and outshining your individual being, these terms remain mere abstractions. Being *is* Consciousness-Power (*Siva-Shakti*). But until you awaken the power of Being and consciously receive it as *Shaktipat,* the poured-down Holy Spirit, *Siva* and *Shakti* remain estranged, and you cannot coincide with the divine Being. "Is-ness," like "Being," remains a mere concept until you can literally spiritually *be* (consciousness-power). It's cool to acknowledge the *being-ness* of things, but until you awaken to your own true spiritual (or *Shakti*-empowered) *being-ness*, "is-ness" is no more than a mental projection.

All Problems Are in Your Mind

What about problems? They never seem to end. When I meditate, my problems are forgotten. But they return after I'm done. Am I just temporarily escaping from them?

There are no problems in reality. Reality is simply what exists, and what exists is never problematic—except to a mind that identifies an aspect of it as a "problem." Is it a problem if America doesn't secure its borders and is overrun with illegal aliens? Not if you're an illegal alien. Is it a problem if your house loses fifty percent of its value in a real estate bust?

Not to the guy who buys it from you at a bargain-basement price. One man's "problem" is often another man's "solution." You call a particular situation a problem simply because you're unhappy with it and want to change it.

You have problems because you have an ego. An ego is all about getting its needs met and its desires satisfied. And because it is impossible to fulfill all your needs and desires, your ego is confronted with one obstacle or "problem" after another in its quest for personal happiness and fulfillment. Again, there is no such thing as an objective problem. From the universe's viewpoint, life is never a problem. But from the ego's viewpoint, life is full of problems. A man with a mature ego attempts to meet his needs and satisfy his desires in an "enlightened" way that does not harm, and which can even benefit, others. But that doesn't remove his problems; it just makes him a better human being.

When you meditate and experience oneness with Being, your ego and its problems disappear in the radiance of divine Light-energy. But as soon as you retract from Being and revert to your ordinary state of consciousness, they reappear. And when they reappear, they can seem worse than before. You were in the penthouse with your gaze fixed on the divine Being, and now you're back in the outhouse with your own shit staring you in the face. This is called "being humbled." It is also a goad to practice oneness more intensely. For until you can permanently rest in Being, your ego will continue to make your life problematic.

It took the Buddha, a prodigious spiritual talent, six years of intense ascetic practice to conquer his suffering (or problems and pain) and attain *Nirvana*. The Buddha, a forest-dwelling renunciant, practiced celibacy, ate one meal per day, and meditated incessantly, practicing the Vipassana-type moment-to-moment mindfulness that Tolle advocates.

Luckily for us, we don't have to live like monks and devote six years of our lives to the nonstop practice of Vipassana in order to free ourselves from our self-created problems and pain. This is the New Age! And the preeminent New Age guru, Eckhart Tolle, informs us that getting rid of suffering and pain comes down to a "simple choice." As Tolle puts it, "All it takes is a simple choice, a simple decision: no matter what happens, I will create no more pain for myself. I will create no more problems."

Just think: if Tolle had been around 2,600 years ago, he could have saved the Buddha six years of unnecessary austerities with his advice to just stop creating pain and problems for himself. And if somehow we could transport Tolle back to the time of Jesus Christ, he could let Jesus know that forty days of fasting and prayer is unnecessary, that merely by making a "simple choice," He could end his suffering and realize Heaven here on Earth.

In fairness to Tolle, he does add a caveat to his "simple choice" statement. He says that "you won't be able to go through with it unless you access the power of Now." But Tolle, three chapters and twenty-five percent into *The Power of Now*, has yet to discuss or expand upon Chapter Two's terse definition of the power of Now—"the power of your conscious presence." Perhaps, at this point, it would be appropriate to recycle Zen master Rinzai's question: "If not now, when?"

The bottom line concerning your pain and problems is this: As long as you are fettered by clinging and craving, your suffering, to one degree or another, will persist. And because your clinging and craving stem from your separation from the divine Being (the Now and its power), until your habit pattern of retracting from the Divine (and contracting into the mundane) is utterly obviated, you cannot "exorcise" your primal (ego-originated) pain and derivative problems.

According to Tolle, in a life-or-death emergency situation, "the mind stops; you become totally present in the Now, and something infinitely more powerful takes over." Did this also hold true for the Zen monks in Imperial Japan's war machine, or for Hitler's Nazis in life-or-death battles with American troops and allies? Does it also hold true for gang members involved in shootouts with the police and for Islamic terrorists who regularly risk their lives to blow up "infidels"?

If a true spiritual dimension were implicit in life-or-death emergency situations, then why do so many men involved in these situations *mindlessly* engage in cruel and callous murder? Because they truly *are mindless* in such situations—on automatic pilot, so to speak, with no conscious feelings about their actions. The fact is, how a man acts in a life-or-death situation is determined by his "programming," the premises and value judgments ingrained in his subconscious mind *prior* to the situation. A man "programmed" with an altruistic mindset becomes a humanitarian in the "Now" of a life-or-death emergency situation, while an Islamic terrorist brainwashed to hate "infidels" becomes a cold-blooded killing machine.

Being momentarily present in the Now—whether due to a life-or-death emergency or the contemplation of a Zen *koan*—hardly amounts to a spiritual experience. Real spiritual experiences do not, and cannot, begin until your plugged-in presence, or fused contemplation, is full enough and intense enough to initiate the infusion of spiritual Energy (*Shakti*) into and through your bodymind.

A Quantum Descent of Consciousness

I've had glimpses of the spiritual dimension, but they don't last for long. The past and future quickly intervene, and I'm evicted from the Now.

Again, without "Divine intervention," the descent of *Shakti*, no real Spirit-full experience is possible. Moreover, the only way anyone can lock into the spiritual dimension for a sustained period of time is through absorption in the Divine current, the Holy Spirit, or power of Now. Every profound *samadhi* (protracted engrossment in the spiritual dimension) has its basis in Grace, the poured-down power of Now. In other words, the only way to sustain a connection to the Now is by allowing the power of Now, the Divine current, to carry you, to meditate you.

Eckhart Tolle does not share my belief that tapping into the Divine current is the only way to sustain a connection to the Now. Tolle is convinced that he and his acolytes are involved in a "profound transformation" in the "collective consciousness of the planet and beyond" that will enable humans to transcend the "time-bound mode of consciousness deeply embedded in the human psyche." Consequently, if you currently find yourself unable to abide in the Now for any length of time, all you have to do is wait for the "quantum leap in evolution of consciousness" that Tolle envisages, and you'll then be able to end time and effortlessly lock into the Now.

Pardon my cynicism, but all I can say is that Tolle either has a vivid imagination or knows that this kind of cosmic malarkey will help him sell more books to New Age utopians, who adore a guru with an idealistic social message. When Tolle boldly declares that, "We are breaking mind patterns that have dominated human life for eons," a rational person has to wonder what planet he's talking about.

Is the breaking up of the old mode of consciousness inevitable, or do we have to work to make it happen?

If we are to believe Tolle, "a quantum leap in the evolution of consciousness" is "our only chance of survival." In other words, unless mankind moves beyond the time-bound mind that is currently destroying the planet, humanity is headed toward destruction. Tolle's position, then, is that mysticism—meaning connectedness to the Now, or communion with Ultimate Reality—is the solution that will save the world.

Like Tolle, I am a spiritual mystic. But unlike Tolle, I do not see mysticism as the solution that will save the planet. The ideal of living in the Now, or communing with Ultimate Reality, is a wonderful one, but I do not believe that it is the answer to the terrible problems that now threaten mankind's existence. The idea that somehow a "critical mass" of people will begin accessing the Now, radiating the power of Now, and then magically, somehow, transform the world into Heaven on earth is nothing short of laughable. A few decades ago Transcendental Meditation (TM) marketed the idea of spreading peace and transforming the world through meditation, but the only real transformation that I ever noticed was in the organization's bank account.

What Tolle fails to mention is that mysticism has already been tried and found wanting as a sociopolitical solution. It failed in India, in the form of yoga, and it failed in Japan, in the form of Zen. Mysticism, in whatever form it takes, is an inherently esoteric *Dharma* that is always inaccessible to the masses. And as the case of Zen in Imperial Japan illustrates, a protean mystical *Dharma* leaves itself open to "shaping," or exploitation, by the powers that be. In short, mysticism is *only* about awakening to a Reality, or Heaven, outside of space and time; it isn't about transforming space and time into a Heaven on Earth.

If mysticism isn't the answer to the world's sociopolitical problems, then what is? In my opinion, the *rational*, time-bound mind. The truly rational mind understands that man must be free, that the state exists for man and not vice-versa. Therefore, the truly rational mind is a moral mind that creates a limited state, or government, that, via a "sacred" Constitution, guarantees the sanctity of the individual. This kind of government is called a "constitutional republic"—what the United States of America is *supposed to be* and *would be* if evil and irrational people hadn't, in effect, reduced the country's putatively sacred Constitution to a mere piece of paper.

A moral and rational constitutional republic protects its citizens' inviolable rights by delimiting its own authority. This means separation of church and state and separation of economy and state. The government's function is reduced to protecting individual rights, which, necessarily, include private property rights. If everyone's rights were protected worldwide, then war, as well as the destruction of the environment, would be universally illegal. In a constitutional republic, government officials are elected via a democratic process, but because a majority cannot vote away individuals' inviolable rights, the state functions first and foremost as a republic, and only secondarily as a democracy.

The Bliss of Being

When you honor the present moment with your total presence, then bliss becomes a possibility. Because the present moment is a portal to the Now, the "Other Side," you can allow Grace, the power of Now, to flow into and through you simply by remaining present to it. You receive the Benediction from above, and the *Sambhogakaya*—the Bliss Body, or Holy Spirit—makes you happy and whole.

The present moment is not sacred. It is just the arising pattern of existence that you perceive in a particular moment. It is simply phenomena superimposed on the eternal Now. If, as Tolle recommends, you attempt to "give your fullest attention to whatever [each] moment presents," you will quickly find out that such a task is not only arduous, it is impossible. Being present to the present moment is not the same as focusing your attention on it. When you are simply present, you are present as *free attention*. When you focus your attention on something, you contract, or narrow, the field of awareness. When you are merely present to the moment, you can give your attention to phenomena when necessary, but the fundamental spiritual practice is not tethering your attention to the ephemeral now; it is connecting to the timeless Now and receiving its bliss-inducing Power.

The *Bhagavad Gita*, the Hindu Bible, is, as Tolle says, one of the "most beautiful spiritual teachings in existence." And one of the yogas (or ways to God-union) it emphasizes is karma yoga, the yoga of selfless service. Karma yoga is simply action for the sake of action rather than for the fruit of action. Such "consecrated" action entails no binding karma, because the ego is not seeking to gain anything from its pure acts of kindness. Tolle is correct when he says you should not be attached to the fruit of your action. Simply do what's right and kind, and the real fruit will be the peace and wonderful meditation that result from your life of right action.

When you're not attached to the results stemming from your right effort or action, then you're free of the pairs of opposites. Praise and blame and "success" and "failure" no longer affect you. You're rested in, or surrendered to, the divine Being, and you allow Providence, the Higher Power, to determine the course of events. You're complete in the Now, and you allow the power of Now to shape the destiny that is always beyond the grasp of the human mind.

In that state of completeness in the Now, would we still pursue or want to pursue external goals?

Certainly. Your actions don't cease, but your attachment to the results does. Each of us is born with creative karma that yearns to express itself on this Earth plane, and the expression of that karma is in no way antithetical to enlightenment.

When you are rooted in Being, becoming (or change of state), no longer implicates you. Thus, you can freely pursue goals without worrying about the results. Being, the deep immutable "context," is never affected by becoming, the superficial, mutable "content." Therefore, when you're established in the timeless Now as your context, your time-bound mind can "play" with the passing now, but never, for a single moment, are you bound by it.

CHAPTER FOUR

The Avoidance of the Now

Separation from the Now: The Core Problem

Even if I accept that time is really an illusion, what good is that going to do me in a world dominated by time?

You shouldn't accept anything that you don't find to be true. Real spirituality isn't about blind faith, belief, or acceptance; it's about direct and immediate experience of a Reality beyond this time-dependent world. The mystic, like ordinary people, lives in this time-based world, but unlike ordinary people, he is not of this world. The mystic is established in the Now, which lies outside of space and time. And because he views the world from the meta-position of the Now, he knows that time, though apparently real, is an illusion in the sense that it masks the vision of Ultimate Reality from the eyes of the ignorant.

The bottom line is this: It doesn't make an iota of difference whether you consider time a reality or an illusion. All that matters is transcending it. For unless you can access the Now, you'll wallow forever in the misery of the not-Now.

But I've still got bills to pay, and my body is going to rot and die like everyone else's. How, then, can I ever say that I'm free of time?

Only *Nirvana*, or Heaven, the Divine Domain of Being, is outside of time (and space). The extent to which you can dwell *in* the Divine Domain of Being instead of dwelling *on* time-based becoming is the extent to which you can transcend your problems. Problems are part of life. But when you're established in the transcendental context—the timeless and spaceless Now—the content, or "problems," of the passing now does not impinge on your all-surpassing spiritual bliss. For a Buddha, a being permanently rested in timeless Being, even the dissolution or death of his body does not compromise his Divine happiness.

According to Tolle, to be free of time "represents the most profound transformation of consciousness that you can imagine." This is true, but Tolle doesn't provide any details about this transformation. He leaves it entirely to our imagination. He says that in some rare cases "this shift in consciousness happens dramatically and radically, once and for all." But most people, he says, "have to work at it." Tolle is wrong. *Everyone* has to work at it. Even in the famous case of the great Hindu sage Ramana Maharshi, who at the age of sixteen spontaneously experienced his Self-nature, intense *sadhana* (practice) was thereafter required before he was able to sever his heart-knot and permanently abide as the Self. Perfect and permanent spiritual awakening is a "once and for all" "event" for *every* fully enlightened being—and as Ramana Maharshi states in *Sri Ramana Gita,* "Once the knot is cut, one is never bound again. This is considered the state of power supreme and peace supreme."

Once you've glimpsed the timeless state of consciousness, the challenge then becomes to sustain your connection to the Now. Spiritual discipleship, in a nutshell, is simply the moment-to-moment discipline of maintaining this connection. Whenever, and as soon as, you notice that you've retracted from the Now, reassume the "position of presence" relative to the moment. Because this "position of presence" connects you to the moment, and through the moment to the Now, it is more accurate to describe it as *plugged-in presence* than as mere presence. *Plugged-in presence* translates into *presence plus oneness.* And *presence + oneness = relationship,* or *communion.* In other words, your habit pattern of disconnecting from the Now can be summarized as the avoidance of relationship, or the ignoring of communion. Therefore, to counteract your habit pattern of disconnecting from the Now, the moment-to-moment discipline you must practice is direct and immediate relationship, or Holy Communion. And when relationship, or communion, is unqualified, it spontaneously morphs into *Sat-Chit-Ananda*—radiant, blissful, nondual Being-Consciousness.

Because Tolle is a two (rather than a three)-dimensional mystic—meaning that his *Dharma* is limited to self and consciousness and ignores Spirit—he is incapable of describing in spiritual terms the process of sustaining a connection to the Now. He says that "You lose the Now, and you return to it again and again. Eventually, presence becomes your predominant state." What Tolle doesn't say, and should, is that the only way to maintain a connection to the Now for a protracted period of time is through absorption in and reception of the Spirit-current, the poured-down power emanating from the Now. The spiritual process involves the effort, or discipline, of connecting to the Now, but it also involves Grace, the reception of the power of Now. And unless you can receive and rest in this God-given down-pouring current (that leads to the spiritual Heart-center and the eventual severing of the Heart-knot), you will not be privy to the profound mystical *samadhis* (states of spiritual absorption) that spring from a connection to the Now.

Levels of Consciousness and Unconsciousness

Can you explain the differences between ordinary and deep consciousness and ordinary and deep unconsciousness?

Consciousness is neither deep nor ordinary; it just is. But when someone is aware of something that lies beneath the surface of mundane existence, that consciousness is considered "deep" relative to one's ordinary, or "superficial," consciousness. Because ordinary consciousness involves placing one's attention on gross, conventionally acceptable objects and objectives, it leads to gross and conventional states of awareness. When one's attention is focused on more subtle phenomena—such as abstruse concepts, repressed feelings, or non-physical energies—the result is deeper states of awareness. When one's attention is utterly free (meaning not bound or implicated by objects), and consciousness apprehends, or beholds, itself as the radiant, transcendental Subject (or Seer) underlying all phenomena (gross and subtle), then, relatively or hierarchically speaking, consciousness is deepest. But absolutely or non-hierarchically speaking, consciousness is not deep; it just *is*.

Just as there are levels of consciousness, there are also levels of "unconsciousness," meaning states of obliviousness relative to different levels of phenomena. Tolle is correct when he describes "ordinary unconsciousness" as "a state not of acute pain or unhappiness but of an almost continuous low level of unease, discontent, boredom, or nervousness—a kind of background static." This chronic unease, or psychic background static, is really a symptom of the primal, existential disease (or *dis-ease*)—separation from Being. Because mainstream society doesn't acknowledge this primal dis-ease of separation from Being, it programs its members to treat "ordinary unconsciousness" as part of "normal life" and doesn't encourage them to seek the real cause of this chronic low-level disturbance. Instead, mainstream society offers its members every type of escape imaginable from this disorder—including drugs, sex, alcohol, TV, and the Internet. But these diversions only numb, distract, or fascinate an individual—and once their spell wears off, the psychic background static starts again.

Truly speaking, there is no such thing as the "unconscious" that Freud posits. Any psychic content that an individual isn't aware of in a given moment is best classified as "subconscious," meaning that it exists beneath the threshold of actively functioning consciousness. But if particular psychic content is very painful to an individual, something he doesn't want to face and consciously process, then it can be said that his act of suppressing and avoiding that content is an act of "unconsciousness." Because this suppressed psychic content is buried deep within one's psyche, it can be said to represent "deep unconsciousness."

When an individual begins true spiritual life, meaning true *conscious* life, he must confront both "ordinary unconsciousness" and "deep unconsciousness." And this confrontation engenders a painful crisis in consciousness—what St. John of the Cross calls the "dark night of the soul." The moment conscious Light-energy awakens in a disciple, it encounters "darkness"—dense resistance in the forms of ordinary and deep unconsciousness. And for this awakened Light-energy to penetrate to the heart of the disciple's soul (or spiritual Heart-center), it must cut through this unconscious darkness. This "cutting through" can be likened to "psychic surgery," and because no anesthetic is available for this painful "operation," the process is often analogized to "crucifixion."

In Christian mysticism, there are three distinct phases or stages in the "way" that leads to permanent at-one-ment with the divine Being: 1) *purification*, 2) *illumination*, and 3) *divine union*. When the disciple devoted to the foundational mystical practice of Holy Communion is baptized by the Holy Spirit, the down-pouring Light-energy initiates a two-sided illumination, or divinization, process in him. On one side, the descending divine Power bathes the disciple in radiant Light, and on the other, it brings to the surface and forces him to confront everything unpleasant that he has ever avoided or suppressed. And because the divine Light is so bright, it not only exposes the disciple to all his fears, regrets, and hatreds, it also dramatically intensifies his experience of them! Consequently, "purification," the "dark side" of the "illumination" process, can be exceedingly painful, which is why Christian mystics refer to it as "purgatory."

What Is Civilization Seeking?

"Resistance to the Now," says Tolle, is a "collective dysfunction" and "forms the basis of our dehumanized industrial civilization." Statements like this, which Tolle makes throughout *The Power of Now*, sound as though they were derived from a neo-Marxist pamphlet, and make me wonder to what extent Tolle has been influenced by the European inheritance of Marxism and primitive communistic tribal society.

Contrary to Tolle's claim, resistance to the Now is *not* a collective dysfunction. It is entirely an individual one, as is the process of overcoming it. Spiritual collectives and communities throughout history and around the globe have produced sparingly few great sages. In fact, the renowned Indian guru Swami Sivananda of Rishikesh (1887–1963) instructed serious yogis to stay away from ashrams, including his own. The greatest spiritual adepts—such as Buddha, Jesus, and Ramana Maharshi—have almost always been rugged individuals who trod the spiritual path alone, in solitude.

Tolle is also off-base in his depiction of industrial civilization as "dehumanized." By historical standards, modern industrial society is hardly dehumanized. People can freely live, work, play, study, and worship alone or together. They can choose among privacy, fraternity, and community, and can mix and match them to their heart's content. They have constitutionally guaranteed individual rights, including the right to own property. Contrast this with preindustrial society, in which man was nothing but an indentured servant to the tribe, the chief, or the ruling cult, whose dictates controlled virtually every aspect of his life.

If modern industrial civilization is as dehumanized as Tolle claims, then why don't millions of Americans drop out and form "humanized" communes in the peaceful countryside, away from what Tolle calls our "extraordinarily violent civilization?" The fact is, in the 1970s, tens of thousands of young Americans did drop out and form hundreds of hippie-type and spiritual-type communes throughout the country. I visited a few of them. For several years, a spiritual community guidebook (I don't remember its name) was published yearly, containing information on each of these communes. By the end of the 1980s, however, virtually all of these communes had failed, and the majority of the disillusioned ex-members had returned to mainstream society to seek their fortune.

What does Tolle recommend as an alternative to modern industrial civilization? Predictably, and pathetically, he doesn't say. He just takes potshots from the peanut gallery and never mentions the inconvenient truth that the small-scale cooperative experiment failed miserably in America. It would also be enlightening if he mentioned his points of view on capitalism versus socialism and individualism versus statism. But if Tolle dealt in specifics instead of in broad generalities, his popularity would be compromised; he would no longer be Everyman's mystic, and his book sales would no doubt plummet.

Tolle makes millions of dollars hawking his books, CDs, and DVDs, but without modern industrial civilization this wouldn't be possible—unless you think a hippie living in the Now in a commune could invent, manufacture, and market computers and other electronic devices that play CDs and DVDs. What I don't understand about Tolle is this: Why does a rich guy like him who hates modern industrial civilization continue to "robe" himself in a confining suit and tie, the signature symbol of the uptight, life-destructive civilization he so despises? You'd think a guy like him, putatively outside the zeitgeist and floating in the Now, would ditch the mainstream monkey suit for less formal attire that reflects his anti-establishment point of view. But what do I know? Maybe GQ pays him to model the formal but stylish threads.

Getting back to serious matters, I want to counter Tolle's indictment of modern industrial civilization with a quote from *Capitalism: The Unknown Ideal*, by Ayn Rand. Rand's picture of pre-industrial Europe makes you wonder why Tolle, who hails from Europe, rails so passionately against the current state of civilization. As Rand points out, until the institution of serfdom was abolished and supplanted by modern capitalism's emergence in the nineteenth century, a man's life and property were not his own; they belonged to the chief of the tribal state, the king.

> The concept of man as a free, independent individual was profoundly alien to the culture of Europe. It was a tribal culture down to its roots; in European thinking, the tribe was the entity, the unit, and man was only one of its expendable cells. This applied to rulers and serfs alike: the rulers were believed to hold their privileges only by virtue of the services they rendered to the tribe, services regarded as of a noble order, namely, armed force or military defense. But a nobleman was as much chattel of the tribe as a serf: his life and property belonged to the king. It must be remembered that the institution of

private property, in the full legal meaning of the term, was brought into existence only by capitalism. In the pre-capitalist eras, private property existed *de facto*, but not *de jure, i.e.,* by custom and sufferance, not by right or by law. In law and in principle, all property belonged to the head of the tribe, the king, and was held only by his permission, which could be revoked at any time, at his pleasure. (The king could and did expropriate the estates of recalcitrant noblemen throughout the course of Europe's history.)

Tolle's rant against the "machine" comes to a head in his "state-of-the-planet" summary statement: "The collective dysfunction has created a very unhappy and extraordinarily violent civilization that has become a threat not only to itself but also to all life on the planet." Tolle's sophomoric statement is flush with rhetoric and devoid of substance. If modern industrial civilization were as violent and dysfunctional as Tolle declares it to be, why do most underdeveloped nations still seek to emulate the U.S., Europe, and Japan? Finally, regarding the "extraordinary violence," on the planet, most of it stems not from modern *civilized* countries, but from backward, *uncivilized* nations that do not recognize and/or protect individual rights. Perhaps Tolle hasn't noticed that the current hotbeds of violence in the world—Africa, Mexico, and particular Middle East countries—hardly qualify as bastions of modern civilization. Yes, the very existence of life on planet Earth is in question. But the reason for this isn't modern civilization; it's the enemies of modern civilization: brainwashed Islamic extremists who would gladly blow up the world in the name of Allah.

I have no idea what subject Tolle concentrated on while at Cambridge, but I would be shocked if it were political science, sociology, or economics. To put it bluntly, Tolle is utterly clueless when it comes to the world's political, social, and economic situation. In fact, if he were to give me a call or join me for some tea and crumpets, my advice to him would be this: avoid pontificating on the state of the world. Stick to what you know best—pop mysticism and sharp suits and ties.

Irradiating Ordinary Unconsciousness

How can we be free of the affliction of unconsciousness?

Simply *be* consciousness relative to life. You cannot be conscious and unconscious at the same time. Therefore, when you assume the "position" of consciousness, unconsciousness is automatically vanished. In order to fully vanish unconsciousness, you must be fully present as consciousness—and you can only be fully present as consciousness when you are in direct and immediate relationship to, through, and beyond the moment. To be (unqualifiedly) related is to *be* (consciousness). Therefore, the root consciousness discipline is to establish yourself in the position of relationship, or communion, relative to existence.

The root discipline of relationship, or communion, is an arduous one. The reason this is the case is because the root egoic tendency is to retract from relationship to the moment into self-contraction—mental abstraction and becoming. But it is not possible to *willfully* establish yourself in Holy Communion, protracted connectedness to the Spirit. Your willpower, or concentrated effort, enables you to assume the position of relationship to the moment, but *only* Grace transforms this relationship into true, or Spirit-empowered, Communion.

But Grace is a subject that Eckhart Tolle avoids discussing in *The Power of Now*. Perhaps he avoids the subject because he knows that Grace is not a popular theme with the New Age self-help crowd. Perhaps he avoids the subject because he is ignorant regarding it. Either way, it is nothing short of incredible that a "spiritual" text entitled *The Power of Now* never broaches the role of Grace, or *Shaktipat*, in the enlightenment process.

According to the Hindu tantric traditions, perfect, *divine* consciousness is *Siva-Shakti*. Conscious Presence is *Siva*, and the descent of divine Power (or Grace) is *Shaktipat*. Thus, in order for a yogi to abide and radiate as perfect, divine consciousness (the Self), he must be not only unobstructedly present (as *Siva*), but also infilled with divine Light-energy (or *Shakti*) from above. When the union of *Siva* and *Shakti* is consummated at the spiritual Heart-root (just to the right of the center of the chest), the yogi awakens as the *divine* Self, as enlightened Consciousness (or conscious Light).

Siva-Shakti in Hinduism can be likened to the *Eucharist* in Christianity. In other words, complete God-consciousness, or full enlightenment, is not possible through communion alone. Communion, or conscious presence + oneness, establishes the divine connection, but for your relationship to God to be full, the Holy Spirit must empower it. Conscious presence is true prayer—consciously presenting yourself to (or being present to) God and asking, and allowing, Him to bless you with his Spirit-power. Thus, for your God consciousness, or relationship with God, to be whole (or holy), you must not only practice true prayer, but also receive the Benediction, the Blessing Power from above, the down-pouring Holy Spirit.

If you monitor your mental-emotional state through self-observation, as Tolle recommends, you will notice that it is essentially one of chronic dis-ease. And you will observe that your fundamental habit pattern of dealing with this dis-ease is to constantly change your state of being—to *become*. Because no state of being is *Nirvana*, or Being itself, your organism's automatic, or unconscious, response is to seek another state of being... and another, ad infinitum. Conscious, spiritual life is about breaking this vicious cycle of becoming and instead establishing Being as the fundamental principle of your life. Being is Consciousness-Energy, or Presence-Power. Therefore, for you to be *spiritually* one with Being, you must not only be consciously present, but also unite your conscious presence with the Spirit-power, or Light-energy, emanating from Being. When this emanated Spirit-power, or Light-energy, merges with, and outshines, your presence, then, spontaneously, you are *spiritually* present as an en-Light-ened being.

Unhappiness and Resistance to the Moment

According to Tolle, "Negativity is never the optimum way of dealing with any situation. In fact, in most cases it keeps you stuck in it, blocking real change." Tolle is absolutely correct. Negativity is a form of resistance to the moment, and because it blocks the flow of life energy, it only makes you, as well as others, unhappy. This isn't to say you shouldn't ever be negative or critical; it simply means you should do so within a positive, constructive framework that offers the possibility of real change. If real change isn't possible, then you should drop your negativity, because continuing to harbor negative energy with no positive outlet will damage you not only emotionally, but physically, too.

Buddhism is, on the surface, seemingly very negative and critical. It describes human life as suffering, due to constant craving and clinging. But because Buddhism offers a way beyond suffering, a path to *Nirvana*, eternal happiness, it is truly a positive religion. Early Buddhists used to meditate in cemeteries, where they would contemplate the death and decay of the body. Such contemplation could be construed as dark and negative. But because it served as a goad to spiritual practice, it was really a positive form of meditation. Spiritual growth as well as personal growth involves creatively transmuting the negative into a positive.

Negativity, as Tolle points out, is contagious and pollutes the psychic environment. Furthermore, if you start giving off bad vibes, because of the law of karma—the law of cause and effect—your negative psychic action will not only infect others, but it will be mirrored right back at you. There is nothing wrong with deep suffering and internal negativity—they are, in fact, an integral part of the awakening process; but you should not spread your psychic dis-ease and unnecessarily inflict your pain and complaints on others. Whenever you acknowledge and accept your own suffering and negativity, your resistance to life and the Now is diminished. You have, in effect, confessed your "sinful" activity, and the "*absolution*" that results opens a portal to the *Absolute* for you.

How can we get rid of our negativity?

What is negativity? It is a resistance pattern on one level or another. As you progress spiritually, one level of resistance after another confronts you as the "clenched fist" of consciousness attempts to open. But regardless of the level of resistance that confronts you, there is only one way to get rid of it: let it go. In order to let it go, you must first recognize it by seeing it or feeling it for what it is: mental-emotional garbage. As soon as you recognize it as garbage, you will throw it away, or at least attempt to.

As Tolle alludes, not all patterns of pain and resistance are equal in intensity. For example, if a loved one dies or your long-time girlfriend or boyfriend dumps you, unless you're the Buddha reincarnated, you're not going to be able to just throw away the emotional pain once and for all in a nanosecond. You will have to process the situation and gradually make peace with it. The fact that you are able to wrestle with the grief in meditation will help you to process the pain and enable you to let it go more quickly.

The easiest and most effective way to get rid of pain and negativity is to access the power of Now, the Holy Spirit. The Holy Spirit is the great Healer and Comforter, and when you are able to tap into its down-pouring Power, your "sins," including your pain and negativity, are washed away in the torrent of Spirit-"water" from above. The term "sin" means to "miss the mark." And when you wallow in misery, you do so because you've missed the mark by retracting from the divine Being into self-contraction. When you reconnect to the divine Being and receive Its Blessing Power, the Holy Spirit, you are absolved of all sin by the Grace of the Absolute. The Lord bears all burdens, and if you are unable to throw away your mental-emotional garbage, even after you recognize it, then give it to God and let Him, via His Spirit-power, heal your wounds and make you whole again.

If some emotions are considered negative, doesn't that create a mental good-bad polarity?

An emotion is negative to the degree that it creates resistance to the power of Now. The only "emotions" that are wholly positive, or truly

holy, are *divine* love and *divine* bliss, which, strictly speaking, aren't
emotions. *Divine* love-bliss is simply the natural, spontaneous feeling-
energy of Being. Whereas emotions are conditioned responses based on
psychological value judgments, divine love-bliss is simply the
spontaneous feeling-radiance stemming from oneness with the *divine*
Being (*Siva-Shakti, or Dharmakaya-Sambhogakaya*). Oneness with the *divine*
Being means that you are fused with the Now and receive its infusion, or
power, without measure. The nature of the power of Now is radiant
happiness, or love-bliss, and because this love-bliss emanates directly
from the singular Absolute (Being), it is beyond duality and consequent
"good-bad" polarity.

*But if you consider emotions other than divine love and divine bliss as negative
because they are forms of resistance to the Now, don't you fall victim to duality
and judgment? Shouldn't all emotions—such as anger, resentment, and
jealousy—be accepted as okay, so we don't subject ourselves to repression, inner
conflict, or denial? Shouldn't our spiritual attitude be that everything is okay as
it is?*

Whatever exists is real, including negative emotions. Negative emotions
contract open, blissful Being into painful, enclosed becoming. If you
don't eliminate them after they arise, they can infect you like a virus
infects a computer. If they get a foothold in your mind, they can destroy
you both psychically and physically. If you had cancer, would you accept
your cancer cells as okay, as part of your singular, "nondual" organism?
Or would you cut them out? Your deeply-entrenched negative emotions
are like mutant cancer cells that must be excised. The essential question
isn't whether or not to judge your emotions, but rather, how to free
yourself from these "mutinous" mind-forms. Once negative emotions
infect you, they are no longer just superficial negative emotions; they
have mutated into deep "mutinous emotions," and these mutinous
emotions want to take over your mind.

Mutinous emotions can literally "possess" us, making our lives miserable.
If we deny the reality of the pain they cause, we deny reality, which

leads to delusion, not enlightenment. These deep-seated toxic emotions are often referred to as the "demons" within us. Fundamental Christians sometimes call these pernicious emotions the "work of the devil." But no matter what we call them, we are bedeviled by these "evil spirits" and must find a way to "exorcise" them.

Before we consider the treatment options available for our disease of mutinous emotions, it is essential to understand the etiology of the disease itself. In other words, how do negative emotions originate, and what causes them to morph into cancer-like mutinous emotions?

Emotions are automatic feeling-reactions to life that reflect our value judgments. Therefore, as long as we maintain set value judgments, or premises, we have no choice about the emotions that life situations will evoke in us. For example, if you believe in the sanctity of private property, and your maid steals your precious jewelry, you will be very upset. If you consider marriage a sacred bond and your spouse cheats on you, you will suffer a host of unpleasant emotions. These emotions are unavoidable if we maintain value judgments, and if we don't, then we aren't connected to the "real world."

As *civilized* human beings, we must maintain rational moral values; otherwise we'll end up like the Japanese Zen monks who mindlessly lived in the Now and mindlessly killed people. And if we or others violate our rational moral values, we will, automatically, judge the violator and the violation and experience unpleasant emotions. These emotions, then, are natural, and often appropriate, responses to life, and unless we want to abdicate our humanity and morality, we need to accept them and deal with them.

Appropriate negative emotions are not a real problem. For example, any American who didn't experience immediate anger when Bin Laden and his boys blew up the World Trade Center buildings clearly lacks rational moral values. But individuals who allowed 9/11 to fill them with perpetual fear and worry became victims—not of terrorism, but of mutinous emotions.

What causes superficial negative emotions to mutate into deep-rooted, mutinous emotions? Habitual, unnecessary dwelling on things. Emotions reflect the mind. And if you continually dwell, or "meditate," on negative life events, then, sure enough, you are planting the psychic "seeds" (what Hindu yogis call *samskaras*) for the growth of mutinous emotions. Once these emotions take root, they are difficult to eradicate because their roots run deep (into the spiritual Heart-center). And unless these insidious emotions are cut off at the source, they will sprout forth again and again, in one form or another, making your life miserable.

Tolle says that unless you are able to access the power of Now, you have no choice about experiencing negative emotions. He says that without the power of Now, you are just a "bundle of conditioned reflexes." He is partially correct. Because you have a free will (to some extent) and a mind, you can consciously reprogram your subconscious mind with different values or premises and thereby modify, or "re-condition," your reflexive emotional responses to stimuli. But even if you do, you will still experience negative emotions when your new values are violated. And if your existing values and premises are already rational and moral, why would you want to reprogram them?

Once you're able to access the *true* power of Now (which means you've been baptized by the Holy Spirit), you have a real choice about the experience of negative emotions. This is so because your experience of life is then recontextualized, with all your experiences now taking place within the context of awakened Spirit. Although you can still experience negative emotions, you no longer will unnecessarily "meditate" on the events that triggered them. When you dwell in the radiant force field of the Spirit-current, thanks to its Grace-full power, you are able to obviate the habit pattern of incessantly dwelling on negative life events, which is what creates deep-rooted mutinous emotions.

Acceptance of negative emotions or other problems can often amount to irrationality. Here's a story that illustrates this point: A man started wetting his bed every night. He told his friend about his problem, and his friend suggested that he see a psychiatrist. A few weeks later, his friend asked him if the psychiatrist had taken care of his problem. The man replied that he had. His friend said, "Well, I guess that means you're no longer wetting your bed." The man replied, "No, I'm still wetting my bed every night, but now I'm proud of it."

A fat man who accepts being fat instead of cutting down on his calories and hitting the gym is just ignoring his problem. A drug addict who accepts his addiction but refuses treatment is probably doomed. The point is this: acceptance of reality does not mean acceptance of problems. Acceptance of reality means acknowledging its existence, but such acceptance does not preclude positive action to alter that reality.

The spiritual attitude of "I'm okay, you're okay" is New Age nonsense. Your *spiritual* attitude should be: "I'm not okay unless I'm directly connected to the divine Being and allow Its power to bless me." And your "real-world" attitude should be: "I'm not okay unless I rationally and ethically deal with *real* problems."

But dealing with real problems does not mean dwelling on negative emotions. When negative emotions arise within the context of your connectedness to the divine Being, neither accept nor reject them. Instead, simply allow the Divine's power to dissolve them. Real surrender is real acceptance—of the Divine's power or "will." And unless you're conformed to the Divine's will, things cannot be truly okay.

Whether or not things are okay is also okay.

You're like the man wetting his bed every night and thinking it's okay. You've read too many pop, New Age psycho-babble books, and the result is that you're now suffering from cognitive delusion.

Wherever You Are, Be Totally Present

Can you give some examples that will help us deal with unconsciousness?

Bring the body into the act of being present. Be present as the body. When you're consciously present as the body, you heal the body-mind split and feel whole and integrated.

Briefly and randomly focus your attention on your hands and your "third eye" area (the area immediately below the middle of your forehead). This will help you to establish and maintain whole-bodily presence.

When you're present, you can intensify the force of your consciousness by being in direct relationship to the moment. When you plug in to the moment by being in direct relationship to it, your "plugged-in presence" transforms presence into oneness. You are consciously conformed to the moment, and this leads to the experience of coinciding with existence.

Spiritual life is a moment-to-moment test. In every moment, you have the choice of either communing with existence or retracting from it. A great aid, or goad, to maintaining your conscious connection to life is a verbal enquiry, in the form of a question. For example, in my own case, I have found it very helpful to randomly question myself via the enquiry, "Avoiding relationship?" This enquiry, which I learned from studying the early teachings of Adi Da, reminds me to reassume the position of being present and connected to the moment. Experiment with this enquiry, as well as with ones of your own making, and see if they intensify your practice of plugged-in presence.

Prayer is an excellent way to establish presence that leads to infused communion, or contemplation. Simply be whole-bodily present, and repeatedly and intently ask God to bless you with His Power, the Holy Spirit. True prayer is simply saying Grace in its purest form—asking the Divine to bless you with Its Spirit-power.

Whatever method(s)—such as bodily awareness, enquiry, or prayer—

you use to help establish your holy, or wholistic, connection to the moment, the goal is to break through to the "other side," the Now, and receive its Benediction, the descent of divine Power. When this poured-down Power intersects with your plugged-in presence, the union of the two results in fused oneness with the divine Being. For your consciousness to fully awaken and shine with radiant power, it must become divinized—and without *Shaktipat*, the descent of divine Power, this isn't possible.

Spiritual life is all about merging with the supreme, or divine, Being. The divine Being has two aspects: consciousness (or presence) and energy (or power). Consciousness expresses itself most fully and intensely when you are wholly present. The pressure of your whole, or *unified*, presence generates palpable force that pulls down pure, *unified* Energy from above. Because your pure, whole presence, or *unity*-consciousness, serves to channel pure, *unified* Energy, this Energy is best described as *Power*. When this channeled divine Power merges with your pure presence, the alchemical result is oneness with the supreme, or divine, Being.

To channel spiritual energy as pulled-down Power, you must first plug into the Now via the practice of presence. When the force of your presence generates enough pressure to invoke the descent of Power, you must "surrender," meaning let go and allow yourself to be penetrated by the flow of Light-energy from above. Integral spiritual life involves two principal modes of practice: *penetrating* (through the moment to the Now) and *being penetrated* (by the power of Now). And unless you practice both of these modes—the *Siva* mode and the *Shakti* mode—you cannot attain total, or Divine, presence.

Because the practice of presence is fundamentally an intense *yang* practice, it can block the flow of life-energy and generate tension. Consequently, to counteract or reduce this tension, you should randomly, periodically, totally relax and utterly let go. This *yin* practice will loosen your bodymind and instigate the flow of *Shakti* into and through it.

You will find not only that the *conductivity practice* of "letting go and letting flow" complements your *consciousness practice* of presence, but also that without it you cannot awaken to, and as, total presence.

Self-improvement is something we should all strive for. As imperfect human beings, we are born in "sin" and plagued with selfish desires and carnal cravings. Bedeviled with insidious and pernicious defilements, we should devote ourselves to extirpating our adventitious taints and *becoming* better human beings—but not at the expense of *being* (free and pure Buddhas).

Endless books have been written, and will continue to be written, about how you can become a better you. Prescriptions for behavioral improvement are legion, and these normative, often spiritual, texts exhort you to act in ways that will purify your affections and makes you more conscious. But no amount of *becoming* will enable you to *be*, and the reason for this is simple: *Being* is always already the case. You cannot become what you always already are—the divine Self—and all your striving to become a better you will not transform you into a Buddha.

Moral, or right, behavior can be practiced as a means to an end, such as self-improvement or spiritual enlightenment. But if we really want to improve ourselves and attain enlightenment, we should practice right behavior for the right reason: it is simply the right thing to do—for ourselves and for humanity. If we're rational and objective, which we should always strive to be, our conscience will tell us what is right, or moral. When right behavior is practiced simply as a matter of course rather than as a means to an end, it serves to curtail becoming and opens a portal to Being. But when it is practiced as a means to an end, karma is generated, which further implicates us in becoming.

Mother Teresa devoted her life to serving the poor and the sick. But at the end of her life, she admitted that she was unhappy and suffering from spiritual doubt. She was an altruistic soul, but because she never learned how to contact the Deity and channel the Holy Spirit, her spiritual life was a failure. The moral of her story is clear: Unless you can mystically connect to the divine Being, all your saintly behavior will not translate into enlightenment. Your practice of selfless service, or karma yoga, can open a portal to Being, but unless you have the "skillful means" to take advantage of it, you'll remain estranged from the Divine, and your life, like Mother Teresa's, will be less than divine.

If you are like most people, you devote a good part of your life to improving your life situation. Whether your goal is better health, a better job, more money, more free time, or whatever, you're striving to improve your life situation. But as Eckhart Tolle properly puts it, "You can improve your life situation, but you cannot improve your life." In other words, you cannot become truly, or spiritually, happy and fulfilled through external changes in your life. You can certainly derive superficial pleasure and joy from positive improvements in your life situation, but only by establishing a holy, Spirit-blessed relationship to the Deity can you attain deep bliss and enduring peace.

You were born a creative being with unique karma, and your destiny is to express your inborn tendencies on this earth plane. But unless you establish a relationship to the living Spirit as the foundation of your life, all that you create will end up nothing more than a "Tower of Babel." If you want your life to be divine, then you must base it on, and in, the underlying Divine Life-Consciousness. Otherwise, your destiny will be nothing more than another turn of the Wheel of Birth and Death.

The Dual Purpose of Your Life's Journey

Our life's journey must have a purpose, and a purpose implies a future. How, then, do you reconcile living in the present moment with our life's journey, which involves a purpose and a future?

Your life's journey is twofold: metaphysical (or spiritual) and physical (or material). Your metaphysical, or spiritual, journey is a pilgrimage into Being, and your physical, or material, journey is a peregrination into becoming. The former involves the "vertical" (or spaceless, timeless) dimension of existence, while the latter implicates you in the "horizontal" (or space-time) continuum. The two journeys are complementary, not contradictory. But the pilgrimage into Being leads to eternal peace, while the peregrination into becoming—when divorced from the journey into Being—leads to suffering.

The purpose of your "inner," or metaphysical, journey is to transcend your karma and achieve *Nirvana*—perfect and permanent oneness with spaceless, timeless Being. And the purpose of your "outer," or physical, journey is to manifest and refine your karma in space and time. When your karma (your bundle of psycho-physical tendencies) manifests in the context of your spiritual presence, it isn't binding, because, as Tolle says, you then have a "choice" (meaning the spiritual power to transcend your conditioning). But when your karma is un-consciously lived, it leads to binding karma—further entanglement in the "web of *samsara*."

When you live in the context of the Now, *being-ness* subsumes becoming, and the present moment is seamlessly integrated with future moments (which exist in your mind). But when you drop context by losing your connection to the Now, your outer life's purpose (of becoming) is then at odds with your inner life's purpose (of *being*). A fully enlightened being never experiences a contradiction between *being* and becoming, the Now and the future. *Nirvana* (*being*) and *samsara* (becoming) are ultimately one because *samsara* is simply *Nirvana* (the *Noumenal* Condition) temporarily modified into finite, transitory conditions.

Certain schools of yoga postulate that when the universe was born (as an emission from Being-Consciousness), for Divine sport (*lila*), Being-Consciousness embedded itself in its emanated matter via a process of involution. And the evolutionary "goal" of this embedded, or implicated, Being-Consciousness is to explicate itself from the confines of matter. But in order for Being-Consciousness to explicate itself from its bondage, matter had to evolve into life-forms, and life-forms had to evolve into conscious beings capable of recognizing their original nature as Being-Consciousness, or *Siva*.

From the perspective of yoga philosophy, the purpose of your outer journey through space-time is evolutionary refinement of your psycho-physical vehicle. Once your psycho-physical vehicle, through innumerable incarnations, becomes a refined medium through which Being-Consciousness can recognize itself, then Being-Consciousness is free and the "Dance of Siva" ends for you. Some mystics, however, such as the Hindu sage Sri Aurobindo (1872–1950), envisage a world in which Self-realized beings glorify the world by virtue of their creative, enlightened presence and purpose. According to Aurobindo, the ultimate goal of spiritual life isn't realizing the Self; it's transforming the world by manifesting the glory and splendor of the divine Being on the earth plane.

Is it important that we achieve our outer purpose? Does it matter whether we succeed or fail in the world?

If it were truly important to achieve one's outer purpose, then life would dictate that everyone achieve success. But the game of life is a Darwinian one, and this means there will be winners and losers. Ten thousand people might have their hearts set on winning American Idol, but only one champion is crowned each year. If your goal is in conflict with Joe Blow's, it's not possible for both of you to be successful in your respective quests.

Furthermore, "success" is entirely subjective and relative. For example, if this book sells ten thousand copies, I'll break out a bottle of Dom Perignon and celebrate. But if Tolle's next book sells less than a couple million copies, he'll probably be on the horn with Deepak Chopra, trying to figure out how he lost some of his audience.

From an Eastern spiritual perspective, it is precisely your craving for ego-based "achievement" and "fulfillment" that keeps you tethered to the Wheel of Birth and Death. Your desire for more and more in your life might lead you to further gain, but from the spiritual point of view, it all amounts to naught. In the classic text *The Zen Teaching of Huang Po,* the great Zen master Huang Po (circa 825 CE), in a pithy directive, compares the value of spiritual attainment to material gain:

Exert your strength in THIS life to attain!
Or else incur long aeons of further gain!

Even if your outer purpose is a "success," it's doomed to eventual failure simply because everything in time and space is impermanent. The outer games of life, such as "achievement" and "fulfillment," can be fun to play, but the most challenging and rewarding game is the inner one. In this "game," you work to free yourself from your self-imposed bondage in space-time and to secure a permanent "place" for your soul in Heaven, the Divine Domain.

The Past Disappears in Your Presence

The unconscious past that conditions our lives—childhood experiences, cultural upbringing, religious indoctrination, etcetera—is so deep-seated in us, how is it possible to ever become conscious of all that or to get rid of it? And if we do get rid of it, what would be left?

If you turn on the light in a dark room, what happens to the darkness? It instantly disappears. Likewise, the instant you're radiantly present, your spiritual Light vanishes your so-called deep, dark, unconscious past.

Conditional existence is all about conditions and conditioning. You can become aware of past conditioning that shaped, and continues to shape, your life and behavior today. But from a conventional standpoint, all you can do about it is to recondition yourself. For example, you might have been brought up as a conservative Republican, and now you might reject your upbringing and become a liberal Democrat. You might have been raised as an Orthodox Jew, but might convert to Christianity and become a Jew for Jesus. You can *change* your conditioning, but none of these changes is radical (or gone-to-the-root); none of them enables you to *transcend* your conditioning and realize your true, *unconditioned* Buddha-nature.

As Tolle says, your past is a bottomless pit. You can delve into it forever, and you can make mindset and life changes in response to your experiences and conditioning. But none of those changes will set you free. Only by recognizing your underlying, *changeless* Buddha-nature can you *be* free. And the secret to recognizing your Buddha-nature (or Christ-consciousness) is the power of Now, the Holy Spirit. Learn how to access the power of Now, and your *personal* presence will morph into *spiritual* presence—and in your spiritually empowered presence, you will recognize yourself as a Buddha (or Christ), as a divine manifestation of the supreme Being.

What, exactly, is the power of Now?

It is the same thing as Hindu *Shakti*, the Christian Holy Spirit, the Jewish *Ruach HaKodesh*, and the Buddhist *Sambhogakaya*. God, the supreme Source, or *divine* Being, is at once immutable Presence and dynamic Power. If God were just changeless Presence (or transcendental Consciousness), He wouldn't be a living or spiritual Being. But God, like the sun, is constantly, changelessly present and yet simultaneously, dynamically active. God's essence is Presence (or universal Awareness), and His nature is Power (or Light-energy). God's eternal Presence is the timeless Now, and the Light-energy emitted from His Presence is the power of Now. God's absolute Light-energy creatively expresses itself, via stepped-down vibrations, as the universe, the manifest full spectrum of non-spiritual light, energy, and life forms. And when a highly evolved life form, such as man, seeks a direct and immediate way back to God, he discovers—underneath the layers of non-spiritual light, energy, and life—the Holy Spirit, the power of Now.

Eckhart Tolle's answer to "What is the power of Now?" is not quite the same as mine. According to Tolle, the power of Now is "None other than the power of your presence, your consciousness liberated from thought forms." Beyond this single-sentence statement, Tolle is mum when it comes to describing the power of Now. And even this statement, sad to say, rings with only partial truth and minimal power.

The eternal, divine Presence *is* the Now, and strictly speaking, it is not *your* presence; it is God's. You can coincide with It, identify with It, and even claim It as your Self-nature, or Being-ness. But in reality, you are no more the Now than a drop of water is the ocean. Similarly, to claim that the power of *your* presence is the power of Now, the divine *Shakti*, borders not only on heresy, but on solipsistic idiocy. The true power of Now, the power of the divine Being, created the universe. If Tolle, via *his* power of Now, can create even a single cockroach, I'll humbly bow down and kiss not only his feet, but the very ground his personally originated roach crawls on.

When your consciousness begins to liberate itself from thought-forms, energy begins to move through your body. But this energy is not necessarily the power of Now, or the Holy Spirit. Unless you practice Holy Communion (presence + oneness) and have been baptized by the Deity or a *Shaktipat* master, the energy that you experience by obviating your thought-forms is *pranashakti*, or intensified *chi*, moving through your *nadis* (or subtle-body "nerve" channels). This energy can even forcefully ascend from the base of your spine to your crown, through the main central-channel *nadi*, called the *Sushumna*. But even this powerful ascending force-flow of energy, the aroused *kundalini*, is not the Holy Spirit, the power of Now.

The power of Now is the current of *Shakti* that descends into and rises out of the yogi's spiritual Heart-center. As a descending current, the power of Now functions as *Shaktipat*, which means that the yogi *receives* this intense down-pouring torrent. When, in a timeless moment, the *Shaktipat* severs the yogi's spiritual Heart-center knot, he awakens as the Self. Upon the yogi's Self-awakening, the force-current of *Shakti* reverses direction and radiates out of his spiritual Heart-center as Self (or Heart)-radiant energy, or *Cit-Shakti*. (Note: Prior to Self-awakening, the yogi can periodically experience emissional spurts of *Shakti* from the spiritual Heart-center.) *Cit-Shakti* (the power of awakened Consciousness) is the ultimate form of the power of Now because it is *Shakti* as inseparable from *Siva* (or *Cit*). It is the eternal effulgence of Being-Consciousness (*Sat-Cit*) that the now-liberated yogi spontaneously radiates, or "gives" to the world.

◇ ◇ ◇

Isn't it helpful for us to understand our past? If we don't examine our past and past conditioning, how can we understand why we do the things we do, react the way we do, and create the particular life patterns that we do?

The Delphic aphorism "know thyself" counsels us to know our conditional self as well as our transcendental Self. With this in mind, I strongly recommend that spiritual aspirants acquire objective understanding of the psycho-physical karma (or inborn tendencies) they animate. To understand your psychic (or mental-emotional) karma, my suggestion is to get natal chart readings from at least two different professional astrologers. As a former professional astrologer, I know how useful astrological readings by competent professionals can be. Although astro-analysis is an art and not a science, readings by top professionals will provide you with all kinds of insights into your karma. And once you have an objective grasp of your inborn karmic framework, your psychic matrix or blueprint, you then have an objective (though not definitive) context in which to consider and understand your past conditioning and present-life activity and patterns.

To understand your physical karma, your body, my suggestion is to see a top Ayurvedic physician and an expert iridologist. Ayurvedic medicine, which originated in India, will provide you with an objective analysis of your innate physical constitution as well as a reading of the current "elemental" condition of your body. I say "elemental" because the physical body is composed of the same "elements"—fire, air, earth, and water—that, to a large extent, determine your psychic karma. The Ayurvedic physician will "read" your body and prescribe a diet and herbal remedies that will help you balance your physical chemistry. Iridology is the science of diagnosing the body's constitution and health by examining the iris. The iris is a reflection of the entire body, and by examining your iris, an expert iridologist can "see" your constitutional weaknesses and diseased tissue, and recommend an appropriate health regimen for you.

Although I recommend that you objectively know your conditional psycho-physical self, and that you understand your past conditioning and present-life activities and patterning in that context, such knowing will not en-Light-en you spiritually. Only spiritual Light, the radiance of the Divine, can en-Light-en you. Knowing your conditional self will simply help you to optimally maintain and service the psycho-physical "vehicle" that you incarnate. And by properly maintaining and servicing your psycho-physical vehicle, you make your bodymind complex a fit "temple" for worshipping and receiving the Spirit.

Once you have an objective grasp of yourself, karmically speaking, and can thereby effectively "minister" to yourself, you don't need to devote undue time to exploring your psychic and experiential past and how it shaped, and continues to shape, your current state and behavior patterns. If something from your past is truly important for you to deal with, it will emerge from your subconscious and make its presence felt in your conscious mind. Spiritual life isn't about researching the history of your "temple" (your bodymind); it's about worshipping (or religiously devoting yourself to) the Now and receiving Its power, the Spirit-energy that will *unconditionally* free you from your past.

CHAPTER FIVE

The Divine State of Presence

Being Merely Present Versus Being Divinely Present

You keep talking about the state of presence as the key to enlightenment. I think I know what you're talking about, but I'm not sure if I really understand it and I don't know if I have ever truly experienced it.

Presence means being whole-bodily present to the moment—like a baseball infielder in his stance when a pitch is thrown. The infielder isn't merely aware of the moment; he is fully present to it. Tolle uses the analogy of a cat watching a mouse hole. Like the infielder, the cat is whole-bodily present, ready to pounce on the mouse the way the infielder pounces on a ground ball.

When you are truly present, you aren't merely aware of the moment, you are directly and immediately plugged into it. When your plugged-in presence generates enough "voltage," enough conscious force, then a current of energy begins to flow—and you conduct this current of energy by receiving it, by allowing it to penetrate you.

When you not only penetrate the present moment to the Now, but allow yourself to be penetrated by the power of Now, the current of Spirit-energy, then you no longer are merely present, you are *divinely* present,

Now, try a simple experiment. Pretend you're a baseball infielder and crouch down in an infielder's stance. But instead of focusing your attention on an imaginary batter, direct your attention to your mind and be ready to receive the first thought that enters it. If you make an "error" and miss a thought, try to "catch" the next one.

Now, try another experiment. Sit up straight in a chair and rest your palms on top of your knees. Direct your attention to your "third eye area" (the area of your forehead between, and just above, your eyebrows), but don't concentrate on it. Now say grace, but instead of asking God to bless somebody with something, ask Him to bless *you* with His Presence and Power. Silently wait for an answer.

Well, what happened?

In both cases I experienced gaps of thought-free awareness. But in the first experiment, even though I was alert and my mind empty, there was an undercurrent of tension because I was willfully working to be attentive. But in the second experiment, there was a sense of peace because I was passively present, waiting to be blessed.

Very perceptive. What you just described is the fundamental difference between *Rinzai* Zen (one of the two major schools of Zen) and mystical Christianity. *Rinzai* Zen practitioners don't believe in Grace; and even though they are Mahayana Buddhists who, supposedly, embrace the *Trikaya* (the Buddhist Trinity of Bodies), they don't have a clue what the *Sambhogakaya* (the Bliss Body) is. It's the Holy Spirit, but in Zen the idea of the Absolute as spiritual Blessing Power is foreign, so instead of waiting to *receive* the Spirit, they physically and mentally torture themselves to remain alert and in the moment. To this end, they'll hit you with sticks and have you intensely practice *koans* (paradoxical conundrums or questions), the practice of which has been likened to "trying to smash your fist through a wall." Given the martial attitude of the *Rinzai* school of Zen, it's not at all surprising that the Japanese Zen establishment aggressively supported the Imperial Japanese war machine for more than fifty years.

Tolle, like many fogged-out mystics, equates thought-free awareness with freedom from time. He says, "The mental noise returns; the stillness is lost. You are back in time." Freedom from the mind is not freedom from time. The clock keeps ticking; you're just oblivious to it.

The following fabled, didactic Zen exchange illustrates just how oblivious to reality some Zen mystics can be:

> Zen Student #1 (observing a flag waving in the wind):
> The flag is moving.
>
> Zen Student #2: No, the wind is moving.
>
> Zen Student #3: No, you're both wrong. The mind is moving.

What this Zen exchange illustrates is nothing less than an utter indictment of man's conceptual faculty. From the Zen perspective, the moral of this story is that Zen Student #3 is correct, that your mind is incapable of accurately perceiving and interpreting objective reality. You see a flag waving in the wind, but it's just an illusion! If your mind is perfectly still, then there is no movement, and hence no time. This type of nonsensical mysticism stems from the wish to assert the primacy of consciousness over existence. In other words, reality is made to conform to your mind (or no-mind) instead of your mind, *properly*, being made to conform to reality. This inane assertion of the primacy of consciousness is exactly what Tolle is guilty of when he claims that your still mind frees you from time.

What does it mean to be "rooted within yourself"?

Tolle is correct when he says, "It means to inhabit your body fully." In Buddhist terms, it means to be "self-possessed." When you occupy your body by consciously coinciding with it, you become whole-bodily present. Being whole-bodily present anchors you in the moment by transforming mere awareness into integral, plugged-in presence.

The Spiritual Meaning of "Waiting"

According to Tolle, the "esoteric meaning of waiting" is being "present with your whole being." "Something could happen in any moment," says Tolle, "and if you are not absolutely awake, absolutely still, you will miss it." This "alert presence," Tolle tells us, "is the kind of waiting Jesus talks about," and in that state, Tolle says, "all your attention is in the Now."

To illustrate the "esoteric" meaning of waiting, Tolle cites, from the Bible, *The Parable of the Wise and Foolish Virgins* (Matthew 25). Here's Tolle's interpretation of it:

> Jesus speaks of the five careless (unconscious) women who do not have enough oil (consciousness) to keep their lamps burning (stay present) and so miss the bridegroom (the Now) and don't get to the wedding feast (enlightenment). These five stand in stark contrast to the five wise women who have enough oil (stay conscious)

Is Tolle's interpretation of this parable truly an "esoteric" one? Let me put it this way: if I were a professor of Biblical Studies at Cambridge and he were my student, I'd flunk him. First of all, *oil* does not represent *consciousness* in the Bible; it represents the Holy Spirit. Noted Biblical scholar Stanley M. Horton, in his book *What the Bible Says About the Holy Spirit,* has this to say about the symbolic meaning of oil in the Bible:

> Oil clearly represents the anointing of the Spirit. Throughout the Bible oil continues to be an important symbol of the Holy Spirit. It speaks of the real anointing, the "unction from the Holy One" (1 John 2:20) which in the New Testament is extended to every believer.

Second, the *bridegroom* is not the *Now*; it's the Son of Man, and this is clearly stated by Matthew himself. The Son of Man, from an esoteric point of view, is the second Person of the Holy Trinity, the human soul (in the Sacred Heart-center), which, upon uniting with the third Person of the Trinity, the Holy Spirit, awakens to its Sonship, its oneness with the Father, who represents the Now, the timeless divine Presence. If the bridegroom is the Now, as Tolle claims, how could the careless women (actually *virgins*, according to the Bible) miss him? If he is the Now, he would be ever-present, but as Matthew says, "Watch therefore, for you know neither the day nor the hour in which the Son of Man is coming." In other words, the reason we do not know when the Son of Man is coming is that the human soul cannot morph into the Son of Man until the Holy Spirit enters the sacred Heart-center and anoints it with its "oil." Third, Tolle equates the *wedding feast* with enlightenment. There is no wedding feast in this parable; there is only a *wedding*, and this wedding signifies the union of the virgin (or Holy) Spirit and the Son. The Now cannot be fully realized until the Holy union between the virgin Spirit and the Son (who dwells in the Sacred Heart) is consummated, but it is not possible for us to know when our spiritual "wedding" is scheduled.

Here's my interpretation of Matthew 25: The five ignorant *virgins* are *pure* practitioners of presence, but because they lack oil (*Shakti*, the Holy Spirit), they cannot keep their lamps burning (sustain their watching, or witnessing, practice), and so they miss the bridegroom (the Son of Man) and the wedding (the Holy union) and thus remain unenlightened (unrecognized by the Lord).

If you want to abide in the kingdom of God, the eternal Now, you must, as Jesus says in John 4, "worship God in spirit and truth." If you practice "alert presence," which Tolle equates with "esoteric waiting," you are worshipping God in truth, but if you want to maintain, and ultimately consummate, your connection to the Now, you must also worship God in spirit. In Acts 1:8, Jesus tells us that the power of the Holy Spirit will make us witnesses. Jesus here is informing us that we cannot practice true and sustained watching, or witnessing, until we receive the Holy Spirit, the power of Now. Unfortunately, Tolle never mentions the Holy Spirit and how it pertains to the practice of being present (or bearing witness). Therefore, the "esoteric meaning of waiting" that Tolle provides us with is really an exoteric one. Hence, when Tolle says that

"Even the men who wrote the Gospels did not understand the meaning of these parables," it's a case of the pot calling the kettle black, a case of an *exoteric* mystic making a fool of himself by grossly misinterpreting the Gospels.

Beauty, Nature, and Presence

This state of spiritual presence and oneness that you have been describing is similar to what I occasionally experience for brief moments when I am surrounded by nature.

Would you experience this presence and oneness if you were in the midst of a violent and destructive form of nature, such as a raging forest fire, a powerful earthquake, or a furious hurricane? How about if your boat did a "Titanic" at sea, and you suddenly found yourself struggling to stay alive in the dark, icy-cold ocean? How about the experience of nature in the form of famine and pestilence? Nature takes many forms; some of them are downright nasty and deadly, and not at all conducive to the type of spiritual experience you're describing.

Any bloke can temporarily experience peace and cosmic oneness in a tranquil, idyllic natural setting. You hike through Yellowstone or stare at a sunset in Maui, and it's easy to momentarily feel like you're one with lovely Mother Nature and the entire cosmos. But when you're alone in the woods and a pack of wolves decides you're lunch, just how spiritual an experience is that?

The real test of spiritual presence is your ability to establish and maintain it in the worst environments, not the best. You might experience a modicum of peace in a Zen garden or in a holy temple, but what happens when you're caught in a rush-hour traffic jam or stuck in a long line at the unemployment office? And even the most scenic environment loses its magic when you're surrounded by it on daily basis. If you park yourself on a tropical island, after a few weeks or so, your senses dull, and the scenery becomes like wallpaper.

The meditation experience of oneness with nature or the cosmos is commonly referred to as "cosmic consciousness." Cosmic consciousness is a form of what Hindu yogis call *savikalpa samadhi* (*samadhi* with form). When your connection to a particular object—anything from a pinhole to the universal whole—is deep and intense, this locked-in state of engrossment is classified as *savikalpa samadhi*. The state of *savikalpa samadhi* can sometimes morph into what Zen Buddhists call *satori*. *Satori*, which Tolle describes as a "moment of no-mind and total presence" is a prized experience in *Rinzai* Zen, but other schools of Buddhism give little weight to these momentary flashes of "enlightenment."

Beauty, no doubt, is a portal to the experience of oneness. But beauty is in the eye of the beholder. For example, one of my two nephews, a surfer, loves the beach and tells me he experiences "oneness with the ocean." His brother hates the beach but says certain music puts him into a "deep meditative state." One man's shrine is another man's sandpit, but the common denominator in refined human beings is finding something pleasing to their senses that they can use as a springboard to the experience of oneness with life.

But even the experience of oneness with life—even to the degree of *savikalpa samadhi* or *satori*—is not sufficient to truly enlighten an individual. Only the Holy Spirit, the radiant Light-energy of the Divine, can en-Light-en you. Only when your practice of plugged-in presence, or Holy Communion, is full and intense enough to break through to the "other side" can you receive That which is Divinely natural and beautiful: the Goddess Power Itself—God's Grace-full Energy, the glorious and splendorous Holy Spirit.

Eckhart Tolle is doubtless a card-carrying member of the Anti-Mind Mystic's Club. Given his success in convincing the New Age crowd of the evils of the human mind, it wouldn't surprise me a bit if he's elected president at the club's next meeting. Everybody needs a scapegoat, and for these mystics, it's the terrible human mind, which, in Tolle's words, can "neither recognize nor create beauty" and which, "when left to itself creates monstrosities." Tolle, ever the social critic, informs us that, thanks to our "mind-dominated culture... no civilization has ever produced so much ugliness."

Well, I've got some good news for Eckhart Tolle. I just got off the horn with an executive at Walmart, and the open-minded suit admitted that it would indeed be cool to beautify Walmart stores. He admitted that a Walmart store looks more like a warehouse than like, say, the Taj Mahal, but said he'd gladly consider adding aesthetic touches to Walmart stores—*if Tolle, or anyone else, agrees to pay for them.* The executive said that he didn't think Walmart would sell any more merchandise if it turned its stores into aesthetic showcases, and he told me that the cost of upgrading the stores' look would cut into the company's profit and cause them to pass the cost on to consumers. But if someone wants to foot the bill for the beautification project, the executive said they'd be glad to join the battle against "civilized ugliness."

It doesn't take a brain surgeon or a rocket scientist to figure out the reason for "civilized ugliness"—money, or the lack thereof. In other words, the urban blight that causes eyesore has nothing to do with the human mind that can't recognize beauty and everything to do with human beings who can't afford to pay for it. For example, I recently resided in Horseshoe Bay, a picturesque resort community just outside of Austin, Texas. Most everything is beautiful around there, because rich people want it that way and are willing to pay for it. The people who live in lovely towns or picturesque communities like Horseshoe Bay don't possess a rare, mystical, mind-transcending ability to recognize beauty; they simply have the means to pay for it.

My point of view on the mind is, of course, in diametrical opposition to Tolle's. In contrast to Tolle, who preaches that modern civilization is insane and loathsome because it is a product of a *mind-dominant* culture, I contend that modern civilization is beset with dire problems because it is a *mind-subordinate* culture. In my opinion, the fundamental problem with modern civilization is that the public education system doesn't teach students the all-important art of rational and logical thinking. If it did, there would be worldwide upheaval, as rational, free-thinking individualists rebelled against the tyranny of *statism* (government-*dictated* collectivism in any of its forms: communism, fascism, socialism, or welfarism).

In my own case, even though I obtained a degree from an esteemed institution of higher learning—the University of California, San Diego—I never learned how to think logically, via objective, reality-based principles, until years after getting my degree. After graduating, I became an expert in Eastern mystical philosophy and an advanced spiritual practitioner, but I wasn't able to think outside of subjectivist boxes until I encountered Ayn Rand's book *Introduction to Objectivist Epistemology*. Although Rand was an atheist, and I'm not, it was thanks to her insights into the nature of the mind that I was finally able to eliminate the contradictions in my philosophical thinking and construct an integral metaphysical/epistemological system.

Now, let's consider the subject of *beauty* more deeply than Tolle does. The first question we need to ask ourselves regarding this subject is: If the human mind is incapable of creating and recognizing beauty, as Tolle claims, then what creates manmade beauty in the form of art (such as paintings, music, and literature)? And the second question is: If the human mind isn't the necessary agent to create these forms of beauty, then why can't animals create them? To my mind, the answers to these questions are clear: Man's mind *is* the faculty that creates and recognizes beauty in the form of art, and because animals lack man's *creative* and *cognitive* mental faculty, they're not only incapable of creating art, but they're also incapable of even grasping the concept of art.

The human mind cannot create something out of nothing. But it is very capable of arranging existing elements into combinations and patterns that are aesthetically pleasing and thus considered "beautiful." Individuals with artistic talent are adept at creating works of art that are beautiful, but their artwork is not a mystical creation; it is a product of their minds. And even if an artist puts little conscious effort into the creative process and his work seems to "mystically" happen on its own, this isn't the case. It simply means the subconscious mind performed the majority of the work necessary to make it "happen."

Realizing Divine Consciousness

Is presence identical to Being?

Here is Tolle's answer: "When you become conscious of Being, what is really happening is that Being becomes conscious of itself. When Being becomes conscious of itself, that's presence. Since Being, consciousness, and life are synonymous, we could say that presence means consciousness becoming conscious of itself, or life attaining self-consciousness."

Here is mine: Presence alone is *not* identical to *divine* Being. The great Hindu formula—*Sat* (Being) = *Siva-Shakti* (Presence-Power)—informs us that for us to coincide with the *divine* Being, we must unite both *vines* (or dimensions) of Being—Presence (or Consciousness) and Power (or Energy)—into a single Self-existing, Self-aware, Self-radiant Intensity. When we are present (or in communion) and channel the Holy Spirit, we are *spiritually* present. When we are present (or in communion) and our presence is united with that of the Holy Spirit, we are *divinely* present—and our *divine* Presence is identical to Being.

Any bloke can be present to the moment with an empty mind and imagine that his presence is pure consciousness, pure Being. But until the great, forceful *Shakti,* or Spirit-power, rips you apart and blows holes through all the knots (or *chakras*) in your subtle, or "inner," body, you cannot be *divinely* present as Presence, or Being.

Being can only become conscious of itself through the Light of its own *Shakti.* Being apprehends itself in the radiance of its own *Shakti,* or Spirit-power, and when your conscious presence unites with the radiant *Shakti*, the *divine* Being is spontaneously present as the Presence-Power that is your True Self.

◊ ◊ ◊

It seems like Being, or God, is incomplete and needs us to complete or realize itself.

Actually, it's just the opposite. You need Being, or God, to complete yourself. You cannot be whole, or holy, until your individual soul, or consciousness, unites with Spirit.

The whole game of evolutionary life is about apparently separate entities evolving over lifetimes until they can, via yoga, merge into the eternal Source. The divine Being has hidden Himself in form, and the ultimate, though usually unconscious, goal of every separate life-form, or soul, is to "locate" God—and this can only happen by uniting *Siva* and *Shakti* within oneself, in the spiritual Heart-center.

When you realize that your suffering stems from your separation, and you're sick of your suffering, then you're ready for yoga, ready to undertake the discipline of Divine Communion and receive *Shaktipat*, the true power of Now.

Eckhart Tolle's tirades are predictable. The enemy, in every case, is the same: man's mind. In another of his apocalyptic rants, Tolle, in a fusillade of fire and brimstone, informs us that the collective egoic mind is dangerously insane and threatens the very existence of life on planet earth:

> Most humans are still in the grip of the egoic mode of consciousness: identified with their mind and run by their mind. If they do not free themselves from their mind in time, they will be destroyed by it. They will experience increasing confusion, conflict, violence, illness, despair, madness. Egoic mind has become like a sinking ship. If you don't get off, you will go down with it. The collective egoic mind is the most dangerously insane and destructive entity to ever inhabit this planet.

What do you think will happen on this planet if human consciousness remains unchanged?

Hide the women and children! Call out the Marines! Forget the War on Terrorism. The real enemy is the egoic mind, and we've got to take action NOW! If the situation is as dire as Tolle claims—and given Tolle's credentials as an "enlightened guru," how could it not be?—then perhaps it's time to line up the people and commence with a mass lobotomy program.

Tolle's modus operandi is empty, hysterical rhetoric. He seems incapable of dealing in specifics. What, exactly, is the major (mind-caused) problem threatening the existence of the planet today? Is it global warming? Communism? Capitalism? Radical Islam? And what, exactly, is his vision for a new Earth? If everyone starts living in the Now, what kind of social, political, and economic system(s) does Tolle envision? Or will the world just somehow, magically, mystically morph into one big hippie love-in, minus the LSD? If Tolle's Brave NOW World is just a few billion empty-minded naked people lollygagging in a giant planetary Garden of Eden, count me in. (Hey, if the female scenery is as breathtaking as I imagine it, I'll even agree to desist from munching on the fruit from the Tree of Knowledge.) But if the NOW Boss (Meet the Now Boss, same as the old boss) decides to pipe in 'round-the-clock tapes of Tolle's talks, then be sure to cancel my reservation.

The worldwide madness that Tolle rags about is not caused by the rational, selfish ego; it is caused by the irrational, self-destructive (and other-destructive) ego. The rational, selfish ego is an ethical ego that believes in every individual's right to life, liberty, and the pursuit of happiness. It believes in the sanctity of both individual rights and private-property rights and in a limited government that protects them. A government that protects these rights cannot initiate force against its citizens or tyrannize them with fascist and/or neo-Marxist policies and laws.

If every country's government were a constitutional republic that protected its citizens' individual and property rights, wars would not (and in fact could not) exist. If we examine the countries that most obviously threatened the planet's existence in the past (Nazi Germany and Communist Russia) and those which most obviously threaten its existence now (North Korea and Iran), we see a common denominator: an aggressive, tyrannical government that denies its citizens individual (egoic) rights. These countries demanded, or demand, *sacrifice* of the ego for the country's "common good." Countries that enslave their citizens always do so via altruistic political doctrines (fascism and/or neo-Marxism) that encourage mind-less, ego-denying existence for the so-called "good of the whole."

It is my contention that the world could be a perfectly peaceful place sans any spirituality, sans any people living in the Now. A planet of selfish, time-bound, non-mystic atheists could turn the planet Earth into a mundane paradise simply by instituting limited governments based on separation of both church and state and economy and state. Individuals would be free to live their lives as they saw fit, provided, of course, they didn't interfere with anybody else's right to do the same. A social system of laissez-faire capitalism within a framework of constitutionally guaranteed individual and property rights would ensure safe and peaceful countries, and thus, a safe and peaceful world.

The *egoic* mind is not the *egotistic* mind. The egoic mind is simply the mind that naturally is concerned with the organism's survival and well-being. Once you make an enemy out of a faculty that should be your friend, you've started an *unholy* inner war. I say *unholy*, because if you devote yourself to genuine *holy*, or Spirit-filled, life, you bypass the unnecessary battle with your egoic mind and simply and naturally release superfluous thoughts into the Spirit-current.

I am not an atheist and I am a mystic—though not of the Tolle ilk—and I believe that the egoic mind should be transcended within the context of Holy Communion and reception of the Holy Spirit. But the egoic mind is not a demonic force that dooms you and the world. It is simply a unique form of *shakti* (energy) with the marvelous ability to measure objective reality from the perspective of embodied existence. If you accept Tolle's viewpoint of the egoic mind as the de facto devil that threatens humanity's existence, you are gravely mistaken. The de facto devil is, in fact, none other than those who collectively, in one fashion or another, attempt to deny the full and free expression of man's egoic mind.

Eckhart Tolle says that the mere fact that we are listening to him is "a clear sign that the new consciousness is gaining a foothold on the planet." I say that it's merely a clear sign that his net worth is skyrocketing. The easiest way for a "guru" to gain market share is to push the cosmic significance of his message. The New Age Crowd—hey, it's not called "New Age" for nothing—loves the idea of the ushering in of a Now World Order. And the less you deal with nitty-gritty specifics and the more you talk in vague, idealistic generalities, the greater the number of bandwagoners you'll attract to your Now Age following.

Tolle states: "I speak from presence, and as I speak, you may be able to join me in that state." Presence is indeed a marvelous spiritual practice—it is, in fact (along with power), the foundation of my own spiritual practice—but in no way does this practice alone represent humanity's salvation. For unless there is a corresponding appreciation of, and allowance for, man's creative, *egoic* mind, humanity will never evolve into a species that can transform planet Earth into a terrestrial Shangri-La.

Christ, Self, and Divine Presence

The term "Christ" is equivalent to the terms "Self" and "Buddha-nature." And as Tolle says, "Christ is your 'God-essence'" and "refers to your indwelling divinity regardless of whether you are conscious of it or not." The only difference between Christ and presence, says Tolle, is that presence "means your *awakened* divinity or God-essence." In other words, you are always already a Son of God, but, according to Tolle, presence signifies that you have consciously awakened your divinity or Christ-consciousness.

Tolle is wrong again. Presence, in and by itself, doesn't signify that you have consciously awakened your divinity or God-essence. Presence, in and by itself, merely signifies that you are consciously present. Until you are initiated by the Holy Spirit, the higher *Kundalini*, your divinity will remain asleep. When Jesus says that you must worship God in truth and spirit, he is telling you that you cannot bear witness to the Father until you receive and channel divine Spirit-power.

It is nothing short of mind-boggling that Tolle can discuss esoteric Christianity without even mentioning how the Holy Spirit and the Trinity relate to the process of spiritual enlightenment. Given that a high percentage of Tolle's students were raised in Christian households, you would think that at least one question in *The Power of Now* would pertain to the Holy Spirit or the Trinity, but not a single one does. And this, in a word, is dis-*Graceful*.

It is utterly *dis-Graceful* because you *cannot* awaken your divinity or God-essence until you are baptized by the Holy Spirit. Jesus makes this clear in the Bible, but to Tolle, Grace, or God's Blessing Power, is not a reality. Merely being present or consciously aware will not, in and by itself, awaken your divinity. Your presence cannot become divine until it is strong enough to pull down Power from above. The divinization (or enlightenment) of the human vehicle only commences upon reception of the Holy Spirit.

According to Tolle, "The 'second coming' of Christ is a transformation of human consciousness, a shift from time to presence, from thinking to pure consciousness, not the arrival of some man or woman." The second coming of Christ is indeed the awakening of the Christ within you. But for this to happen, you first must be *born from above*. (Note: the correct translation from the Greek is "born from above," not "born again.") Jesus states this clearly in John 3:3 (New Revised Standard Version): "Very truly, I tell you, no one can see the kingdom of God without being born from above."

The kingdom of Heaven is a synonym for divine Self-realization, or permanent oneness with the divine Presence. But for a disciple to realize that "I and the Father are one," a four-stage process must occur. First, the disciple must establish himself in intense one-pointed communion, to the degree of pulling down *Shakti*, or Spirit-power, from above. Second, the disciple must empty himself and receive the infusion of divine Energy, allowing it to penetrate to his Sacred Heart-center. Third, the disciple must, spontaneously, rest his attention in the Sacred Heart (or Christ-consciousness)-center and realize his identity as the indwelling transcendental Christ (or Son, or Self). Fourth, the disciple must let go of this blissful *samadhi* of dwelling as the inner (exclusive) transcendental Son or Self and, via the "practice" of effortlessness, allow the Holy Spirit, or *Shakti*, to sever his Heart-center knot and permanently unite with *Siva*, the transcendental Self. Upon consummation of the divine Heart-union of *Siva* (the transcendental Son) and *Shakti* (the Holy Spirit), permanent oneness with the divine Presence, or Holy Father, is established, and the disciple thereafter abides in, and *as*, the *divine*, eternal I AM.

The universal, impersonal Absolute should never be reduced to a particular personal form. No enlightened teacher is the exclusive avatar of the age, and your spiritual quest will be most fruitful if you eclectically consider gurus, Dharmas, and traditions. Therefore, Eckhart Tolle is correct when he tells you to "never personalize Christ" or make him into a "form identity."

A true guru enlightens disciples in three principal ways. First, he functions as a teacher, disseminating the Dharma to them. Second, he functions as a spiritual potentate, initiating and empowering them with *Shaktipat*. Third, he functions as a radiant mirror, reflecting their nameless, formless identities back to them. As Tolle puts it: "Presence is one" and there is "no mine or yours in presence." Therefore, the guru is simply a Light-energy medium who facilitates the disciple's progressive awakening to his own identity as the impersonal divine Presence.

Spiritual groups, or even the company of a single fellow disciple, can magnify the power of your presence. Jesus intimates this when he says, "Wherever two or more are gathered in my name, there I am." Tolle is right when he says, "A group of people coming together in a state of presence generates a collective field of great intensity." In a focused spiritual group, the force field of awareness can transform an ordinary room into a veritable holy site charged with *Shakti*. And once you're *initiated* and can channel *Shakti*, you can take advantage of these empowered environments to accelerate your spiritual evolution.

Although enlightened masters, *satsangs* (group communions), and empowered holy sites are invaluable aids to spiritual growth, you should not become dependent on them. Once you are initiated, you will need to learn how to practice plugged-in presence and reception of *Shakti* under all circumstances and in every environment. If your goal is to "be a Light unto yourself," you must practice communion even when you face conditions that are distasteful. For unless you confront the "distasteful" with your presence, you will never experience the wonderful mystical state of "One Taste."

CHAPTER SIX

The Etheric Body

Being Is Your Divine Self

You earlier mentioned the importance of inhabiting the body, of being deeply rooted within it. Can you elaborate on this?

The body is the manifest point of contact through which Being is realized. By consciously occupying and coinciding with your body, you transform it into a living temple or holy abode through which Being shines.

I'm still not clear on what you mean by Being.

Being is *pure* conscious existence, meaning consciously existing (or being consciously present) without grasping hold of thought-forms. As soon as you grasp hold of thought-forms, Being mutates into becoming.

Being is Consciousness-Energy (or *Siva-Shakti*). Thought-forms contract consciousness into forms, or states, of consciousness, thereby attenuating the natural intensity, or radiant energy, of Being. When you are unobstructedly present, free of mental grasping, then Being is no longer modified or fragmented by thought-forms, and It shines as Consciousness-Energy.

Tolle says that "subject and object merge into one" in Being. This is a crude and inaccurate description of awakening to Being. Being is actually the transcendental Subject, or Seer, behind and beyond all mental and physical objects that it perceives. When Being (the transcendental Self) awakens, standing free of all objective superimpositions, then all objects are intuited as mere modifications of Itself, the transcendental Subject.

Because Being is not an object, a great "Other," it cannot be dualistically known or perceived. It can only be (spontaneously) felt, or intuited, as your true nature—Self-aware, Self-radiant existence.

Only Being is Truth, and only Truth can set you free.

Free from becoming?

Yes—free from identification with your mutative bodymind. Being is the immutable, or changeless, Existent that frees you from attachment to your manifest form, which changes and dies. Your sin is to limit your illimitable true Self to this ephemeral form.

The Limitation of Words

I have a problem with the word sin. I don't like judging others or being judged.

Then find another word for your habit pattern of separating from Being and contracting into becoming and suffering. As Tolle says, "Don't get stuck on the level of words. A word is no more than a means to an end... an abstraction... a signpost."

What's great about living in the twenty-first century is that we have access to the greatest spiritual traditions in history. So if you're unhappy with how a particular tradition, such as Christianity, describes your habit pattern of avoiding the Divine from moment to moment, you can easily find a more amenable term in another tradition. For example, instead of referring to your activity of ignoring Truth as *sin*, simply adopt the Buddhist approach and label it *ignorance*. If you prefer a psycho-energetic description of your separative activity, you can, like a Daist or Kashmir Shaivite, describe your retraction from Being as *self-contraction*.

◊ ◊ ◊

I don't care for those terms either. They still imply judgment and tell me I'm not okay.

Listen! You're not okay. And that's simply fact, not judgment. If you see a guy a hundred pounds overweight and tell him he's fat, that's not judgment; it's just an objective fact. Likewise, it's clear that you're suffering from separation. Otherwise, you wouldn't be seeking Truth and asking spiritual questions.

If you want to continue in denial and cling to your "I'm okay, you're okay" nonsense, be my guest. I won't judge you. It's your life, and you're free to live it as you see fit, as long as you don't deny other people the same freedom. However, until you acknowledge your dis-ease of separation, you cannot cure it. For example, if you go to a doctor and he tells you that you have VD, he's not judging you; he's just diagnosing your condition. Likewise, I'm not condemning you. I'm just diagnosing your condition and prescribing spiritual medicine—divine yoga—as the cure for your existential disease.

Eckhart Tolle, however, is worse than judgmental. He lumps all egoic (or rationally self-interested) people in with those relatively few members of what he calls "the human race that killed over a hundred million of its own species in the twentieth century."

So we're all guilty by association?

If you believe what the histrionic Tolle says. As Tolle puts it: "As long as you are run by the egoic mind, you are part of the collective insanity." The fact is, a true egoist staunchly upholds the individual rights of all people and would never initiate force against another human being. The mass exterminations perpetrated by the likes of Stalin, Hitler, and Mao Tse-tung were executed not by egoists but by cold-blooded despots with no regard for human life. Estrangement from the Divine is the root existential disease, but to equate this separation, or "unconsciousness," with insanity, as Tolle does, is unconscionable.

Awakening to Your Invisible Inner Reality

You've said that identification with the physical form prevents enlightenment. So how can this body, this physical form, lead to a realization of Being?

According to Tolle, "The body you can see and touch cannot take you into Being." But even though the gross physical form cannot enlighten you, Tolle insists that the "invisible inner body," the "animating presence within you," can bring you to a realization of Being. Tolle states that this "inner body lies at the threshold between your form identity and your essence identity, your true nature." Tolle considers this inner energy field so important to the enlightenment process that he enjoins us to "never lose touch with it."

What, exactly, is this "invisible inner body" or "animating presence" that Tolle is directing us to? Very simply, it is what Hindu yogis term the *prana-maya-kosha*, the second of the five hierarchically ordered (from grossest to most subtle) *koshas,* or "sheaths," that encase or envelop (and veil) the indwelling Being-Consciousness. In his monumental text *The Yoga Tradition*, Dr. Georg Feuerstein, the foremost authority on yoga today, describes the five sheaths thus:

1. The *anna-maya-kosha*, or sheath composed of food; that is, of material elements: the physical body.

2. The *prana-maya-kosha*, or sheath composed of life force: the etheric body in Western occult literature.

3. The *mano-maya-kosha*, or sheath composed of mind: The ancients considered the mind (*manas*) as an envelope surrounding the physical and the etheric body.

4. The *vijnana-maya-kosha*, or sheath composed of understanding: The mind simply coordinates the sensory input, but understanding (*vijnana*) is a higher cognitive function.

5. The *ananda-maya-kosha*, or sheath composed of bliss: This is that dimension of human existence through which we partake of the Absolute. In later Vedanta, however, the Absolute is thought to transcend all five sheaths.

The "animating presence" or "invisible inner body" that Tolle enjoins us to focus our attention on is *not* the indwelling Spirit-force; it is simply the vital life-energy that animates all living and breathing creatures. In humans, the *prana-maya-kosha,* or vital life-energy sheath, manifests itself in three primary forms: 1) as an etheric body, the energetic correlate of an individual's astral (or soul, or psychic-matrix) body; 2) as a network of non-physical meridians, or *nadis*, through which subtle life-energy (*prana,* or *chi*) moves and enlivens the organism; and 3) as the process of breathing air (which, when yogically, or consciously, done, intensifies the movement of *prana-shakti*, or life-force energy, in the disciple).

Can focusing your attention on your animating presence or invisible inner body take you directly into spiritual Being? Not according to Dr. Feuerstein. He informs us that the "dimension of human existence through which we partake of the Absolute" isn't, as Tolle asserts, the *prana-maya-kosha* (or life-force sheath). Rather, it is the *ananda-maya-kosha* (or bliss sheath).

The bliss sheath (or dimension) is a synonym for *Shakti, Ananda,* the *Sambhogakaya*, and the Holy Spirit. When *Shakti* is apprehended independently of *Siva,* when *Ananda* is experienced as separate from *Cit,* when the *Sambhogaka* is enjoyed as distinct from the *Dharmakaya*, and when the Holy Spirit is beheld apart from divine Presence, then the Blessing Power, or radiant Light-energy, of the Absolute is *objectified*, which, in effect, reduces it to a *sheath*—albeit a blissful one—that prevents the nondual realization of the *divine* Being.

The divine Being, or Absolute, can only be realized when the in-pouring Holy Spirit, *Shaktipat,* unites with the immanent Son, indwelling *Siva,* in the Sacred Heart. In other words, only Spirit (or Light)-energy, and not mere life-force energy, can en-Light-en a disciple and bring him to a realization of nondual spiritual Being.

Because Tolle places so much emphasis on the inner energy field without differentiating it from the Holy Spirit (the Bliss Body, or Blessing Power, of the Absolute), I believe that it is important to further elucidate the distinction between the *pranic* life-current and the divine Spirit-current. To this end, the following definition of *prana*, excerpted from the glossary of Adi Da's *Santosha Adidam*, provides a clarifying summary of the difference between cosmic life-energy and divine Spirit-power:

> The Sanskrit word "prana" means "life-energy." It generally refers to the life-energy animating all beings and pervading everything in cosmic Nature. In the human bodymind, circulation of this universal life-energy is associated with the heartbeat and the cycles of the breath. In esoteric Yogic Teachings, prana is also a specific technical name for a number of forms of etheric energy that functionally sustain the bodily being.
>
> Prana is not to be equated with the Divine Spirit-Current, or the Spiritual and Always Blessing Divine Presence... The finite pranic energies that sustain individual beings are only conditional, localized, and temporary phenomena in the realm of cosmic Nature. Even in the form of universal life-force, prana is but a conditional modification of the Divine Spirit-Current.

Tolles's point of view on the animating life-force is diametrically opposed to Adi Da's.

Tolle calls this invisible, inner *pranic* sheath a "deeper reality," but if it truly is a deeper reality, then why do all the classical hierarchical spiritual models (including the five-sheath one) list the life-energy body below the human mind in the spiritual-evolutionary continuum? And if the life-energy body, or "vital," truly pertains to a deeper, "indestructible," reality, why then do all living creatures—including lowly cockroaches and rattlesnakes—possess such a body while lacking man's higher cognitive functions? Tolle believes that you can become conscious of Being simply by focusing your attention on your inner energy field. He says, "Direct [the focus of your attention] away from thinking and direct it into the body, where Being can be felt in the first instance as the invisible energy field that gives life to what you perceive as the physical body." The truth is, simply being consciously present to *any object* (including your inner energy field), and arresting your thought process, temporarily stops becoming and results in the experience of *being*—but not in the experience of *spiritual* Being, not in the experience of the *divine* Being. Although focusing your attention on your bioenergetic field is a fine form of meditation, you can only be truly conscious of the divine Being when you are blessed with spiritual Energy from the Deity. The classic Hindu formula: *Sat* (Being) = *Cit* (Consciousness)-*Ananda* (Blessedness) informs us that only *Cit-Shakti*, not *prana-shakti*, can directly awaken us to the Divinity.

To summarize: Tolle is both correct and incorrect in his assessment of the physical form's role in enlightenment. He is correct in stating that the gross (insentient) physical body cannot bring you into Being, but he is incorrect in claiming that the invisible (bioenergetic) subtle body can. The truth of the matter is that only the Bliss (Light) Body—the *Sambhogakaya* (or Holy Spirit)—can lead you to spiritual enlightenment. Yes, it's true that the physical body can be "remodeled" into a "holy temple" that can serve as a receptacle for the Holy Spirit. And it's true that focusing your attention on your life-energy body can help you to control your *prana,* arrest your mind, and awaken your *kundalini.* But only the *Sambhogakaya*, the Bliss Body itself, can (via its re-union with the *Dharmakaya* in the Sacred Heart) bring you to a realization of the radiant, divine Being.

Connecting with the Inner Body and the Bliss Body

The key to connecting with the "inner" (or *pranic*) body is the same as the key to connecting with the Bliss (or Light) Body—whole-bodily relationship. Feel yourself as the whole body, and *as* the whole body, be in direct relationship to either the space inside or the space outside your body. This psycho-physical "stance" of whole-bodily relationship not only puts you in the right "position" to connect with both the inner body and the Bliss Body, it also enables you to *truly connect*, or *commune*, with anything and everything in your field of awareness.

The disposition of whole-bodily relationship automatically translates into the feeling of occupying, or consciously conforming to, the physical form. And because "to be related is to *be*," when your relationship to the space in front of you (or to any object in that space) is direct and unqualified, this state will morph into the feeling of *being*.

The mind is ordinarily curled upon itself, absorbed in inward abstraction apart from the physical form. This results in a body-mind split and a feeling of disunity. You can heal this split and feeling of disunity via the wholistic (or holy) gesture (or act) of relationship (or communion). Simply be in direct, immediate relationship to the space inside or outside your body. Relationship = presence + oneness (or plugged-in presence), and this translates into no-boundary awareness, or unity-consciousness.

Here are a few recommendations that may help you to establish and maintain your conscious connection, or relationship, to the space in front of you: 1) Practice with both open and closed eyes. Periodically alternating between these two modes helps dissolve the boundary between "inner" and "outer." 2) Randomly focus your attention on your hands and on your "third eye area." This "triadic" form of focusing will help you to feel, and stay, whole-bodily present. 3) Use a verbal enquiry to help reestablish yourself in relationship. In my own case, I periodically, randomly ask myself: "Avoiding relationship?" This reminds me to reassume the "position" of whole-bodily presence relative to, and through, the moment.

The yoga "posture" of whole-bodily relationship puts you in the proper position to directly connect with and feel your life-force. But more than that, it also (by virtue of the conscious force it engenders) intensifies the flow of *pranic* energy, which, in turn, intensifies your sensitivity to *prana* and its relationship to consciousness and the mind. What you'll notice is the extent to which *prana*, in the form of your breathing, affects your thought process and emotions.

In his Yogic Commentary in W.Y. Evans-Wentz's classic text *Tibetan Yoga and Secret Doctrines*, professor Chen-Chi Chang states, "Every mood, thought, and feeling, whether simple, subtle, or complex, is accompanied by a corresponding or reciprocal *prana*." And Dr. Evans-Wentz himself writes, "The thought process and the breathing process are found to be interdependent, and the control of the latter gives control over the former." In other words, by connecting to, and controlling, your inner *prana*, you can (temporarily) prevent your mind-stuff from fluctuating—and this is the goal of yogic *pranayama* (or breath control).

I have experimented with virtually every form of yogic *pranayama*, and in my opinion, the most efficacious and natural one is what I call *electrical pranayama*. Here is the practice: After you assume your whole-bodily *asana* of relationship, simply be in direct relationship to your breathing cycle. Direct relationship (awareness + oneness) = maximal consciousness-force (pure consciousness plugged directly into life). And because *pranayama* is simply (and only) *conscious* breathing, the result of combining maximal conscious force—via relationship—with the breath is the most powerful form of *pranayama* possible.

According to Walter Russell (1871–1963), the renowned spiritual polymath, there are just two primary forces in the universe: *charge* and *discharge*. When you consciously breathe in, you effectively charge (or infuse) your organism with *prana*, and when you consciously breathe out, you discharge (or circulate and radiate) *prana*. Charge and discharge are akin to voltage (force) and amperage (flow) in an electrical cicuit; therefore, if (in the context of conscious whole-body relationship) you practice full inbreathing (all the way down to your navel) and full outbreathing (utterly emptying your lungs, and your mind, too), you will maximize the force (+) and flow (-) of *prana* in your "body electric."

Pranayama, the conscious exercise of charging and circulating subtle life-energy, is a wonderful discipline that should be practiced by all yogis. But, again, *pranic* energy should not be equated with the Holy Spirit, the divine Spirit-current. Only when your practice of direct and immediate relationship (or true Holy Communion) is full enough and intense enough will you be *initiated* by the Holy Spirit, Mother *Shakti*. How will you differentiate between the Holy Spirit (the Baptist Fire) and *pranic* energy? It's very simple: the Baptist Fire literally crashes down on you. The definition of *Shaktipat* is the "descent of divine Power," and when this *Shakti* (or Holy Fire) pours (or rages) through you, its intensity will rock your body, periodically causing it to jerk or shake with *kriyas*, spontaneous purifying movements.

Life-force contemplation and *pranic*-energy exercises are yoga practices that *you perform*; *Shaktipat* yoga *is performed on you*, by the Deity. All you do is receive the Benediction, the Grace-full invasion of the inpouring divine Power. Contemplating your inner energy-field and circulating *prana*, or *chi*, will vitalize and balance your body and help you to silence your mind, but these practices are only preliminaries to receiving the Blessing Power of the Bliss Body, the "body bright."

According to Eckhart Tolle, "The feeling of your inner body is formless, limitless, and unfathomable. You can always go into it more deeply." If your inner body (or your feeling of it) is, as Tolle says, truly "formless, limitless, and unfathomable," how can you tell that you are actually going into it "more deeply?" And if it is formless, it must be the same on the surface as deep underneath, so what is the point of going into it more deeply? And if it is indeed formless and limitless, how can you even feel "it," since there is no "thing" to feel?

The truth of the matter is that the inner body is not formless. It has a specific, subtle (or non-physical) form, or "structure," that great mystics have mapped out. For example, the acupuncture meridian network and the *prana* flow patterns were "seen" or "felt" by gifted yogis. Even the Holy Spirit, the divine Spirit-current, has a specific pathway (independent of the *chi* and *prana* channels) through which it flows in the human body.

When Tolle says, "The inner body lies at the threshold between your form identity and your essence identity, your true nature," he is implicitly presenting, but actually misrespresenting, the Mahayana Buddhist Threefold Body (*Dharmakaya, Sambhogakaya, Nirmanakaya*) of Buddhahood. He is correct in identifying your essence identity (the *Dharmakaya*) as your "true nature" and your form identity (the *Nirmanakaya*) as your manifest body. But he is incorrect when he implicitly identifies your inner body (the *prana-maya kosha,* or *pranic* body) as the *Sambhogakaya,* the Bliss (or Light-energy) body. The *Sambhogakaya* is not the *pranic* or *chi* energy body; it is the Holy Spirit, the true power of Now, which is not reducible to your inner bioenergetic field.

Transformation through, versus Denial of, the Body

Why have most religions condemned or denied the body, regarding it as sinful and as a hindrance to spiritual life?

First, as Tolle points out, humans did not want to admit they were animals with the same primitive biological drives as other creatures. So they invented myths, like the Garden of Eden, to explain their fall from Grace. Instead of perceiving themselves as risen apes, they could now imagine themselves as fallen angels, corrupted by "sinful" carnal cravings. And because these carnal cravings stemmed from the flesh, by regarding the body as the evil, devil-infused cause of their fall from Grace, they became estranged from their physical vehicles and at war with their own biology.

Second, as Tolle does *not* point out, even if you befriend your body and embrace your animal nature, the physical vehicle still remains problematic spiritually. For unless you can master your "vital"—your animal within—your spiritual life will be impeded by the constant demands of your undisciplined flesh. And disciplining, or controlling, your fleshly cravings, your food and sex urges, is not a lot of fun. The truth is that unless you eat small, simple, easily digestible meals, your mind will "feed on the food" and disturb your meditation. And unless you completely cease, or at least drastically limit, your orgasms, you will lack the subtle life-force essential for communing with the Divine and conducting its Spirit-current.

To emphasize that denial of the body is not the way to find God, salvation, or enlightenment, Tolle cites the Buddha's experience: "Even the Buddha is said to have practiced body denial through fasting and extreme forms of asceticism for six years, but he did not attain enlightenment until after he had given up this practice." What Tolle conveniently fails to mention is the fact that *after* the Buddha renounced extreme asceticism, he still lived as a hermit, practiced celibacy, ate only one meal per day, and meditated virtually nonstop. The Buddha termed his post-extreme ascetic life the "Middle Path," but by modern standards the only way to describe it would be *extreme*.

Tolle is guilty of a disputable statement when he says, "Of the ancient teachings concerning the body, only fragments survive." Anyone who has studied Indian Hatha yoga, Taoist yoga, or Tibetan tantra knows that this is not the case. These holistic systems clearly embody and represent far more than mere fragments. Tolle is also barking up the wrong tree when he blames the belief that "you are not your body" as the reason so many seekers never achieved enlightenment. According to Tolle, because of non-identification with the body, "countless seekers have thus been prevented from attaining spiritual realization for themselves and becoming finders." The fact is, two of the greatest Indian sages, the Buddha and Ramana Maharshi, as well as untold other Buddhist and Hindu yogis, *successfully* emphasized non-identification with the physical vehicle as a means to achieving enlightenment. When Tolle says that you aren't your mind, but you are your body, he in effect fosters the body-mind split, a split antithetical to integral spirituality and a wholistic vision of life.

Great mystics do not foster the body-mind split. They are in either one camp (that of strategically disidentifying from *both* the body and the mind) or the other (that of directly transforming and transcending *both* the body and the mind). Tolle fosters a body-mind split because he can't decide which camp he is in. The result is a disintegral spiritual teaching. In short, if transformation is through *your* body, then it must also be through your mind.

Would it be helpful to recover and piece together the fragments of the lost teachings on the body?

First, if such fragments actually exist, I would love to hear Tolle detail which fragments in which spiritual traditions he is talking about. Second, although I agree with Tolle's statement that "there is no need to [piece together the fragments]," I disagree with his reason: the limited value of signposts and words. According to Tolle, because "all spiritual teachings originate from the same Source," all teachings are merely "signposts," "no more than a collection of words." This is reductionism carried to an irrational extreme. All spiritual signposts are not reducible to an equal collection of words. Some spiritual teachings, or "signposts," point in the wrong direction, while others lack coherence and depth. But when your finger points toward your pocketbook instead of the "moon" (the Source-Light), it's always easy to reduce all teachings to one unerring finger: your own.

Tolle instructs us to "feel [our] inner body" while he informs us that he will summarize the "lost teachings of the masters" for us. But before he enlightens us, maybe he could finally let us know if our inner energy field, the animating presence within us, is identical to the power of Now, and if the power of Now is simply another name for the Holy Spirit. Seriously, is this asking too much from a book entitled *The Power of Now*?

Sermon on the Inner Body

Eckhart Tolle says, "You are your body." And he is convinced that the way into Being, or God, is through, rather than away from, your body. Your gross physical form is "only a thin illusory veil," he tells us, and "underneath it lies the invisible inner body, the doorway into Being."

Unsurprisingly, not all the *unlost* teachings of the masters concur with Tolle's claim that the way into Being is through the body. In fact, the Buddha's *Dharma* and the teachings of classical Hindu Advaita Vedanta emphasize that both the gross physical shell and the *pranic* (or etheric) inner body are veils that hide the Absolute. Consequently, both teachings emphasize disidentifying from these elements, which condition, and apparently limit, the Absolute, or Unconditioned.

Thus, the Buddha taught that in order to achieve *Nirvana* (or Self-realization), the yogi should disidentify from the five *skhandas* (causally conditioned elements): 1) *Rupa* (form or shape: the physical body and the etheric body); 2) *Vedana* (feeling or sensation: the emotional body); 3) *Sanna* (perception: awareness of sensation); 4) *Sankhara* (the mental impressions resulting from emotions and perception); and 5) *Vinnana* (dualistic, or subject-object, consciousness). And traditional Advaita Vedanta instructs the yogi to disidentify from the previously-described five *koshas*, or sheaths (physical body, etheric body, lower mind, higher mind, and apparently separate bliss body), that veil the Self. In the case of both the Buddhists and the Advaita Vedantans, the goal is the same: to negate identification with anything and everything that is not the Self, the nondual transcendental Being-Consciousness.

The Buddhist hierarchical schema lumps the inner, or etheric, body in with the physical form, and the Hindu model gives it its own category. But in either case, the inner, or etheric, body is to be rejected as a conditioned element leading to *samsara* (becoming). According to renowned Buddhist scholar Christmas Humphreys (1901–1983), *Rupa*, the first of the five *skhandas*, is usually considered "as the material body composed of physical and etheric matter." In other words, though the inner body cannot be seen or touched, Buddhists still classify it as a material, or *non-spiritual*, constituent. Therefore, from the Buddhist perspective, the inner body *cannot* be "the doorway into Being [or *Nirvana*]."

Even though I have presented the Buddhist and the Advaita Vedanta positions relative to both the gross physical and subtle inner bodies, I am not an advocate of these spiritual traditions. I have presented these positions only to counter Tolle's claim that the inner body is the direct spiritual link to God. My position, which I have made clear throughout this book, is that the only direct link to Being is the Holy Spirit. Although I agree with Tolle's approach of transformation through the body rather than the Buddhist and Advaita Vedanta approach of rejecting the body, I believe that this radical transformation can only take place when the human vehicle is blessed by *Shaktipat*, the descent of divine Power.

Have Deep Roots in the Deity

Eckhart Tolle tells us to "have deep roots within." And to attain this deep-rootedness, he enjoins us to establish a permanent connection with our inner body:

> The key is to be in a state of permanent connectedness with your inner body—to feel it at all times... See if you can be in touch with your inner body at the same time [you are peripherally aware of your surroundings].

Establishing a connection with your inner, or *pranic*, body is an important step in the yogic process. By intensifying your *pranic* "electricity" and sensitizing yourself to the etheric dimension of existence, you naturally open yourself to *Shaktipat*, the descent of the Holy Spirit. Protracted connectedness with the inner body leads to *initiation*—baptism by the Holy Spirit. And once you've been baptized, the amount of *pranic* force that you can summon and command will increase dramatically.

Pranic energy, it must again be emphasized, is not the highest form of *Shakti*. Because Tolle doesn't make this clear, I have made it a point to present excerpts from notable spiritual sources that stress the distinction between the life-force and the higher *Shakti*. Here is what the eminent Sri Aurobindo, in his text *The Synthesis of Yoga*, has to say about *pranic* Shakti:

By yoga, we become aware of a greater life-force, a pranic Shakti, which supports and fills the body and supplies all the physical and vital activities—for the physical energy is only a modified form of this force— and supplies and sustains too from below our mental action. This force we feel in ourselves also, but we can feel it around us and above, one with the same energy in us...

The pranic Shakti can be directed not only upon ourselves, but effectively towards others or on things or happenings for whatever purposes the will dictates. Its effectivity is immense, in itself illimitable, and limited only by defect of the power, purity, and universality of the spiritual or other will which is brought to bear upon it, but still, however great and powerful, it is a lower formulation, a link between the mind and body, an instrumental force. There is a consciousness in it, a presence of the spirit, of which we are aware, but it is encased, involved in and preoccupied with the urge to action. It is not to this action of the Shakti that we can leave the whole burden of our activities; we have either to use its lendings by our own enlightened personal will or else call in a higher guidance; for of itself it will act with greater force, but still according to our imperfect nature and mainly by the drive and direction of the life-power in us and not according to the law of the highest spiritual existence.

The ordinary power by which we govern the pranic energy is that of the embodied mind. But when we get clear above the physical mind, we too can get above the pranic force to the consciousness of a pure mental energy which is a higher formulation of the Shakti.

By all means practice connecting with and feeling your inner body, but remember that the life-force (*prana*, or *chi*) is not the Holy Spirit, the highest *Shakti*. Establish deep roots in your inner body to help you stay rooted and present, but know that the goal is to awaken to and rest in the divine Spirit-current from above, which will lead you to the Sacred Heart, where you will realize yourself as a Christ. Your yogic efforts can only take you so far. When they fail, as they will, call on Grace, and unconditionally surrender to the Higher Power.

Eckhart Tolle believes that when Jesus (in Matthew 7) instructed his listeners to build their houses on the rock rather than on the sand, he was really telling them to dig deep roots within by consciously contacting their inner bodies. This simply isn't the case. Jesus himself likens adherence to the *entirety* of his sayings in the Beatitudes (Matthew 5 to 7) to building a house on the rock, and he never mentions anything about the inner body in his Sermon on the Mount. In fact, the rock, or spiritual foundation, he is talking about is essentially twofold: the lamp of the body (or eye) and submission to the will of the Father. The *eye* signifies one-pointed awareness; and *doing the will of the Father* refers to the act of letting go, or self-surrender. In other words, the real Christian rock is the *Eucharist*, the act of focusing your attention (via Holy Communion) on the Deity and then letting go and allowing His "Will" (the Holy Spirit) to enlighten, or "save," you.

Before You Enter into Communion, Forgive or Forget

When I attempt to put my attention on my inner body, I experience agitation and some tightness in my stomach. I don't experience the deep-rooted connection with the inner body that you talk about.

When you put attention into your body, you're going to be confronted with negative emotions and physical unease. The bodymind is a multi-sheath (or layered) entity, and before you can penetrate to the underlying inner body, you must cut through levels of psycho-physical resistance. Consciousness in an advanced meditator is like a diamond-blade knife that cuts right through the dross to the pure substance underneath. In a beginner, however, consciousness is like a butter knife, and gets stuck in surface patterns of emotional and physical resistance. The more you practice being present to your inner body, the sharper your "tool of consciousness" will become, and the more easily you'll be able to slice through the outer dimension of existence to the inner one.

Simply be present to your interior and "confront" disturbing emotions and uncomfortable physical sensations with non-resistance. In other words, merely be present and do nothing about them. You can dissolve thoughts and emotions by directly observing them, or you can simply remain present and allow them to "self-liberate" (meaning "dissolve of their own accord"). As Tolle says, "Full attention implies acceptance," which means you don't have to do anything about your psychic content except be consciously present to it.

When Tolle says, "Attention is like a beam of light—the focused power of your consciousness that transmutes everything into itself," he is actually describing the essence of *tantra* (or spiritual alchemy). Your thoughts and emotions are psychic formations that contract consciousness (into limited states), but when you assume the position of full and focused consciousness, the formations spontaneously dissolve in the force field of your awareness, and only consciousness itself remains. But what Tolle fails to tell you is that without Grace, the infusion of the highest *Shakti*, your consciousness—contracted *Siva*—will lack the power to sustainedly transmute mutable mind-forms into immutable awareness. Therefore, unless you are plugged into the divine Spirit-current, you will struggle mightily to remain fully attentive and free of resistance.

When you attempt to enter into communion or connect to your inner body, the most disturbing emotional patterns that confront you will likely involve grievances of some sort. These grievances can take the form of blame, self-pity, or resentment—and entire meditation sessions can be spent wrestling with these "demons." That is why Jesus said, "Before you enter the temple, forgive." Because if you don't consciously forgive, or at least forget, before you commence the practice of presence, you will be inviting these insidious emotions to arise while you meditate.

Eckhart Tolle says, "The mind cannot forgive." If the mind can blame, then why can't it also forgive? Obviously, it is much easier to forgive in some circumstances than in others. For example, if your kid breaks a few windows playing baseball in the house, you'll blame him for his mistake. But if he apologizes and offers to do extra chores to pay for the damage, you'll probably forgive him in a flash. But if a mean neighbor shoots your beloved dog, how easily will you be able to forgive him?

When Tolle says, "Forgiveness is to offer no resistance to life," he is conflating forgiving with forgetting. But his advice is good. In a case where you're incapable of consciously forgiving a wrongdoer—yourself or someone else—you must, for your own sake, simply let it go. Otherwise, you will succeed only in making yourself miserable and possibly compromising your health.

Spirit Is Your Link with the Unmanifested

What is the relationship between presence and the Holy Spirit?

"Presence," according to Eckhart Tolle, "is pure consciousness—consciousness that has been reclaimed from the mind, from the world of form." I beg to differ with Tolle. You can empty your consciousness of all content, but the resulting "pure consciousness" is not necessarily equivalent to "presence." Presence simply means being consciously present to existence. If binding thought-forms arise in the context of your presence, your presence can be said to be "impure," and if no binding thought-forms arise, then it can be said to be "pure." In either case, you are still practicing "presence."

The practice of presence is the foundational practice of real spiritual life. But in order for your presence to be *divine*, or *spiritually pure*, it must be plugged into the divine Spirit-current, which "purifies" it by incinerating your thought-forms. In other words," pure *spiritual* consciousness" is synonymous not with an empty mind, but rather with a mind that is outshone by the true Virgin Mother, the pure, radiant Consort (or Power) of the Holy Father (the Divine Being).

"The inner body," says Tolle, "is your link with the Unmanifested, and in its deepest aspect *is* the Unmanifested: the Source from which consciousness emanates, as light emanates from the sun." As I've continually emphasized, the inner body is *not* your direct link with the Unmanifested; the Holy Spirit is. Tolle says your inner body, or life-energy field, is *chi;* but I repeat that *chi,* which is the Chinese equivalent to Indian *prana,* should not be conflated with the Holy Spirit, the Bliss, or Light-energy, body. The Holy Spirit is the power of the Unmanifested, the "first reflex," or direct emanation, from the Source. The *essence* of the Source is Consciousness, and its *nature* is radiant Light-energy, the Holy Spirit, or *Sambhogakaya.*

"Awareness of the inner body," Tolle claims, "is consciousness remembering its origin and returning to the Source." Contrary to what Tolle says, consciousness cannot "remember its origin and return to the Source" via awareness of an object, even if the object is a subtle, invisible one such as the inner body. Consciousness remembers, or recognizes, itself as the Seer and Source only when subject-object duality is transcended. And subject-object duality can only be transcended when the act of placing attention on an object, or "other," is obviated. The inpouring *Shakti* initially appears as a great Object, or "Other," to consciousness, contracted *Siva,* but when the divine Spirit-current penetrates to the Source-center within—the Sacred Heart—the habitual act of placing attention on objects is spontaneously transcended, and consciousness then stands free as the radiant Source. In reality, *Siva* and *Shakti* are never separate; they are merely two aspects—essence and nature—of the same Source, or Being. Consequently, it can be said that when you place your attention on *Shakti,* the Holy Spirit, you are not really meditating on a separate Object; you are simply being *Siva,* contemplating, or enjoying, your own radiant, blissful Nature.

Is the Unmanifested equivalent to Being?

Yes. As Tolle says, the word *Unmanifested* is just a negative term for Being. In most religions, positive terms are used to describe the

Absolute, but in Buddhism there is an emphasis on negation. For example, the definition of *Nirvana* isn't "Being"; it's the "end of becoming." Because the Buddha was an *apophatic* (or negative) mystic, he regularly used the terms "the Unborn," "the Uncompounded," and "the Unmanifested" as synonyms for the Absolute.

Who reclaims consciousness from the mind? Who recognizes himself as the Seer?

You *apparently* do—by being consciously present and transcending thought-forms, which contract consciousness into limited mental states. But in reality, the divine Being-Consciousness, via Its *Shakti,* outshines your mind and reveals and recognizes Itself as your true Self, the transcendental Seer. From an individual perspective, you seem to reclaim your consciousness. But because you are, in essence, divine Consciousness, the Seer, it can from a spiritual point of view be said that it is *really Siva* who sees and recognizes Himself.

From a mystical perspective, reclaiming consciousness from the mind involves both individual effort and divine Grace, or *Shakti.* The false, individual "I," the ego-self, puts itself into position to allow its consciousness, contracted *Siva,* to unite with the inpouring *Shakti.* When this union takes place, contracted *Siva*—the individual consciousness— awakens and shines, spontaneously recognizing Himself as Being-Consciousness, the real, transcendental "I."

What you're saying is way beyond my comprehension. And yet, I can intuitively feel the truth of it. Am I just deceiving myself?

Truly, mystical spirituality is not complex or difficult to comprehend. Its fundamental principles can be easily grasped by almost anyone. From a Christian perspective, mystical spirituality is simply the *Eucharist*: the integral act of Holy Communion, which includes receiving the Holy Spirit. In other words, it is just fusion and infusion—being consciously plugged into life and allowing the divine Power to flow in and en-Light-en you. Prior to being baptized by the Holy Spirit, you can intuitively feel that you are being consciousness when you are in direct and immediate relationship (or communion) with life. But until the Holy Spirit, the divine *Shakti,* crashes down on you, you cannot intuitively feel, or radically apperceive, that you are *divine* Being-Consciousness.

The Aging Process and the Inner Body

Eckhart Tolle believes that awareness of the inner body can "significantly slow down the aging of the physical body." He may be right, but offers no scientific evidence to back up his claim. It stands to reason that by stimulating the movement of *chi* through the meridians (or *nadis*), the intensified, or more freely flowing, subtle life-energy would enliven the gross physical structure and renew the body's cellular matrix. But reason and reality do not always coincide.

The health benefits of contemplating your inner body may be debatable, but it is a proven fact that vigorous physical exercise and a natural-food diet high in fruits and vegetables can significantly slow the aging process and help the body ward off disease. A prominent example of this is Jack LaLanne, who died in 2011 at the age of ninety-six. Jack, the "godfather of fitness," did two hours of "violent exercise" (Jack's term) every morning, and ate only natural food the last eighty years of his life. The question we must ask is: If Jack had devoted two hours each morning to, say, hatha yoga, tai chi, and inner-body awareness instead of to weight training, cardio, and swimming, would he have enjoyed the same great health, energy, and vitality that he did? In other words, even if hatha yoga, tai chi, and inner-body awareness promote health and retard aging, do they do so to an extent that equals or exceeds that of conventional vigorous exercise?

Another question we must ask is: When it comes to intensifying the invisible life-force, is there such a thing as too much of a good thing? For example, moderate drinkers, on average, live longer than teetotalers, but anyone who drinks heavily is more than likely facing an early checkout time. I raise this question of "too much of a good thing" because if awareness of *chi* is indeed the Fountain of Youth that Tolle claims it is, then we would expect spiritual gurus—radiant beings teeming with *chi*—to be beacons of health who live extraordinarily long lives. But, unfortunately, spiritual gurus seem to be subject to the same physical maladies that plague ordinary folk, and they do not, on average, live any longer.

To prove that spiritual mastery does not translate into radiant health and longevity, I have compiled a death-age list of arguably the twenty most prominent spiritual gurus who passed away in either the twentieth or twenty-first centuries. Gurus who died in accidents (Meher Baba and Swami "Rudi" Rudrananda) or whose birth data is unavailable (Neem Karoli Baba) have been excluded from the list. Although "guruphiles" will no doubt disagree with some of my selections, I believe that most of them will agree that, overall, my list is fair and accurate and proves my point. The list follows, with the age of death in parentheses: Sri Aurobindo (78); Sri Chinmoy (76); Adi Da (Franklin Jones) (69); Georg Gurdjieff (73); J. Krishnamurti (90); Murshid Samuel Lewis (74); Osho (Bhagwan Shree Rajneesh) (58); Sri Nisargadatta Maharaj (84); Ramana Maharshi (70); Swami Muktananada (74); H.W.L. Poonja (Papaji) (86); Swami Ramdas (79); Ramakrishna (50); Suzuki Roshi (66); Swami Satchidananda (87); Swami Sivananda (75); Chogyam Trungpa (49); Swami Vishnudevananda (65); Swami Vivekananda (39); Paramahansa Yogananda (59).

The average age of death for the "twenty most prominent spiritual gurus" is 70, virtually the same as for ordinary men. Consequently, before I can accept Tolle's claim that "if you inhabit the inner body, the outer body will grow older at a much slower rate," I would need to see scientific evidence that supports it.

So there isn't any scientific evidence that supports Tolle's claim?

None that I'm aware of. And I'd love to see scientists try to prove my favorite Tolle statement on aging: "When you become identified more with the timeless inner body than with the outer body, when presence becomes your normal mode of consciousness and past and future no longer dominate your attention, you do not accumulate time anymore in your psyche and in the cells of the body." Anybody naive enough to buy this hokum probably believes that there are gurus who live on air alone and that the "ageless," five hundred-year-old Mahavatar Babaji is still trucking around in the Himalayas.

The Immune System and the Inner Body

When you consciously inhabit your body, you will notice that you feel more alive and whole. And this inner-body presence *probably* strengthens your immune system and helps protect you from disease. But there is no hardcore proof of this. For example, when I checked out Tai Chi at Wikipedia, I found the following information pertaining to a research study on meditation's therapeutic benefits:

> In June, 2007, the United States National Center for Complementary and Alternative Medicine published an independent, peer reviewed meta-analysis of the state of meditation research, conducted by researchers at the University of Alberta Evidence-based Practice Center. The report reviewed 813 studies (88 including Tai Chi) of five broad categories of meditation, mantra meditation, mindfulness meditation, yoga, Tai Chi, and Qi Gong. The report concluded that "the therapeutic effects of meditation practice cannot be established based on the current literature," and firm conclusions on the effects of meditation practices in healthcare cannot be drawn based on the available evidence.

Eckhart Tolle provides a simple but beneficial self-healing meditation that he says will boost the strength of your immune system:

> Close your eyes. Lie flat on your back. Choose different parts of your body to focus your attention on briefly at

first: hands, feet, arms, legs, abdomen, chest, head, and so on. Feel the life energy in each part for fifteen seconds or so. Then let your attention run through your body like a wave a few times from feet to head and back again... After that, feel the inner body in its totality, as a single field of energy. Hold that feeling for a few minutes. Be intensely present during that time, present in every cell of your body. Don't be concerned if the mind occasionally succeeds in drawing your attention out of the body and you lose yourself in some thought. As soon as you take notice this has happened, just return your attention to the inner body.

Tolle's self-healing meditation is very similar to the one that I used to practice in the 1970s, when I was experimenting with various East Asian energy-balance systems. Then, in the early 1980s, Mantak Chia, a master of Taoist Esoteric Yoga, arrived on the spiritual scene. Chia introduced Westerners to the Microcosmic Orbit, a meditative and internal energy practice for awakening and circulating *chi* in the inner body. Chia's groundbreaking teachings on self-healing and spiritual development are detailed in his first book, *Awaken Healing Energy Through the Tao: The Taoist Secret of Circulating Inner Power*. This book and subsequent ones by Chia provide in-depth information about using *chi* to open the "routes," the energy channels of the inner (etheric) body.

For a guru who emphasizes the inner body to the extent that he does, Tolle's teachings on the cultivation and circulation of *chi* are shockingly superficial. If you're interested in the deeper aspects of internal energy, I suggest you go to Amazon.com and check out the many fine books on Taoist yoga.

Breathe Your Way into the Body

At times my mind becomes quite anxious and restless, and I'm unable to feel the inner body. Do you have any suggestions?

Yes. My suggestion is the same as Tolle's: conscious breathing. I have already detailed the practice of *pranayama* that I recommend (*electrical pranayama*, described earlier in this chapter in the section "The Inner Body and the Bliss Body"). And you can compare it with Tolle's technique, which is simply to follow the expansion and contraction of the abdomen. Once your mind is quiet and you feel connected with your inner body, you can temporarily dispense with the practice. At times, it will only take a few breaths to charge your body with *prana* (which you can feel as an internal, expansive pressure) and connect with your inner body; and at other times, it will take a sustained effort. Because conscious breathing is more art than science, more a "feel" thing than a mechanical method, you should feel free to experiment with it and to implement it in whatever way best serves your meditation practice.

Creative Thinking

If you've ever wondered what the secret to creative thinking is, Eckhart Tolle has an answer for you: "Whenever an answer, a solution, or a creative idea is needed, stop thinking for a moment by focusing attention on your inner energy field. Become aware of the stillness. When you resume thinking, it will be fresh and creative."

Earlier in *The Power of Now*, Tolle claims that "[the mind] is not at all creative," but now he is telling us how to use the mind creatively. This is a blatant contradiction, but Tolle, sad to say, never addresses it.

The fact is that the human mind is very creative. But because this creativity involves the interplay between the conscious mind and the subconscious mind (which performs the majority of mental work on some problems), the conscious mind must periodically shut down in order to allow time for the subconscious mind to do its job. Creative thinking—contrary to what Tolle says—does not stem from stillness; it stems from the relationship between the conscious mind and the subconscious mind. Awareness of stillness is simply a means of turning off the conscious mind so the subconscious mind can freely do its work.

The Secret to Listening

If we are to believe Eckhart Tolle, the inner body is the key not only to creative thinking, but also to the art of listening. Tolle advises us: "When listening to another person, don't just listen with your mind, listen with your whole body. Feel the energy field of your inner body as you listen. That takes attention away from thinking and creates a still space that enables you to truly listen without the mind interfering."

I've been a meditating mystic for four decades, and if I thought that listening with the whole body and feeling the energy of the inner body were the secrets to the art of listening, I'd say so. But they aren't. In fact, attempting to feel the energy of your inner body while you are listening to someone actually distracts you from fully listening to that person. An ex-girlfriend of mine used to get very upset when we conversed while my attention was partially on my *chi*. She could always tell when I wasn't giving her my undivided attention. Perhaps this is why we are no longer together. Interestingly enough, this woman had her Sun in Aquarius and Moon in Taurus, just like Eckhart Tolle.

Unsurprisingly, Eckhart Tolle's concept of "listening" goes beyond just hearing what the other person has to say. Tolle says, "Most people don't know how to listen because the major part of their attention is taken up by thinking. They pay more attention to that than to what the other person is saying, and none at all to what really matters: the Being of the person underneath the words and the mind." For more than one reason, I do not second Tolle's point of view on listening.

First, if you're paying attention to both your inner body and the other person's Being, as Tolle advises, how much free attention will you have left to listen to what the other person is saying? Unless you're a world-class mystic, you will not automatically be able to continually focus your attention on your inner body and the other person's Being. And your ongoing struggle to do so in the midst of interpersonal exchanges will detract from your ability to listen to the other person. Second, if your inner body is the link to your Being, as Tolle claims, then how can you be aware of the other person's Being without using his or her inner body as the link to it?

Tolle emphasizes being in touch with your own inner body, but he never mentions your contact with the other person's inner body and how this contact impacts relationships. Tolle says, "Most human relationships consist mainly of minds interacting with each other, not of human beings communicating, being in communion... Being in touch with your inner body creates a clear space of no-mind within which the relationship can flower." The truth is that if you are in communion with another person, what you will experience behind his mind is his inner body, his etheric energy field, which emanates from his physical form as his aura. Unless you're psychic, you won't see his aura, his etheric presence, but you *will* subconsciously, and *can* consciously, feel it. And regardless of the mental content exchanged between you and the other person, your respective energy fields will, to one degree or another, either mesh or clash. This interaction of complementary or contradictory energy fields precedes and supersedes any words exchanged between the two of you. Consequently, when Tolle blames the mind and disregards the inter-inner body dynamic, as the cause of conflict in relationships, he displays just how shallow a psycho-metaphysician he really is.

As a long-time professional astrologer (now retired from formal practice), I have done hundreds of relationship readings for couples involved with mind-transcending spiritual disciplines. Regardless of their common interest in going beyond their minds, these couples experienced harmony or disharmony in their relationship directly in accordance with the harmony or disharmony between their respective inner bodies, or etheric energy fields. Because an individual's etheric body is the energetic correlate of his *astral body* (his psychic matrix of *samskaras*, or pre-mental seed tendencies that "sprout" into thoughts), astrology, which provides a blueprint of an individual's astral body, can accurately predict how one individual's energy field will interact with that of another. Hence, contrary to what Tolle says, it is mainly disharmonious inner, or etheric, bodies, and not the human mind, that engender most of the strife in interpersonal relationships.

In short, the "art" of listening is much simpler than Tolle makes it out to be, and doesn't involve unnecessary concern with the inner body and Being. The art of listening is essentially a matter of *wanting* to hear what someone has to say. You will win friends and influence people if you are a patient listener who takes a genuine interest in what others have to say. But if you believe that most people have nothing interesting or important to say, then you will not be a good listener. It's as simple as that. And if your goal is to be a good listener, you probably will learn more about this art from studying Dale Carnegie than you ever will from listening to Eckhart Tolle.

CHAPTER SEVEN

Openings into the Absolute

Consciously Penetrating the Body

I can feel the energy inside my body, but my meditation doesn't go any deeper than that. What should I do?

First, make sure that your *asana*, or "seat," is conducive to deeper meditation. To this end, Tolle's recommendation is: "Sit on a chair, but don't lean back. Keep the spine erect. Doing so will help you to stay alert. Alternatively, choose your own favorite position for meditation."

Tolle's recommendation is fine, and I'll add a couple more suggestions: 1) Rest your palms on top of your thighs (which will facilitate the feeling of being at one with the body); and 2) tuck your chin in slightly (which will help keep the spine erect).

Tolle provides further meditation instruction: "Make sure the body is relaxed. Close your eyes. Take a few deep breaths. Feel yourself breathing into the lower abdomen, as it were. Observe how it expands and contracts slightly with each in and out breath. Then become aware of the entire energy field of the body. Don't think about it—*feel* it. By doing this, you reclaim consciousness from the mind."

My instructions for "going deeply into the body" differ somewhat from Tolle's: Take a few deep breaths. Totally let go in concert with the exhalations. Close your eyes. Briefly feel yourself as the whole body. Then, be present (or in relationship) to the space inside your body. In the context of being present (or in relationship) to your interior space, neither grasp nor reject thoughts. Allow them to appear and disappear of their own accord. By doing this, you liberate awareness from thought-forms and put yourself in position to receive the Benediction from above.

Tolle enjoins you to become one with the energy field that you now feel: "Merge with the energy field, so that there is no longer a perceived duality of the observer and the observed, of you and your body. The distinction between inner and outer also dissolves now, so there is no inner body anymore. By going deeply into the body, you have transcended the body."

According to Tolle, simply by merging with the perceived field of energy, dualistic distinctions are obviated and the inner body is rendered nonexistent. This is mystical poppycock. First, the observer and the observed never become one. You might be absorbed in a state of intense oneness with the energy field and thus temporarily oblivious to the distinction between the perceived and the perceiver, but this distinction remains an existential reality. Second, your inner body does not mystically dissolve and disappear. Your inner, or etheric, body continues to exist, just as your outer, or physical, body does. Just because you transcend your body by going deeply into it does not mean that you existentially become one with everything.

My invitation to you is to receive and embrace the Holy Spirit. Merging with the inner energy field will not bring you into divine Being. Only the union of *Siva* (your plugged-in presence) and *Shakti* (the down-pouring Spirit-power) will enable you to awaken to the all-encompassing Presence of God. Tolle exalts the inner body, deeming it the great link to the Unmanifested. Well, if it's truly the great link to *Nirvana*, then why isn't it mentioned in most Buddhist literature? And true Christianity isn't about connecting to the inner body; it's about receiving the Holy Spirit. But Eckhart Tolle, New Age salesman nonpareil, is intent on packaging the inner body and peddling it to seekers as the golden bridge to Heaven, a.k.a. the timeless Now.

◊ ◊ ◊

Eckhart Tolle is *partially* correct when he states, "Having access to that formless realm is truly liberating. It frees you from bondage to form and identification with form." Yes, the formless realm does provide temporary respite from the incessant arising of thought-forms, which contract your field of awareness into states of suffering. *But*, as the Buddha himself made clear, mystical absorption in the void, in the formless realm, is a temporary *state*, and not equivalent to Nirvana, the *non-state* of pure Being.

Who sees form and formlessness, objects and the void? You do. Who are you? The Self, or Seer—*Siva-Shakti*. But you can only awaken to your transcendental position as the *illumined* Seer when your individual awareness, or contacted Siva-nature, is irradiated and expanded by *Shaktipat,* the down-poured Light-energy from above.

The Nature of Chi

Is chi *the same thing as the Unmanifested?*

No, it's not. In his book *Science and the Evolution of Consciousness*, Dr. Hiroshi Motoyama defines *chi* as "life-sustaining energy that circulates throughout the physical body." This energy, according to Dr. Motoyama, is "the 'vital force' upon which gross physical life is dependent." *Chi*, as Dr. Motoyama makes clear, is simply universal *bioenergy*. And as such, it should not be conflated with the Holy Spirit, which is divine *Light-energy*. Bioenergy sustains your physical existence, but only Light-energy, the Holy Spirit, can en-Light-en you.

Tolle says, "*Chi* is the link between the Unmanifested and the physical universe." This is true. But *chi* is not the link between the Unmanifested and your *soul*. The Holy Spirit is. If *chi* were the bridge from the Absolute to the human soul, then millions of people who practice *Tai Chi* would be sages, channeling and radiating *Shakti*—but, sad to say, they're not.

According to Tolle, "When your consciousness is directed outward, mind and world arise. When it is directed inward, it realizes its own

Source and returns into the Unmanifested." Tolle, like many mystics, enjoins you to direct your mind inward to find the Source. But the Source is no more within than it is without. The Source is the Condition of all conditions, inner and outer. By directing your attention inward to find the Source, Tolle is promoting an exclusive-reductive realization of Truth rather than an all-inclusive, wholistic one. Implicit in his directive to invert your attention is the idea that the outward realm leads you away from Truth, while the inward realm points you toward It. The message is that the world must be rejected in order to awaken to the divine Source. This is a negative message, one that significantly hindered India's emergence as a modern nation. The Truth, in its totality, can only be realized when your consciousness no longer drops full ontological context by seeking the Source exclusively within or exclusively without. If you can remain unobstructedly (or *Spirit-fully*) present, not seeking for anything whatsoever, you will spontaneously experience the *all-pervading* Source and intuit It as the Condition of all conditions.

Tolle tells you what your spiritual practice should be. His instructions are: "Feel the inner body even when engaged in everyday activities, especially when engaged in relationships or when you are relating with nature. Feel the stillness deep inside." What Tolle doesn't tell you is this: Spiritual feeling follows spiritual *being*. And because to be (directly and immediately) related is to *be*, you must first establish yourself in full-context relationship, or Holy Communion, in order to genuinely feel the inner body and Being. The feeling of Being *spontaneously* arises *after*, not before, you commune with the Divine. Tolle, by directing you to focus on spiritual feeling rather than on spiritual *being*, puts the cart before the horse.

Dreamless Awakening

Hindu spirituality informs us that there are four basic states of consciousness: waking, sleeping, dreaming, and transcendental awareness. The first three basic states pertain to ordinary existence, while transcendental awareness, the "Fourth State," refers to spiritual awakening, to existing outside, or beyond, the first three states.

In deep dreamless sleep, your body is recharged with vital energy as you *unconsciously* plug into the Source. Because your connection to the Source is unconscious when you are deeply, dreamlessly asleep, you cannot awaken to your identity as the Self while in this state. In order to recognize the Self, you must *consciously* merge with it, and this can only be done while you are awake.

In the dream state, it is possible to remain conscious, but as Tolle says, consciousness during this state leads only to lucid dreaming, not to liberation. In Tibetan Yoga, one of the Six Doctrines is the Doctrine of the Dream-State, which prescribes specific meditation exercises to perform during the dream phase of sleep. But in my forty years of experience as a spiritual eclectic, I've yet to meet anyone who has become enlightened through the practice of dream-state yoga.

In reality, the three transitory states of waking, sleeping, and dreaming constitute the illusion of separate, finite, embodied existence. In deep meditation, when you rest in the Fourth State (which Hindus call *Turiya*), you recognize yourself as the Self. You know that, in essence, you are not the One who is subject to the three transitory states. You know that, in truth, you are dreamlessly awakened timeless Awareness, the Real.

The Two Main Portals

According to Eckhart Tolle, "The Now can be seen as the main portal [to the Unmanifested]." But not all the great spiritual traditions support Tolle's view that there is a *single main portal* to Being. The Hindu and Buddhist tantric traditions, for example, have (rightly, in my opinion) identified *two main portals* to the Absolute: Consciousness (or Presence) and Energy (or Power).

Spiritual connectedness can be likened to an electrical circuit, wherein voltage (electromotive force) is analogous to presence (plugged-in conscious force) and amperage (electron flow) is analogous to power (spirit flow). The ancient tantric masters, though lacking scientific knowledge of electricity, recognized the electrical-like nature of spiritual Reality. And on the basis of this recognition, they identified Consciousness (or *Siva*) and Energy (or *Shakti*) as the *two* fundamental portals to the Unmanifested.

Every portal to the Unmanifested is simply a form of consciousness-force ("charge") or spirit-flow ("discharge"). In other words, every type of meditation, implicitly or explicitly, involves the generation of conscious force and/or the conduction of spiritual energy. Because Holy Communion (plugged-in-presence, or direct and immediate relationship) generates maximal conscious force, it is the definitive "charge" portal. And because reception of the Holy Spirit is the conduction of maximal spiritual power, it is the ultimate "discharge" portal.

Every portal that Tolle identifies—connecting to your inner body, the cessation of thinking, surrender; awareness of silence, etc.—falls under the category of either a consciousness (or "charge") portal or an energy (or "discharge") portal. For example, awareness of silence is a concentrative, or "charge" portal, while surrender, or letting go, is a relaxant, or "discharge," portal.

Tolle says it's only necessary to use one portal to access the Unmanifested:

> It's up to you to open a portal in your life that gives you
> conscious access to the Unmanifested. Get in touch with
> the energy field of the inner body, be intensely present,
> disidentify from the mind, surrender to what is; these are
> all portals you can use—but you only need to use one.

Tolle is wrong. You need to use two portals—a consciousness (or "charge") portal and an energy (or "discharge") portal. The two great Hindu formulas—*Sat* (unmanifest Being) = *Siva* (Consciousness)-*Shakti* (Power) and *Sat* = *Cit* (Consciousness)-*Ananda* (Blissful Energy)—inform us that both a "positive" (or conscious-force) portal and a "negative" (or spirit-flow) portal must be combined if *Sat*, unmanifest Being, is to be realized.

Is love a portal into the Unmanifested?

No, it isn't. Tolle is right when he says that "Love isn't a portal; it's what comes *through* the portal into this world." Spiritual love, or love-bliss, is simply the Holy Spirit shining through you. You are simply a conduit that feels and radiates the love-energy of Being. Love, the radiant and blissful feeling of Being, naturally manifests through you when you consciously plug into the Unmanifested and receive the Benediction, the Blessing Power from above.

Silence

Are there portals other than the ones already mentioned?

Whatever brings you into the Spirit is a portal. If particular music, images, or environments facilitate your connection to and conductivity of the Divine, then they can be classified as portals. Spiritual music is an excellent portal because it serves to silence the mind, enabling you to more easily connect to the Light-energy beyond thoughts. I personally love to meditate while listening to Merlin's Magic-Chakra Meditation music. You can sample it at YouTube.com.

Focusing your attention on silence is another way to still your mind. If you're intently conscious of the gaps between sounds, you can easily lock into the silent, empty space underlying all phenomena. Once you're engrossed in the formless realm, you're in ideal position to receive the Benediction.

As Tolle says, "A portal opens up every moment." But these *secondary* portals are merely tributaries that lead to the main river, the Holy Spirit. Conscious "charging" (the discipline of Holy Communion) and spiritual "discharging" (the practice of channeling Grace) are the two *primary* portals because they, and they alone, directly, immediately, and wholly establish you in Being, the Unmanifested.

Space

Eckhart Tolle reveals his existentialist roots when he states, "Every physical object or body has come out of nothing, is surrounded by nothing, and will eventually return to nothing." This is utter nonsense. The truth is, it is impossible for *something* to come out of *nothing*. It cannot happen. Existents, in the form of physical objects or bodies, can only come from some Thing, or Existent, and this Existent—the Self-radiant, Self-existent Being—is hardly a nothing.

To support his position that "the essence of all things is emptiness," Tolle quotes the *Heart Sutra*, a prominent Mahayana Buddhist text. The *Heart Sutra* famously declares, "Form is emptiness, emptiness is form." Is this true? No, it's not. If form were emptiness, then we could walk through walls and a knife plunged into a man's heart would not kill him. Emptiness is a derivative concept that has no meaning unless there is some thing or Thing (such as God) that can be empty, or void of content. Presence, not absence, is the foundational essence of all things, and emptiness simply refers to the nonappearance of objects, or content, in the context of divine Presence.

The Big Bang did not begin the expansion of the universe into space. The Big Bang itself was the beginning of space (and time). Prior to the Big Bang, there were no objects or space; there was only the spaceless, timeless Unmanifested, pregnant with the potential Energy for manifestation. Without the manifestation of objects, there can be no space. Space is the interval or area between objects, and without objects, the concept of space is meaningless. The universe is not expanding into space. Existents (such as galaxies and stars) are separating from each other, and this creates more space, or area, between them, which results in the so-called expanding universe.

◊ ◊ ◊

What is this "emptiness" or "nothing"?

Eckhart Tolle responds to this question by negating its validity. He says, "You cannot ask such a question. Your mind is trying to make nothing into something. The moment you make it into something, you have missed it."

Tolle can't answer the question, but I can. My response is that there is not, and cannot be, such a thing as absolute "emptiness" or "nothingness." The truth is, emptiness, or nothingness, cannot come from "Thingness," the Absolute Being. The fact that scientists cannot create an absolute vacuum devoid of subatomic particles and energy proves that Thingness and things cannot be reduced to nothingness. All things can be reduced to energy, but not to nothingness. The maxim "nature abhors a vacuum" holds true metaphysically as well as physically. If you empty your mind, you are flooded with spiritual energy. This is why mystics often refer to Ultimate Reality as the Vacuum-Plenum. Yes, Presence and absence can be viewed as a mystical dialectic. But whereas divine Presence is the *absolute* Context, emptiness is merely the *relative* lack of content. The more you empty your mind, the more the Unmanifested shines through you, as the dissolved mind-forms transmute into spiritual energy. In other words, consciousness *is* energy, not an empty nothingness.

Tolle sees the problem as "trying to make nothing into something." But Tolle and the apophatic Mahayanists have their own problem: trying to make something into nothing. And as the universe proves, this is impossible.

Tolle says, "'Nothing' can only become a portal into the Unmanifested for you if you don't try to grasp or understand it." I say, "Nothing" can only become a portal into the Unmanifested if you realize that it pertains to the process of mind-emptying and not to an ineffable spiritual Reality.

It's difficult to grasp "Nothing."

Only that which exists can be grasped. Because "nothing" doesn't exist, it can't be grasped, except as a concept appertaining to the absence of existents.

Spiritual life isn't about "something" or "nothing;" it's about awakening to the divine Being, the "Thing-in-Itself," which is Consciousness-Energy, not an impossible Zero.

Tolle says, "Space has no existence." This is patently untrue. Prior to the birth of the universe, there was no space or time. As soon as the universe manifested, space and time came into existence. If space has no existence, why can we measure it? The spaceless Unmanifested is immeasurable, but space, as a manifested dimension, is a measurable existent. Tolle says, "You cannot understand space because it doesn't stand out." If space doesn't stand out, how come everyone is so aware of its existence?

Tolle deifies space, claiming it has no existence, but enables everything else to exist. This is more nonsense. What enables everything—including space—to exist is God, the great Existent, who created the universe by modifying Himself into an infinity of spatial existents.

Tolle says space is "nothing" and that you should "pay attention to nothing" by becoming aware of the empty space around you. Although space is not "nothing," it is an excellent object of contemplation, a wonderful portal to the Unmanifested. In fact, when I teach people how to meditate, I instruct them to "gaze into space" as a means to establishing themselves in plugged-in presence. The contemplative gaze into empty space is a fundamental practice in Tibetan Dzogchen, and it leads to empowered Holy Communion. The "void" is not void, and once you've been baptized by the Holy One, emptiness "dances" as bliss-*full* Light-energy.

Space, Time, and the Universe

According to Eckhart Tolle, "World and space arise simultaneously." If world and space arise simultaneously, then, like the world, space must be a created phenomenon. But Tolle contradicts himself when he also claims that "Space is no-thing, so it was never created." If space is nothing, why do scientists tell us that the gravity of planetary bodies curves it? Moreover, gravity even exists in space, and physicists refer to this minute amount of gravity as "microgravity."

Anything that can be objectified, including space, cannot be a nothing. It is a contradiction to make space an object of meditation and to also claim that it is an uncreated nothing. But Tolle and his fellow foggy mystics revel in contradictions. And because there are not, and cannot be, any contradictions in reality, Tolle and his mystic brethren have, in effect, evicted themselves from reality.

The "basic space" of phenomena (*Dharmadhatu* in Tibetan) is not an empty nothingness; it is timeless Awareness, the universal Buddha-nature, or omnipresent *Dharmakaya* (Essence Body). This timeless Awareness is prior to and beyond space. It pervades ordinary space, but cannot be reduced to it. Empty space is a portal to this "basic space," but unlike empty space, "basic space" cannot be objectified. It can only be subjectively beheld, via the *Sambhogakaya* (Light-energy Body). Contemplation of empty space leads to contemplation of Light-energy, which culminates in apprehension of the universal Buddha-nature, the *Dharmakaya,* the *spaceless* Context, or "basic space," of phenomena.

Eckhart Tolle is so muddled when it comes to esoteric metaphysics that an astute critic could crank out volumes refuting most every sentence he writes on the subject. For example, Tolle states, "And the greatest miracle is this: That stillness and vastness that enables the universe to *be* is not just out there in space—it is also within you." First of all, stillness and vastness do no enable the universe to *be*; God does. Stillness and vastness are derivative *qualities* stemming from God, the *unqualified* Being, and in no way do they enable the universe to *be*. "Vastness" only exists because the distance between objects is extensive. In other words, "vastness" depends on the existence of objects. Thus, it is ludicrous to say that vastness enables the universe to *be*. "Stillness" likewise does not enable the universe to *be;* God's *Shakti*, or dynamic power, does. God as *Siva* is static, but relative to emanation, universal creation, God is pure energy, not stillness.

Tolle says that the "still inner space of no-mind" within you "is vast in depth, not in extension." "Spacial [sic] extension," says Tolle "is ultimately a misperception of infinite depth—an attribute of the one transcendental reality." If spatial extension is indeed a misperception, as Tolle claims, then the implication is that man's senses are invalid and that the universe can only be correctly perceived mystically. Tolle doesn't elaborate on his statement, but by invalidating man's senses, he also impugns his mind. Man's conceptual ability depends on the material provided by his senses, and if his perceptual faculty is flawed, as Tolle implies, then his ability to reason must also be impaired.

According to Einstein, if we are to understand the universe, space and time must be recognized as an integral whole, as a single manifold.

Yes. Space and time must be considered in tandem, as a space-time continuum with four dimensions (three of space, one of time). The beginning of the universe was the beginning of space-time, which came into existence in conjunction with energy and matter. Without the manifestation of energy and matter, space-time would not be a reality.

Tolle says, "Within you, both space and time have an inner equivalent that reveals their true nature, as well as your own." According to Tolle, "Whereas space is the still, infinitely deep realm of no-mind, the inner equivalent of time is presence, awareness of the eternal Now." If space is an infinitely deep realm, then how can it be nothing? And if it is nothing, then how can you tell it is infinitely deep? No-mind simply means the absence of thoughts. When the interval between thoughts is increased, consciousness feels more spacious, and even seems to expand. But in order to recognize the true nature of space—luminous Awareness—you must go beyond the void and channel the continuum of radiant Energy that is the *Sambhogakaya*, the Holy Spirit. Presence does reveal the true nature of time, but only when it is empowered by the Holy Spirit. Tolle rightly recognizes that absence (no-mind) and presence (pure awareness) are two sides of the same coin, but what he doesn't acknowledge is that your awareness can only illuminate the void after you've awakened the Holy Spirit. Tolle's discussing presence and absence while ignoring (Spirit) power is tantamount to a physics teacher talking about voltage (force) and ohms (resistance) while ignoring amperage (flow). Such neglect is inexcusable—especially when the title of your book is *The Power of Now*.

Eckhart Tolle states, "You are here [in the world] to enable the divine purpose of the universe to unfold." If this is true, then it stands to reason that the way to allow the divine Will to live through you is to connect to the divine Source and allow its Power, the Holy Spirit, to direct your life. The Bible says the Holy Spirit is the divine Teacher and Guide. If this is the case, then the key to enabling the universe's divine purpose to unfold through you would be to channel the Holy Spirit and adhere to its directives. But Tolle, negligently, fails to mention the role of the Holy Spirit in aligning oneself with the divine purpose of the universe.

The Death Experience

According to various Eastern spiritual traditions, death affords a final opportunity to achieve immortality. In The *Tibetan Book of the Dead*, the foremost text on conscious death, specific after-death instructions are provided on how to merge with the clear (or white) Source-Light and thereby avoid rebirth. But as Tolle rightly points out, "Unless you have encountered the Unmanifested in your lifetime, you are likely to miss [the opportunity to unite with the Absolute]."

In his acclaimed book *Easy Death*, the spiritual adept Adi Da describes the after-death experience. According to Da, the soul, upon passing, is confronted with a field of light that is white in the center and gold and blue on the periphery. The gold area is associated with gross perception and the blue area with subtle. If your attention is drawn to either of these realms, you'll pass into a *bardo*, or astral plane, that is commensurate with your soul's karma, and you'll eventually reincarnate. But if you can transcend the tendency to associate with the gross (gold) and subtle (blue) planes of phenomena and stay centered on the white Source-Light, you can merge with it and attain eternal rest in the Absolute.

Staying centered on the white Source-Light is exceedingly difficult. Most humans habitually grasp at phenomena while alive, and, according to various Eastern traditions, this grasping tendency continues after death. Consequently, as *The Tibetan Book of Dead* informs us, unless the passed soul was an accomplished yogi in life, his karma will draw him to the non-white light, and he will find himself in a *bardo* that leads to another round of birth and death.

So death doesn't mean annihilation, just a bardo *and then rebirth?*

Yes, unless you practiced communion intensely while alive and can hold fast to the Clear Light after you pass.

Tolle is correct when he states that the "dissolution of the physical form is always a great opportunity for spiritual realization." And he is also right when he says, "This opportunity is tragically missed most of the time, since we live in a culture that is almost totally ignorant of death." If you're interested in learning more about spiritual counseling for the dying, I suggest two books: *On Death and Dying*, by Elisabeth Kübler-Ross; and *Who Dies?*, by Stephen Levine.

CHAPTER EIGHT

Light on Relationships

Be Here Now, Independent of Others

Without a love relationship with a complementary "other," the right man or woman, how is it possible for us to be whole?

If you're dependent on another person to make you whole, then you'll be a suffering fragment when you're alone. Even if you happen to find the "right" partner, your imaginary "wholeness" will disappear whenever he or she fails to satisfy you. And if he or she abandons you, you'll be a basket case.

I believe a love relationship can fulfill us.

Then why are you seeking spiritual salvation? If you truly believe another flawed human being can be your savior, why bother with the discipline of Holy Communion?

What does salvation mean?

Eckhart Tolle describes true salvation in "negative" Buddhist terms when he says it is a "state of freedom—from fear, from suffering, from a perceived lack and insufficiency and therefore from all wanting, needing, grasping, and clinging." In Hindu and Christian yoga, it is described positively as union with God or Ultimate Reality.

Salvation is only in the Now. It is not a state that you can attain in the future by *becoming*, or changing your life circumstances. It is not about finding something or someone to fulfill you. It is about entering the Now, plugging into the divine Presence and allowing its down-pouring Power to liberate you from your fruitless search for fulfillment through an "other."

In every waking moment—whether you are alone or with someone—*be here now*. In other words, simply be utterly and totally present and don't seek for anything, including fulfillment or salvation. When the pressure of your presence is sufficient, the Holy Spirit will pour down through you, divinizing your presence and making you whole. Only this union of your individual soul with absolute Spirit can make you whole. A relationship with another human being cannot.

Dysfunctional Relationships

Eckhart Tolle views non-spiritual human relationships in a negative light. He says, "Unless and until you access the conscious frequency of presence, all relationships, and particularly intimate relationships, are deeply flawed and ultimately dysfunctional." Is he right? Not in my opinion. My long-time experience as a counselor has taught me that spiritually oriented people have the same problems in relationships as everyone else.

Over the past forty years, I've been involved with multiple spiritual groups. I've (astrologically) counseled innumerable individuals and couples within these groups, and I've found that despite a commitment to live consciously in the moment, these people suffer from the same dysfunctional relationships as conventional people. It would be nice if a life devoted to living in the Now automatically translated into harmonious human relations, but from my experience that's not the case. The mass failure of the hundreds of spiritual communities that sprouted up in America in the 1970s graphically illustrates that the practice of conscious life is no panacea when it comes to interpersonal relationships.

According to Eckhart Tolle, "Most 'love relationships' become love/hate relationships before long... Negative, destructive cycles occur with increasing frequency and intensity, [and] then it will not be long before the relationship finally collapses." It is true that a high percentage of romantic relationships degenerate into a classic yo-yo pattern, in which the polarities of love and hate alternate until the negative cycles finally destroy the relationship. But the reason for this pattern eludes Tolle, who, mistakenly, attributes it to a lack of conscious presence.

The truth is this: No matter how idealistic or spiritually evolved a couple might be, if the karmic energy fields of the partners do not harmoniously mesh on multiple levels, their relationship will eventually fail. Romantic relationships are fueled by animal attraction, intense primal bioenergy. At the outset of a relationship, this primal bioenergy drowns out the more subtle mental-emotional energies exchanged between the two individuals. Once the animal attraction subsides, as it inevitably will, the partners' mental-emotional energies begin to predominate. And if those energies are incompatible, then the relationship, regardless of the couple's spiritual maturity, will inevitably reflect this inherent disharmony.

Addiction, Love, and Wholeness

Why do we become addicted to another person?

It's biological. According to researchers, our glands secrete chemicals that fuel romantic infatuation for a period of a few years, just long enough to create a family. Once the chemical addiction to the partner weakens, the relationship depends mainly on compatible mental-emotional energies to make it work. Romantic infatuation is a chemical phenomenon, and the chemicals your body produces are like drugs that addict you to the other person. Physically and psychologically, you become dependent on the other person's presence, and their absence from your life can trigger intense, painful withdrawal symptoms. This is why breaking up is such an ordeal.

Romantic love relationships reflect our powerful need for wholeness. Consequently, the urge for union with the opposite polarity is, as Tolle points out, "almost irresistible." But when you depend on a sexual partner to make you feel meaningful and whole, any perceived breach in the relationship threatens your sense of spiritual security. And when the relationship begins to fail, a psychological crisis invariably ensues. If you're honest with yourself at this point, you'll realize that you're an addict whose dependency on a significant "other" is a disease; and if you're a serious truth-seeker, you'll seek a cure. If your search is fruitful, you'll realize that the only cure for your dependency is the Holy One, for only a relationship with the divine Being can make you truly (or spiritually) whole and set you truly (or unconditionally) free.

When your practice of plugged-in presence bears fruit—down-pouring *Shakti*—you have the means to override the bodily chemicals that addict you to your significant other. Down-pouring *Shakti,* the Holy Spirit, is *Nectar,* ambrosial energy from God. When you're able to rest in the divine Spirit-current, your need for an other to make you whole vanishes. The Spirit-current is not a super opiate that replaces the "drug" of the significant other; it is the inherent bliss of your own Self-nature. At first, it is enjoyed as objective Light-energy; but finally it is recognized as the radiance of your own *Being.*

Because you are a physical being as well as a spiritual one, your urge for a complementary other, the right man or woman, is not going to suddenly disappear just because you begin to practice Holy Communion. But as your relationship with the Divine deepens, your need for a physical partner to make you feel whole will begin to dissipate. And because you'll no longer depend on a human partner to make you feel complete, your relationship with a significant other is more likely to flower sans your neediness. Some advanced spiritual practitioners lose all interest in sex and intimate relations, while others still enjoy the play between the sexes. But what these practitioners have in common is freedom from addiction to an other. They realize that no one but the Holy One can make them complete.

Adyashanti is a prominent contemporary guru who teaches the nondual Advaita Vedanta path to enlightenment. (Google his name and you'll find samples of his teachings.) He is also a happily married man. He once remarked that when his wife said she no longer needed him, he knew that she had "gotten it" spiritually. The moral of this story is clear: Love your significant other, but transcend your addiction to him or her by deriving your sense of wholeness from the Spirit.

The Secret to Enlightened Relationships

How can we change an addictive relationship into an enlightened one?

According to Eckhart Tolle, "The greatest catalyst for change in a relationship is complete acceptance of your partner as he or she is, without needing to judge or change them in any way. That immediately takes you beyond ego."

What Tolle says is utter New Age nonsense. If you're Adolf Hitler's partner, do you accept him as a hateful racist and mass murderer? If your husband is a rapist or a pedophile, do you avoid judging him? If your wife is a drug addict, do you stand idly by while she kills herself?

It's one thing to accept your partner's idiosyncrasies; it's another to accept their violent or destructive behavior. Failure to judge and act with regard to serious issues not only is irresponsible, it's also stupid and potentially deadly.

Common sense is a very useful attribute, but when you replace *intelligent* judgment with mindless non-judgment, common sense is abandoned. When you ignore reality in the name of acceptance, you aren't transcending the ego, you're simply abdicating responsibility and discrimination.

Tolle believes that complete acceptance and non-judgment put an end to all codependency and enable you to either "separate [from your partner]—in love—or move ever more deeply into the Now together—into Being." This raises the question: isn't non-acceptance and judgment implicit in the decision to separate from your partner? And if, for argument's sake, you were free of judgment and beyond ego, how could you ever determine if a prospective partner is right for you?

The secret to enlightened relationships is twofold: 1) right understanding, and 2) right action.

Right understanding means knowing yourself, knowing the other person, and knowing your interpersonal chemistry. Only a mind that is deeply and objectively judgmental is capable of such knowing. The greatest aid to such knowing is astrology—not pop astrology, but real astrology. Anybody seriously interested in understanding himself, others, and interpersonal relationships should study astrology. Astrology provides the blueprint or map of an individual's psyche, and once you have that, it's so much easier to assess your chemistry with another person.

Right action means acting *appropriately* once you deeply understand your relationship with your partner. And you can only act appropriately, or *intelligently*, if you are free of interpersonal addiction. As already emphasized, the way to transcend interpersonal addiction is by establishing a yogic relationship with the Deity; for only at-one-ment with God can make you whole and set you free.

Even though an intimate relationship cannot set you spiritually free, the bond that connects you and your partner can provide a portal to the Absolute. A soul mate, a partner with whom your life energies and psyche harmoniously align, represents a doorway to the "Other Side," but it is up to you to step across the threshold and connect to the Spirit. The right partner can serve as a conduit to the Infinite, but only the infinite Being Itself can liberate you. And if you become dependent on your partner as an exclusive means to Being, to divine love, then you once again become an addict.

When you find someone who, in Tolle's words, "reflects your love back to you more clearly and more intensely than others," then you have made contact with a potential soul mate. And if a love relationship ensues, the challenge is to transmute the romantic connection into a spiritual one. This transmutation of *eros* into *agape* is the essence of tantra yoga, and unless you and your partner are able to transform romantic communion into Holy Communion, your relationship will degrade, rather than elevate, your spiritual life.

Tolle, rightly, says, "True communication is communion—the realization of oneness, which is love." But what Tolle doesn't say is: true (or spiritual) communion, oneness, and love are not possible without *Shaktipat*, the descent of the Holy Spirit. Human love is but a fragment, a stepped-down modification, of divine love. And human love cannot become divine love without the intervention, or descent, of divine Power, the Holy Spirit.

The Transformation of Relationships

Eckhart Tolle specializes in apocalyptic statements, and he even applies his bold sociopolitical predictions to the field of male-female relationships. Tolle asserts that "as the egoic mode of consciousness and all political, social, and economic structures that it created enter the final stage of collapse, the relationships between men and women reflect the deep state of crisis in which humanity now finds itself."

Let's analyze Tolle's assertion. First, he claims that the egoic mode of consciousness is entering its final stage of collapse. This is a laughable statement. In fact, if anyone can introduce me to even one person whose ego is in its final stage of collapse, I'd be nothing short of amazed. Only a fogged-out utopian could take Tolle's assertion seriously. Second, he claims that all egoically created political, social, and economic structures are also on the verge of collapse. This statement raises two questions: What political, social and economic structures is Tolle referring to? And what "non-egoic" political, social, and economic structures will supplant them after the collapse of the egoic mode of consciousness? It is ridiculous to make a statement like Tolle's unless you specify the egoically created structures that you're talking about and the non-egoic, New Age structures that will replace them.

Tolle is correct when he says that dysfunctional relationships are legion in modern society and that "most relationships [nowadays] are not rooted in Being and so turn into a source of pain and become dominated by problems and conflict." Because denying or escaping from the reality of a difficult relationship (one you cannot easily end because of children or other reasons) is not a solution, Tolle advises a spiritual approach. He says, "All you *can* do is create space for transformation to happen, for grace and love to enter."

Tolle's advice, in my opinion, is right. The true spiritual approach to any problem, including a dysfunctional relationship, is to simply be present and allow Grace and Love to enter. Tolle, unfortunately, doesn't elaborate on what, exactly, Grace is. He hardly mentions the term in his book, and he never tells us how Grace relates to the power of Now. What Tolle should have said is: Grace is the Holy Spirit, the power of Now, the descent of Love-bliss into the world of man.

In accordance with his apocalyptic mindset, Eckhart Tolle states that "Never before have relationships been as problematic and conflict ridden as they are now… [and] for those who hold on to the old patterns, there will be increasing pain, violence, confusion, and madness."

But even though human relationships are, according to Tolle, in a terrible state of decline, the solution, he says, is to "accept that the relationship is here to make you *conscious* instead of happy."

Yes, relationships should serve as a vehicle to heighten your spiritual consciousness, but if they're not also agents of joy, why not, if possible, just end them?

Tolle's viewpoint on relationships raises the following two questions: 1) Are relationships really more problematic now than ever before? 2) Can anything other than the practice of conscious presence make them less problematic?

As I see it, relationships are indeed more problematic now than ever before, and this is so for one fundamental reason: the breakdown of traditional roles in society. When social roles, particularly male-female ones, are no longer clearly defined and religiously adhered to, confusion and conflict ensue. But even though relationships nowadays are more difficult, the breakdown of traditional social roles is by no means an entirely negative phenomenon. It has resulted in a freer, more open-ended society. Instead of the "old world's" static and repressive social orders, the "new world's" dynamic and liberating ones offer individuals independence from stifling sociocultural imperatives.

Tolle, a joke as a sociologist, mistakenly views the breakdown of relationships as a sign of impending Armageddon, in which the new-world political, social, and economic structures will all collapse. Here's my advice regarding the demise of modern civilization: don't hold your breath waiting for it to happen. And if you're naïve enough to believe that the human race will self-destruct unless humanity, en masse, begins to live in the Now, then welcome to the Church of Tolle.

To make relationships less problematic, I have two suggestions: 1) cultivate friendships with responsible, high-integrity people, and 2) limit your intimate (non-family) relationships to people with whom you are astrologically compatible. The first suggestion will save you much grief by enabling you to eliminate flakes and low-integrity people from your life. Regarding the second, know that even two spiritually-minded souls cannot happily intermesh if their etheric energy fields are inherently incompatible. By following these two suggestions, you're sure to reduce the problems in your relationships.

My partner is still acting out his old patterns of unconsciousness—jealousy, control, etc. I point this out to him, but he is unable to see it.

Tolle's "remedy" for an unconscious partner is "no-remedy." He repeatedly instructs you to remain present, relinquish judgment, and give your partner space. In other words, he simply tells you to extend your *sadhana*, your spiritual practice, into your relationship.

If you do what Tolle recommends, you become a mirror for your partner. By not reacting to his unconscious behavior, your *clear* consciousness acts as a mirror, reflecting his activity back to him. This will enable him to see and feel what he is doing. If he is spiritually oriented, he will drop, or at least attempt to drop, his negative behavior. But if he is defensive rather than open, your mirroring, or conscious non-reaction, can intensify his negative behavior, and he might, at some point, "explode." Explaining the "mirror effect" to him can help him understand what is happening, but the ball is in his court when it comes to dropping his old patterns of unconsciousness.

Tolle says, "Learn to give expression to what you feel without blaming. Learn to listen to your partner in an open, nondefensive way. Give your partner space for expressing himself or herself. Be present."

Tolle's advice is fine—to a certain extent. But at some point—and your "spiritual intelligence" must be the judge—it is appropriate to blame people, to hold them accountable. To simply remain present and open and allow your partner or anyone else to egregiously "shit" on you or others is patently irresponsible. If you want to take a laissez-faire approach and "do nothing" in response to flagrantly destructive behavior, be my guest. But I certainly don't recommend it.

Men and women are from different planets, and the book *Men Are from Mars, Women Are from Venus* became a bestseller because it details the psycho-physical differences between the two sexes. Although volumes have been written about these differences, they can be summarized in a single statement: Men live in their head and in their cock; women live in their heart and in their body.

The typical man strives to be rational and suppress his emotions. He is concerned with doing and achieving, and this extends to his love life, where he is preoccupied with copulating. The usual female, in contrast, focuses attention on her feelings, and rather than suppressing emotions, expresses them. She is preoccupied with establishing an emotional-physical connection, but not with coitus.

Women typically suffer in relationships when men are emotionally unavailable and lack empathy, while men usually suffer when women are irrational and overly emotional. The practice of spiritual presence helps men to be more sensitive and understanding, and it grounds women, enabling them to curb their fussing and nagging.

Tolle does not believe that a relationship between a conscious partner and an unconscious one can succeed. He states:

> If you are consistently or at least predominantly present in your relationship, this will be the greatest challenge for your partner. They will not be able to tolerate your presence for very long and stay conscious. If they are ready, they will walk through the door you opened for them and join you in that state. If they are not, you will separate like oil and water. The light is too painful for someone who wants to remain in darkness.

I don't fully agree with Tolle. Although it is true that your "mirroring" can provoke negative, or "dark," energy from your partner, this is not always the case. If your partner is open and intelligent enough to appreciate a less problematic you, then regardless of their lack of interest in spiritual life, they will approve of and benefit from your life in the Spirit.

As I stated previously, even if both you and your partner embrace conscious life, the Light, this by no means ensures a successful relationship. Because astral chemistry is more powerful than conscious intent in interpersonal relationships, if you're astrologically incompatible with your partner, no type or amount of *sadhana* will transform your union into a felicitous one. In fact, the Light itself will often intensify your conflicting tendencies, and you will both realize that it is in your mutual interest to dissolve the partnership.

Are Women Closer to Enlightenment than Men?

Is the path to enlightenment the same for a man as for a woman?

Not if we are to believe Eckhart Tolle. His position is that women are closer to enlightenment than men, so their path to Being is more direct. Tolle says, "Generally speaking, it is easier for a woman to feel and be in her body, so she is naturally closer to Being and potentially closer to enlightenment than a man."

Compare Tolle's view on women's spiritual potential to the Buddha's:

> If, Ananda [the Buddha's closest disciple], women had not retired from household life to the houseless one, under the doctrine and discipline announced by the Tathagata [the Buddha himself], religion, Ananda, would long endure; a thousand years would the good doctrine abide. But since, Ananda, women have now retired from the household life to the houseless one, under the doctrine and discipline announced by the Tathagata, not long, Ananda, will religion endure; but five hundred years, Ananda, will the good doctrine abide.

Elsewhere, in response to a question from Ananda, the Buddha replies:

> Women are soon angered, Ananda; women are full of passion, Ananda; women are envious, Ananda; women are stupid, Ananda. That is the reason, Ananda, that is the cause, why women have no place in public assemblies, do not carry on business, and do not earn their living by any profession.

The Buddha's view on the spiritual potential of women is diametrically opposed to Tolle's. These quotes of the Buddha were extracted from

Ananda K. Coomeraswamy's text *Buddha and the Gospel of Buddhism*, originally published in 1916. Dr. Coomeraswamy, the foremost Buddhist scholar of his time, wrote before the advent of the modern feminist movement. Nowadays, in deference to feminism, writers on Buddhism conveniently ignore the Buddha's disparaging commentaries on women.

Before I present my own view on the gender/enlightenment issue, I want to dispute Tolle's claim that the Unmanifested, the Source, is fundamentally feminine in nature. It is important to refute Tolle's claim because his argument for feminine spiritual superiority is based on the erroneous notion that the Divine, like a woman, is essentially yin in nature.

The Divine, the Source Itself, is neither male nor female. It is transgender Presence (or Consciousness) and Power (or Energy), but Its nature can be likened to an androgynous Matrix that is simultaneously *both* masculine and feminine. Because great religions emphasize reception of the Divine's Power, the yin gesture of opening and receiving spiritual Energy can seem to imply that the Divine is feminine in nature. But, in fact, it implies just the opposite. If you allow yourself, like a vagina, to be penetrated by the divine Power, then the implication is that the Power itself is actually phallic, or penetrative, in nature.

The truth is, the enlightenment process *equally* involves the yang gesture of connecting and the yin gesture of receiving. The great Christian mystic Meister Eckhart summarizes the need for both gestures when he says, "I penetrate God, and God penetrates me." True spiritual life demands both an intense penis-like thrust into the Divine (to connect) and an effortless vagina-like opening to the Divine's Energy (to receive). In the Hindu tradition, a Self-realized sage is commonly (and reverently) addressed as Bhagavan. The term Bhagavan, etymologically, means "penis in the vagina." Thus, a Self-realized, or truly holy (or whole), being is an individual who has integrated the yang function of penetration and the yin function of being penetrated into the single, nondual function of radiant, transcendental *Be-ing*. Contrary to what

Tolle asserts, Being is not exclusively feminine. Rather, It is *Siva-Shakti*, meaning that It is equally male and female, both yang and yin.

Though it is clear from Meister Eckhart's teachings and the Hindu representation of God as *Siva-Shakti* that the enlightenment process involves both male (or penetrative) and female (or receptive) elements, how is it that a religion such as Taoism could flourish by emphasizing only the yin ideal of emptying or letting go? The answer is: it couldn't. Although the *Tao Te Ching*, the Taoist Bible, preaches the yin ideal of surrender, real-world Taoism recognizes the need for yang, or concentrative, exercises. If you examine Taoist yoga texts, you'll find that the Taoism of the *Tao Te Ching* is hardly the Taoism practiced by Taoist yogis. But Tolle, fixated on the feminine, is adamant about asserting women's spiritual superiority and yin energy, so he conveniently ignores the importance of male, or yang, energy in enlightenment. The following statement by him illustrates his prejudice against the role of male, yang, energy in enlightenment:

> To go beyond the mind and reconnect with the deeper reality of Being, very different qualities are needed: surrender, non-judgment, an openness that allows life to be instead of resisting it, the capacity to hold things in the loving embrace of your knowing. All these qualities are much more closely related to the female principle.

In the *Bhagavad Gita*, the Hindu Bible, (Lord) Krishna says to (disciple) Arjuna: "Set your mind on me and fight." In other words, the path to God, as represented by Krishna, is warfare. Therefore, the true disciple, or yogi, must be a warrior—and the path of the warrior is hardly a feminine one. But Tolle, conveniently, refers only to the yin-oriented *Tao Te Ching*, while neglectfully ignoring the yang-oriented *Bhagavad Gita*.

The essence of yoga practice is meditation—*dhyan(a)* in Sanskrit. And the term *dhyan* is derived from the Sanskrit root *dhi,* meaning "to bind" or "to hold on." Spiritual life, therefore, involves not only the yin gesture of surrender or letting go, but also the yang act of attaching yourself to or holding on to an object (including the formless Divine as an abstract "Object"). And since the act of attaching yourself to, or connecting to, the Divine *precedes* the gesture of surrender to, or reception of, the Divine's power, it should be obvious to objective thinkers that male energy is just as important as female energy in the enlightenment process.

The Collective Female Pain-Body

Is the pain-body more of an obstacle for women?

According to Eckhart Tolle it is—and this very fact, Tolle informs us, is why women are closer to enlightenment than men are. If Tolle's belief that exposure to the "pure pain" of a collective pain-body serves as a great opportunity for enlightenment, it stands to reason that the most exploited, subjugated, and traumatized groups on the planet would be the ones that produce the most enlightened beings, the most Self-realized sages. But simple observation tells us that this is not the case. A case in point is African Americans, who have suffered untold pain from enslavement and denial of human rights. But despite their prominent collective pain-body, African Americans in no way represent the leading edge of the spiritual enlightenment movement. And the same thing can be said about women.

Tolle, an unabashed champion of feminine spiritual superiority, claims that "The number of women who are now approaching the fully conscious state already exceeds that of men and will be growing even faster in the years to come." My rejoinder is: The number of women participating in the New Age movement certainly exceeds that of men, but this in no way means that women represent the vanguard of the spiritual consciousness movement. And the reason for this is simple: women are not testosterone-driven; they lack the glandular fuel that drives men to relentlessly strive for enlightenment, creatively originate great Dharmas, and iconoclastically engender new social orders and modes of being.

A man's testosterone predisposes him to imbalanced brain function, and imbalanced brain function is a correlate of genius (and retardation). Women, on average, according to studies, are virtually as smart as men. But unlike men, women have balanced brain chemistry that rarely results in extreme cases of intelligence (or stupidity). In other words, although the average woman is almost as smart as the average man, the range of female intelligence is genetically limited compared to that of males. Consequently, according to some researchers, such as psychiatrist Glen D. Wilson, author of *The Great Sex Divide*, only men can be true geniuses (or total idiots).

It can be argued that it takes a genius of sorts to navigate the treacherous waters of the enlightenment process and to be able to articulate the technical aspects of this esoteric process. And in my forty years of study, I have yet to encounter a truly profound technical spiritual guide authored by a woman. And without the presence of such truly profound guides, no genuine spiritual New Age is possible.

In all my reading of philosophy, Eastern and Western, I have encountered only one woman whom I consider exceedingly brilliant, one woman who perhaps qualifies as a true genius: Ayn Rand. And she was a staunch atheist with little regard for the feminist movement. When questioned about her opinion of the feminist movement, Rand's witty reply was: "I'm a male chauvinist." Rand knew that her extreme talent as a philosopher was freakish for a female, and she held that male geniuses were the prime movers, the driving force, behind positive epochal change.

Because pioneering *yang energy* is at the root of positive (as well as negative) social and spiritual revolutions, it's my contention that it is men, not women, who will champion any *true*, world-transforming "New Age" spiritual movement. Although my viewpoint is a controversial one sure to bring me much flak, it is my belief that unless political correctness is supplanted by naked truth, unpopular as it might be, no genuine awakening of humanity is possible.

◇ ◇ ◇

Eckhart Tolle believes that women are inherently more spiritual than men. He says, "Women are regaining the function that is their birthright and, therefore, comes to them more naturally than it does men: to be a bridge between the manifested world and the Unmanifested." It is Tolle's belief that women, because of menses—which every month expose them to the collective female pain-body—possess an inherent biological spiritual advantage over men. "One of the best times [for enlightenment]," Tolle informs us, "is during menses." Accordingly, Tolle believes that "Many women will enter the fully conscious state during that time." Exposure to premenstrual tension, the awakening of the collective female pain-body, Tolle argues, can "then become not only a joyful and fulfilling expression of your womanhood but also a sacred time of transmutation, when you give birth to a new consciousness." The end result, according to Tolle, is that "Your true nature then shines forth, both in its female aspect as the Goddess and in its transcendental aspect as the divine Being that you are beyond male and female duality."

Given Tolle's apotheosis of the menstrual cycle, you have to wonder how many men, after reading *The Power of Now*, have visited their family doctor and pleaded for a menses pill. In Tolle's "Brave NOW World," penis envy has been replaced by pussy envy.

Eckhart Tolle is correct when he says, "Through sustained attention and thus acceptance, there comes transmutation. The pain-body becomes transformed into radiant consciousness, just as a piece of wood, when placed in or near a fire, itself is transformed into fire." But what Tolle doesn't say is this: No particular biological phenomenon, such as menses, is necessary to intensify the experience of the pain-body and to help you transform it into radiant consciousness. The very act of Holy Communion will, *by itself*, automatically intensify your exposure to the pain-body, engendering your very own "dark night of the soul." And when, in the context of your Holy Communion, you no longer recoil from your "dark night" of suffering, the Holy Spirit, the Baptist Fire, will spontaneously incinerate your pain-body and en-Light-en you with its radiant Energy.

Eckhart Tolle fails to address an important question: If women are closer to enlightenment than men, why didn't the greatest avatars, Buddha and Jesus, also recognize this fact? If Jesus, for example, believed that women were inherently more spiritual than men and greater agents for the awakening process, wouldn't he have chosen some—if not all—female apostles? And nowhere in their teachings do the Buddha or Jesus talk about the menstrual cycle as a spiritual advantage for women. It's wonderful that Tolle refers to the words of Jesus and the Buddha throughout *The Power of Now*. But it's lamentable that he fails to consider to them when the subject matter involves the enlightenment of women.

Eckhart Tolle, properly, preaches that the ultimate purpose of male-female relationships is mutual enlightenment. He, rightly, emphasizes the importance of "holding the space of intense presence" between you and your partner. By doing this, he says, "a permanent energy field of a pure and high frequency will arise between you," and "no illusion, no pain, no conflict, nothing that is not *you*, can survive in it."

Tolle's description of the ideal male-female dynamic can be restated as follows: When your relationship to your partner is direct, immediate, and unobstructed, then, spontaneously, your interpersonal communion morphs into Holy Communion, as the Holy Spirit, the power of Now, blesses your union with its living Presence.

This living Presence, this "vortex of consciousness," says Tolle, "represents the fulfillment of the divine, transpersonal purpose of your relationship." In other words, all interpersonal relationships are but a doorway to transpersonal relationship with the Divine—Holy Communion. And when your communion, your enactment of oneness, is whole—not obstructed or fragmented—then the Divine can fully manifest itself in your life, enabling you to fulfill the real, or spiritual, purpose of your relationship(s).

Enlightenment and Relationships

When one is enlightened, does the need for a relationship with the opposite sex vanish?

Sometimes yes and sometimes no, depending on the individual's karma. Some great sages, such as the Buddha and Ramana Maharshi, had no interest in sex or a male-female relationship. Others, such as the late Adi Da and the legendary Tibetan guru Marpa (1012–1097), continued to enjoy the company of the opposite sex after they awakened.

Tolle's point of view is that enlightenment does not obviate the form identity, which is one-half of the whole. In other words, men and women are biologically incomplete, and in his words, "This incompleteness is felt as male-female attraction, the pull toward the opposite-energy polarity, no matter how conscious you are."

But contrary to what Tolle says, many sages and saints throughout history have transcended the urge for a physical "other," which renders his point of view less than accurate. The fact is that certain ascetically inclined beings simply, often spontaneously, lose all interest in sexual relationships.

Realistically speaking, however, for most of us still on the spiritual journey, the need for a significant other is not going to magically vanish any time soon, even if we meditate ten hours a day and live on tofu and veggies. Consequently, for us to feel complete on the outer level of our being, we require the company of our opposite-energy polarity.

But Being, as Tolle points out, has no needs. Therefore, as he puts it, "It is perfectly possible for an enlightened person, if the male or female polarity is not met, to feel a lack of completeness on the outer level of his or her being, yet at the same time be totally complete, fulfilled, and at peace within." In other words, although desires, including sexual ones, may continue to arise in an enlightened being's mind, the Light of Consciousness, the radiance of his Self, outshines them, and these surface "disturbances" do not affect his underlying wholeness and peace.

How does being gay impact one's spiritual quest? Is it a positive or a negative?

If you read nothing but the Great Traditions—the classic Hindu, Buddhist, Taoist, and hermetic Christian texts—you wouldn't even know that homosexuality exists. The ancients had great insights into Ultimate Reality, but relative to mundane reality, they were terribly deficient, offering little wisdom relative to specific matters, such as homosexuality.

Consequently, present-day spiritual teachers are left to their own devices when it comes to discussing controversial matters such as homosexuality. And most New Age gurus, unlike most conventional religious preachers, have no problem with homosexuality and same-sex marriage, sanctioning them as acceptable alternatives to straight life and male-female conjugality.

But the incontrovertible fact remains: gay people are queers, people with a sexual proclivity that defies the biological order: reproduction of the species. And as such, they are abnormal—not members of an equal but merely alternative "lifestyle," but members of a sexually "dysfunctional" group. Even though this is so, I want to make it clear that I have no problem whatsoever with gay people, and in my opinion, they are entitled to all the same rights as straight people.

Because gay people are social outsiders, they are forced, individually and as a group, to confront mainstream society from a position outside the norm. As outsiders, they are blessed in the sense that they must live and think outside the box, which frees their minds from the disinformation and propaganda foisted upon the public by the government and the mainstream media. Moreover, as necessarily creative outsiders, they are, as Tolle points out, more likely to be open to the spiritual dimension of existence than are straight people. Thus, homosexuality can serve as an inducement to enlightenment. But as Tolle also points out, if a gay individual gets egoically caught up in his uniqueness, in his lifestyle and subculture, then instead of serving as an advantage, homosexuality can turn into a hindrance.

Is it necessary to have a good relationship with yourself and love yourself before you can have a fulfilling relationship with another person?

No. Narcissists love themselves, but hardly lead the world in fulfilling relationships. The keys to a fulfilling relationship are good (astral-etheric) chemistry and common interests. If your energy field is compatible with your partner's, you'll both feel good when you're together, and if you share common interests, the relationship will be mentally stimulating.

Eckhart Tolle doesn't believe that it is necessary have a good relationship with yourself. In fact, he doesn't believe that it is necessary to have a relationship with yourself at all. He opines: "But do you need to have a relationship with yourself at all? Why can't you just be yourself? When you have a relationship with yourself, you have split yourself into two: 'I' and 'myself,' subject and object. That mind-created duality is the root cause of all unnecessary complexity, of all problems and conflict in your life."

To my mind, Tolle's dismissal of the need for a relationship with yourself is absurd. If you don't have a relationship with yourself, you can't know and understand yourself. And if you can't know and understand yourself, you are less than human. What separates us humans from lower forms of life is our mental ability to introspect, to split ourselves into two, so we can gain insights into our respective physical, mental, and emotional natures.

Life is relationship, but if you cannot split yourself into two, you cannot understand relationships. All knowledge is gained through a subject-object split, through mind-created duality. But if you are a *via negativa* mystic like Tolle, you will choose to see the (necessarily) dualistic mind as the root cause of all problems and conflicts in your life rather than as a marvelous tool for understanding yourself, others, and relationships. What Tolle and his ilk fail to acknowledge is that conflicts in nature exist independent of the mind. For example, wild animals regularly fight over downed carcasses, territory, and the alpha role. Likewise, much of the conflict experienced by humans is biologically induced rather than just mentally created. In other words, the human mind *recognizes* conflict, but it doesn't necessarily create it. Yes, it can create conflicts, but it can also resolve them—even when it isn't the cause of them. In short, the evidence does not support Tolle's indictment of the mind as the root cause of *all* conflicts in human beings' lives.

Socrates insists that the unexamined life isn't worth living. But Tolle considers the examined (or self-reflective) life a curse. He says that upon enlightenment, "The split caused by self-reflective consciousness is healed, its curse removed." Who is right? Examine the historical social impact of religious and political dogmas that have, implicitly or explicitly, preached against an examined life. Then decide for yourself if self-reflective consciousness is a curse or an integral form of awareness that should be cultivated by members of an enlightened (or free-thinking and progressive) society.

Real spiritual life is *all about* relationship. As Adi Da says, "The [spiritual] discipline is relationship." Relationship is simply another word for communion. Holy Communion is simply an *ontic* (or radical existential) relationship with Being Itself. But prior to establishing an ontic relationship with Being, you must establish an *epistemic* (or knowing) relationship with yourself, the manifest complex of *becoming*, or flux, that you are. In other words, before you can "know" (or recognize) your Self, you must know (or cognize) your self. And you cannot profoundly know your self without self-reflectively examining yourself via a dualistic relationship with yourself. Establishing a direct and immediate relationship with your self not only enables you to gain profound insight into your self-event, it also positions you to receive the Holy Spirit. And this "position to receive the Holy Spirit" will morph into empowered Holy Communion (or Divine Relationship) once the Spirit "touches" you.

CHAPTER NINE

Happiness and Inner Peace

The Bliss Beyond Peace and Suffering

What is the difference between happiness and inner peace?

Eckhart Tolle says," Happiness depends on conditions being perceived as positive; inner peace does not." I say that true happiness, the Bliss (or Spirit)-current of the Self, depends on nothing; it is spontaneously Self-generated when you effortlessly rest in Being. Inner peace can refer to any self-satisfied state, spiritual or non-spiritual. Simply accepting reality as it is results in inner peace. But unless the acceptance is unconditional—to the degree of pulling down the Holy Spirit, the *Sambhogakaya* (or Bliss Body)—the inner peace cannot be classified as truly spiritual (or Spirit-full).

Is it possible to only attract positive conditions into our life? By thinking only positive thoughts, we would manifest only positive events in our life.

As Tolle says, "Do you know what is positive and what is negative? Do you have the total picture?" Some of the seemingly worst experiences in life can result in positive outcomes, while some of the seemingly best experiences can end in disaster. In other words, be careful of what you wish for, because you may end up getting it. And for argument's sake, if everything in your life did turn out "positive," in accord with your thoughts or affirmations, you would never develop humility or grow as a person by having to confront and overcome difficult challenges. True prayer or affirmation is not to petition the Divine for what you egoically consider a positive outcome; it is to ask to live in accord with the Truly So, the spontaneously arising Absolute.

This does not mean that truly "positive" (or "good") and truly "negative" (or "bad") do not exist as objective realities. They do, if you accept a rational "standard of value" (Ayn Rand's term) to judge what is good or evil. It simply means that the result of your *experience* of them is not always predictable in a world that likewise is not always predictable.

Tolle asserts that "when you live in complete acceptance of what *is*—which is the only sane way to live—there is no 'good' or 'bad' in your life anymore. There is only the higher good—which includes the 'bad.'" The fundamental problem with this "spiritual" perspective is that it contradicts the rational viewpoint of man's life as the proper standard of value. If you accept man's life—his survival and well-being—as the standard of value, then, clearly, certain things (actions, circumstances, and events) must be judged as "bad." For example, smoking is bad because it kills you. Rape is bad because it grossly violates a woman's well-being. To adopt Tolle's "spiritual" perspective is to deny the existence of objective "good" and "bad."

According to Dr. David R. Hawkins, the renowned psychiatrist, spiritual guru, and author of *Power vs. Force: The Hidden Determinants of Human Behavior*, "good" and "bad" can be objectively measured with applied kinesiology. Dr. Hawkins has devoted himself to calibrating (via a logarithmic scale) the levels of goodness (or light) and badness (or darkness) of almost everything in existence, spiritual and mundane. In fact, he has even calibrated Eckhart Tolle, and according to the scores (available on the Internet if you Google the subject), Tolle does not rate very high. Perhaps this less than stellar rating stems from the faulty moral relativism Tolle preaches.

The (unmanifest) "higher good" that Tolle speaks of certainly transcends (manifest) "good" and "bad"—but it does not negate them. To accept true badness (by not condemning or rejecting it) is to practice a form of world-denying, solipsistic mysticism. True spiritual life is all about channeling or radiating spiritual energy—but you do *not* have to surrender your power of *rational* judgment and "accept what is" to live a true spiritual life. You can live in accord with the spontaneously arising

Absolute, radiate spiritual power, and continue to sagaciously pass judgment.

To quote Tolle, the Book of Genesis says that "Adam and Eve were no longer allowed to dwell in 'paradise' when they 'ate of the tree of the knowledge of good and evil.'" In other words, according to the Old Testament, man's rational, discriminating mind, which is his essential tool of survival, is God-forsaken and is the reason for man's fall from Grace. But the Old Testament does not stop at condemning man's mind; it also condemns his body, his "depraved" carnal nature. Thus, man is born with two strikes against him—a "sinful" mind and a "sinful" body, and all he can do to save himself is to mindlessly get down on his hands and knees and worship an "angry and jealous God." Tolle, of course, fails to mention this when he conveniently, but out of full context, quotes the Book of Genesis to support his view that man's discriminating mind is his major impediment to enlightenment. And of course, Tolle also fails to mention that the Old Testament, like *The Power of Now*, is, hypocritically, replete with the very mental judgments that it condemns.

It seems like denial and self-deception to pretend something isn't bad when it actually is. If something is bad—such as an accident, illness, pain, or death—it makes no sense to deny it.

Eckhart Tolle's response to this argument is: "You are not pretending anything. You are allowing it to be as it is, that's all. This 'allowing to be' takes you beyond the mind with its resistance patterns that create the positive-negative polarities."

My rebuttal to Tolle's response is: When does non-reactive allowing cease and reactive action start? For example, if you're being robbed and mugged, do you just allow it to be as it is? If you see a woman being raped, do you simply allow it to be instead of attempting to stop it? Positive-negative (or good-bad) polarities are a reality; they are *not* created by the mind's resistance patterns. The rational mind, properly, identifies objective good and bad. Tolle demonizes the mind by reducing it to a mere resistance pattern that is the cause, rather than the identifier, of positive and negative. The rational mind, properly, identifies and *resists* clear-cut negative reality, and, properly, it identifies and *does not resist* clear-cut positive reality. For example, if your "guru," *a la* Jim Jones, tells you to drink cyanide-laced Kool-Aid, your rational mind would rightly resist his pathological demand. But if your guru told you to practice Holy Communion to realize spiritual Truth, your rational mind would rightly not resist his life (and Light)-positive directive.

Tolle says that the emanation of Being is "the good that has no opposite." This is very true, but the *manifestation* of Being (as the world) is the play of opposites, and again, the rational mind doesn't create these opposites via its resistance patterns; it simply recognizes their existence (within the context of a life-positive standard of value) and, appropriately, embraces the good while rejecting the bad.

If I'm able to do something about a situation, should I? How can I do something about a situation and let it be at the same time?

Tolle's answer is: "Do what you have to do. In the meantime, accept what *is*. Since mind and resistance are synonymous, acceptance immediately frees you from mind dominance and reconnects you with Being."

My answer is: The very fact that you even need to ask if you should do something in response to a situation indicates that you have already abdicated a portion of your rational faculty. Not taking appropriate action in response to a situation is irrational, and in no way spiritual. If you reconnect with divine Being, and rest in the Spirit-current, your thought-processing will no longer dominate your consciousness, and from this surrendered position, you can do what you have to do.

At-one-ment with divine Being, what IS, is true *spiritual* acceptance. If you first, directly and immediately, commune with the divine Being, your mind and body are free, within this divine context, to function as necessary, enabling you to do what you need to in response to life situations.

Did Jesus accept what *is,* the status quo? Hell, no. He was a political rabble-rouser who entered the temple precincts to drive out those engaged in buying and selling. Mystical communion and rest in the Spirit-current constitute true *spiritual* acceptance of what IS. Any other form of "acceptance" is simply mind-based toleration of existing circumstances. Therefore, until you can connect with Being and channel its Power, true spiritual acceptance of what IS cannot be a reality for you.

Eckhart Tolle says that by "allowing the present moment to be as it is, the miracle of transformation happens not only within but also without... You dissolve discord, heal pain, and dispel unconsciousness—without doing anything—simply by *being* and holding that frequency of intense presence." First of all, you don't dissolve discord, heal pain, and dispel unconsciousness; the Holy Spirit, the power of Now, does. Second, Tolle and his fellow apophatic mystics err when they claim that this "miracle of transformation" happens "without doing anything." In reality, for this "miraculous" transformation to occur, you must "hold that frequency of intense presence," and this only happens by *doing something very specific*— practicing the sacred act, or spiritual discipline, of Holy Communion. Once your Holy Communion, or plugged-in presence, is sufficiently unobstructed, you pull down the power of Now and can rest—"without doing anything"— in the Spirit-current. In other words, before you can receive the descent of Grace, you must make a conscious effort to connect to the divine Source. If you don't generate sufficient conscious force (or voltage) through your connection, then the Spirit-current (or amperage) will be too weak for you to rest in it, and even if you attempt to "do nothing," your (out-of-divine-context) attempt at non-resistance (or minimizing ohms) will *not* result in natural, effortless, radiant *beingness*.

Drama, the Ego, and Bad Things

According to Eckhart Tolle, most of the bad things that happen in a person's life are ego-created, and the term he uses to refer to these bad things is "drama." In other words, the ego is the evil culprit, the "devil," that causes conflict and misery, or "drama," in an individual's life. Moreover, the ego's damaging, or "damning," effects aren't just limited to oneself; they also infect relationships, society, and the entire human collective. In Tolle's words, "When egos come together, whether in personal relationships or in organizations or institutions, 'bad' things happen sooner or later: drama of one kind or another, in the form of conflict, problems, power struggles, emotional or physical violence, and so on. This includes collective evils such as war, genocide, and exploitation."

Given the ego's God-awful damaging effects on every level of human existence—individual, social, and collective—what can be done to save humanity? I say, Praise the ego! Yes, accept it (for all intents and purposes) as an irremovable reality that can be a force for good just as much as it is a force for bad—and emphasize its positive side. Existentially speaking, the ego is neither good nor bad; it just is, and as such, it can be a tool for either positive creation or negative destruction. But for hypocritical spiritual moralists like Tolle, who preach acceptance while damning the ego, it is only evil, the devil disguised in the form of the human mind.

Even if you accept Tolle's premise that the ego is the God-awful evil destroying individual lives and humanity as a whole, a big problem remains: the ego just won't go away. In fact, I have yet to meet a spiritual guru or practitioner who has managed to rid himself of his ego. Is Tolle ego-free? Check his lifestyle, investment portfolio, and seminar price-structuring, and decide for yourself. Maybe the greatest spiritual masters in history—such as the Buddha and Ramana Maharshi—were totally ego-free, but even if they were, the odds of a particular individual's permanently obviating the primal separate-self sense along with inborn egoic self-interest is far less than one in a billion. Hence, if you are naïve enough to believe that the solution to humanity's problems is to extirpate the ego, my suggestion to you is this: first rid yourself of you own ego before you attempt to convince others that ego-eradication is the remedy for worldwide suffering.

Interestingly enough, as I am writing this rejoinder to Tolle's condemnation of the ego, I have just picked up a book, *From the Profound to the Profane*, by Jaime T. Licauco, a venerable Filipino writer on occult matters who lives in Manila, where I am temporarily residing. Licauco, a long-time spiritual seeker, has this to say about gurus:

> I have a strong bias against gurus in general and Indian ones in particular. I have met several and they all had bloated egos while preaching love, humility, and spirituality. They all basked in the admiration of credulous people and expected everyone to worship them. So I have avoided them like the proverbial plague.

If the spiritual gurus can't rid themselves of their egos, what hope is there for mere spiritual seekers like the rest of us? Not much if your goal is ego-eradication. But if the ego is defined as self-interest (and the mature ego as *rational* self-interest), why would you want to eliminate it? The ego, as self-interest (or self-preservation), is biological in nature, a natural and life-positive, rather than a spurious and life-negative, psychic survival mechanism that seeks to ensure one's well-being. Because the ego is biological, ingrained in our very DNA, even the gurus who preach against it fall victim to it. Unlike the hypocritical gurus who demonize the ego, I can't fault a biological mechanism that aims to secure my survival and well-being. I can fault irrational, egocentric, and destructive forms of the ego, but not the ego's life-positive function.

Tolle's definition of the ego—"the false self created by unconscious identification with the mind"—is not satisfactory (or adequately descriptive), even when the ego is (disparagingly) defined from a spiritual perspective. From the radical (or gone-to-the root) spiritual perspective, the ego is simply the moment-to-moment activity of retraction from (or avoidance of) the Divine, and this activity creates a separate-self sense, a self-contraction. The ego's act of retraction is in the form of abstraction—cognition via concept-formation that contracts one's field of awareness. And this contraction, this formation of awareness into successive, and always limited, states of consciousness, is perceived as suffering by sensitive souls. From this radical spiritual perspective, the ego is seen not as an entity, but as an activity—the activity of retraction from (or avoidance of) the Divine. Because it is the ego as mental abstraction that generates the self-contraction (or "pain-body"), it is the ego-mind, as a resistance pattern, that is demonized by Tolle and other gurus. But Tolle and other gurus obviously continue to think after enlightenment. So the ultimate goal is not getting rid of the mind; it is establishing yourself in the transcendental field of nondual Being, the divine Context that renders thoughts non-binding and the self-contraction (or pain-body) obsolete.

Adi Da and radical Buddhists have likened the ego to a fist clenching in the midst of empty space. Once the clenching (or mental grasping) ceases, so does the ego, the separate-self sense caused by the hand curling into a closed fist. Viewed from this perspective, the ego is illusory and disappears once the mental clenching stops. But only the rarest beings in history have been able to sever the spiritual Heart-center knot and permanently rest in open Being, the Divine Condition that is *prior* to and beyond the ego. And as soon as any spiritual practitioner—no matter how advanced he is—retracts from the Divine, the ego-self—or self-contraction—re-forms into its usual karmic, or conditioned, pattern. Consequently, the self-contraction, or "illusory" ego will, for all but a few of the world's population, still remain a reality. Hence, Tolle's and other utopians' dream of an ego-free Shangri-La on planet Earth is, sad to say, nothing more than a pipe dream.

It is my contention that even if a rare being is able to permanently eradicate his ego, as Tolle or Adi Da and the radical Buddhist define it, he is not thereby automatically free of his biological ego. The biological (or hardwired DNA) ego dictates that an un-brainwashed human be interested in his own well-being, however he consciously or subconsciously defines it. Thus, it should come as no surprise when we see one big-name guru after another—including the late mega-luminaries Chogyam Trungpa, J. Krishnamurti, Bhagwan Shree Rajneesh (Osho), and Adi Da (who I believe cut the spiritual Heart-center knot)—exposed as all too human, saddled with the same egoic self-interest as the rest of us.

Tolle informs us that "Many types of illnesses are caused by the ego's continued resistance, which creates restrictions and blockages in the flow of energy through the body." But, he says, "When you reconnect with Being and are no longer run by your mind, you cease to create those things." This is very true. But what Tolle doesn't say, and should, is that when you reconnect with Being (*Siva-Shakti*, or Consciousness-Energy), the awakened force, or power, of Being—*Shakti*, in the form of *kundalini* energy—can create all kinds of bodily disorders. The body can become over-amped from the force-flow of Being, and the "stalk", as the Tibetan Buddhists refer to the physical vehicle, can "wilt" or "bend" from the pressure of this power. A number of books—including *Kundalini: The Evolutionary Energy in Man*, *Krishnamurti: The Years of Awakening*, *The Mystique of Enlightenment*, and the earlier-discussed *Wild Ivy: The Spiritual Autobiography of Zen Master Hakuin*—detail some of the physical effects stemming from the awakened *kundalini*, and individuals interested in the subject are invited to refer to these texts.

Tolle contends that "When you live in complete acceptance of what *is*, that is the end of all drama in your life. Nobody can even have an argument with you, no matter how hard he or she tries." The Buddhists in ancient India lived in complete acceptance of what *is*, and the invading Muslims, by exploiting their pacifism, killed them and drove them out of the country. The Vedic Hindus, in direct contrast, fought the Muslims bravely, refusing to accept this invasion as the "Divine Order" (or what *is*). If you're an Eckhart Tolle devotee, would you, like the Buddhists, passively accept the violent invasion of your country and have no argument with the invaders? Or would you, like the Hindus, resist and fight back?

Tolle says, "An argument implies identification with your mind and a mental position, as well as resistance and reaction to the other person's position." I say, an argument can, *but does not necessarily*, imply identification with your mind and mental position. It can simply imply the identification of reality. For example, if you insist that the Earth is flat (as members of The Flat Earth Society do), and I argue against your absurd point of view, my argument has nothing to do with identification with my mind and everything to do with the pure and simple recognition of reality.

There can be no doubt that the greatest sages engage in arguments. And Jesus was no exception. For example, in Mark 12:28, the Bible reads: "One of the teachers of the law came to Jesus. He had heard Jesus arguing with the Sadduces and the Pharisees." In India, Adi Shankara (788 CE–820 CE), the renowned consolidator of Advaita Vedanta, traveled from one end of the country to the other, debating and defeating his Dharma opponents. And in China and Japan, the ancient Zen masters regularly engaged in Dharma battles and argued whether enlightenment was sudden or gradual. Ask yourself this: Doesn't the very fact that you even *choose* to argue against a point of view contrary to your own imply resistance to it on some level? And if there is some resistance, how can there be *complete* acceptance of what *is*?

Resistance and the Cycles of Life

Eckhart Tolle rightly differentiates between physical pain and suffering, which is mental-emotional in nature and always involves resistance on some level. As he says, "All suffering is ego-created and due to resistance." But what he neglects to say is: Not all resistance results in suffering. For example, when you're on a strict diet and you resist eating a piece of chocolate cake after your healthful salad and grilled fish, your *positive* resistance prevents suffering—the emotional pain caused from gaining weight and failing to adhere to your diet.

Eckhart Tolle is hardly an original thinker, and much of his spiritual teaching is derived from the late J. Krishnamurti. Like many of the simplistic New Age and Advaita Vedanta gurus on the scene nowadays, Tolle loves to emphasize the Krishnamurti maxim that "all effort [or resistance] is the avoidance of what *is*." Thus, Tolle's Dharma "mantra," in effect, is: "surrender to (or accept) what *is*." But this mantra has multiple problems, which I will touch upon.

First, the hypocrisy of those, including Krishnamurti himself, who push it. If you listen to gurus like Tolle and Krishnamurti—and I used to regularly participate in Krishnamurti groups—you soon realize that they are filled with the same kinds of resistance, or judgments, as the rest of us. Whether it's the insane political system, the conventional religious establishment, or whatnot, they constantly rail at the all-pervading madness in the world. There is nothing wrong with this—I do the same thing myself—but please don't push *complete* acceptance of what *is* if you've got a closet full of axes to grind.

Second, the foundational spiritual practice—that of conscious presence—involves *resistance* (to unconsciousness). In other words, being present to what arises is a discipline that demands an integral counter-unconsciousness effort. Exclusive of this context of integral presence, effortlessness, or non-resistance, does not translate into the Benediction, the descent of divine Blessing Power. Put another way, wholistic (or holy) spiritual practice is a dialectic, involving effort (the practice of presence) and effortlessness (the practice of absence). And integrating these two poles results in the flow of Grace from above. True surrender to what *is* is not the mental acceptance of life conditions; it is utterly letting go and *accepting*, or *receiving*, the Flow from above. "Going with the flow" does not mean that you no longer resist or criticize aspects of conditional existence; it simply means that you rest in the Current from above and confront life from a Spirit-empowered position.

In *Krishnamurti's Notebook,* a revealing journal of Krishnamurti's spiritual experiences, there is a single recurring theme: the Benediction. Krishnamurti repeatedly uses the term "Benediction" to describe his mystical experiences of the sacred "Other." But Tolle never mentions the Benediction, the spiritual Grace that blesses disciples of the Divine. For Tolle, spiritual life is essentially about silence and stillness, not the power emanating from (what Krishnamurti calls) the "Highest." Non-resistance is the means to create an inner vacuum that allows the

"Plenum," the Spirit-full power of Now, to penetrate a devotee. But for Tolle, discussion of this Plenum, this Benediction, is seemingly verboten.

Tolle explains that life is cyclical in nature and that the down cycle is as necessary as the up cycle. He tells us, "Dissolution is needed for new growth to happen... The down cycle is absolutely essential for spiritual realization." Very true. But Tolle never mentions any way to understand or predict these cycles. Is there one? I say there is—astrology. As the Emerald Tablet of Hermes Trismegistus declares: "As above, so below." In other words, a powerful correlation between the position of the planets and human behavior exists. And for those with "divining" ability, the understanding of this synchronous relationship enables them to decipher and predict (to an impressive degree) individual and collective cycles of becoming. For those interested in the subject, I suggest two books: *Planets in Transit*, by Robert Hand, and *Cycles of Becoming*, by Alexander Ruperti.

If you're interested in warmed-over Buddhism, then Eckhart Tolle might be your cup of tea. Tolle repeats ad nauseam, in one form or another, the Buddhist Noble Truth that life is suffering. But aside from some rudimentary instructions pertaining to a beginner's practice of mindfulness, he offers no insights into the higher aspects or dimensions of Buddhist spiritual practice. Yes, all compound things are subject to decay and dissolution, and yes, clinging to these ephemeral forms results in suffering. But when it comes to the essence of Buddhist mindfulness—how right (or perfect) concentration culminates in right (or perfect) *samadhi,* and then *Nirvana*—Tolle is inexcusably silent. If you're interested in a first-rate presentation of the Buddha's teachings on the practice of mindfulness and the attainment of *Nirvana*, pick up a copy of *Some Sayings of the Buddha, According to the Pali Canon*, by F.L. Woodward.

Eckhart Tolle says, "Your happiness and unhappiness are in fact one... Only the illusion of time separates them." I say, conventional happiness and unhappiness are one only in the sense that each state arises as a modification of Being, the non-state. Conventional happiness arises as either *joy* (a relatively sustained state of positive, expansive feelings due to the achievement of one's goals) or as *pleasure* (a very temporary state of relief or excitation due to the satisfaction of one's desires). And unhappiness, whatever form it takes—anger, sorrow, jealousy, and so on—arises when your attempt to achieve your goals or satisfy your desires is frustrated. The "illusion of time" does not separate happiness and unhappiness; what separates them is the degree to which your thoughts contract the field of awareness. When you are conventionally happy, your mind (or consciousness modification pattern) is not significantly compressing the field of awareness, so you feel relatively good. But when you are unhappy, your thoughts are intensely contracting the field of awareness, and the corresponding feelings that arise from this activity are sad.

Regardless of my incessant criticism of Tolle's Dharma, I must give the man credit for a sense of humor. For example, when he says, "The whole advertising industry and consumer society would collapse if people became enlightened," only a complete idiot or oblivious fool could take him seriously. After all, anyone who has paid any attention to the procession of prominent spiritual gurus ever since Maharishi Mahesh Yogi (the founder of TM) hit the scene in the '60s knows that most of these guys have enjoyed decadent lifestyles that the rest of us can only dream about. From Rajneesh's (Osho's) ninety-nine Rolls Royces to Wayne Dyer's mansion in Maui, most of these guys have exhibited levels of materialism akin to those of rock stars or hedge fund managers. When Eckhart Tolle trades in his pricey threads for a Goodwill loincloth and his private limo for a Pinto, I'll finally stop laughing at his statement that mass enlightenment spells the end of our consumer society.

According to Tolle, "Things and conditions can give you pleasure, but they cannot give you *joy*. Nothing can give you joy. Joy is uncaused and arises from within as the joy of Being." Actually, what gives you true joy, divine bliss, is the Holy Spirit. And this joy, or bliss, is "caused" when you allow the Holy Spirit to bless you. The Holy Spirit is the power of

Being, and the nature of this power is Bliss. But you cannot receive and enjoy this Bliss-current, this Benediction, until you commune with the Holy One and allow Him to bless you with his Spirit-power, his *Shakti*.

Eckhart Tolle says, "To offer no resistance to life is to be in a state of grace, ease, and lightness." The path of least (or no) resistance, in and by itself, is hardly the spiritual panacea that Tolle makes it out to be. If it were, we'd see the great sages recommending deep sleep and relaxing massages as the keys to *Nirvana*. The Buddha, in fact, instructed his disciples *not* to practice exclusive effortlessness. He taught that meditation is like playing a string musical instrument: if the strings are too tight, they will break, and if they are too loose, there will be no sound. The Buddha's Noble Eightfold Path includes Right Effort as one of its constituents, so the Buddha certainly wouldn't second Tolle's one-dimensional directive to abandon all resistance.

Non-resistance is an essential component of real spiritual practice. But just as reduced resistance is meaningless in the circuit of an unplugged lamp, it is also less than potent in a yogi disconnected from the Source. The first principle of mysticism is direct contact with Ultimate Reality. Once this contact is established, it becomes appropriate to let go and receive Grace, the flow of *Shakti*. In other words, if you want to be in a state of Grace, the exclusive, contextless "practice" of non-resistance won't enable you to achieve it. Only within the full context of Holy Communion will non-resistance enable you to receive and integrally channel Grace, the Holy Spirit, or the true power of Now. Until the Heart-knot is cut, effort—in the form of countering (or resisting) unconsciousness by attempting to remain present and plugged-in—is necessary. The force, or "voltage," of your plugged-in presence creates a palpable pressure, and when you feel this pressure, the appropriate gesture at that point is to yield to it. And when you yield to it, relinquishing all resistance, the pressure translates into the flow of *Shakti*. Only this *Shakti*, this *Kundalini*, is Grace and Light; but this Grace and Light cannot be realized without effort. Spiritual life involves an intense holding-on (to the Source) as well as a total letting-go (of resistance), but for yinned-out New Age gurus like Tolle, it simply isn't cool to emphasize the *work*, or *pressure*, side of spiritual life.

Resistance and Negativity

Nowadays in spiritual preaching the big money is in pushing the positive and putting down the negative. In the contemporary Christian community, no one exemplifies this better than Joel Osteen, author of the *New York Times* bestseller *Become a Better You*. Osteen has shrewdly abandoned the traditional Christian message of fire and brimstone for one of New Age-inspired self-improvement. In the New Age movement itself, Tolle qualifies as Osteen's counterpart, as he incessantly condemns negativity, essentially equating it with egoic resistance. Other New Age gurus, of course, also emphasize the positive while eschewing the negative, but what makes Tolle so successful is his ability to expertly package the New Age ethos in combination with serious, yet simplified mysticism.

Tolle informs us that "All inner resistance is experienced as negativity in one form or another" and that "All negativity is resistance." In this context, he says, "The two words are almost synonymous." Tolle intensifies his attack on negativity when he states that "Its only 'useful' function is that it strengthens the ego, and that is why the ego loves it."

These statements not only are nonsensical, they also contradict earlier statements. Tolle previously said that "Happiness and unhappiness are in fact one. Only the illusion of time separates them." Well, if happiness and unhappiness are one, then positive and negative have to be one, meaning that there is no reason to rag on the negative as Tolle does. Moreover, if only an "illusion" (time) separates the two, then why even bother making a distinction between them? Finally, Tolle even questions our ability to distinguish between positive and negative when he asks, "Do you truly know what is positive and what is negative?"

Imagine that you are a professional film critic and a Tolle disciple. Because he has convinced you that negativity is negative, that it only strengthens the ego, you decide to only write positive reviews of movies. When you get fired from your job for being an uncritical critic, your self-esteem will no doubt take a hit. But think of the positive side: you will have achieved Tolle's goal of weakening your ego.

Tolle declares that "Negativity is totally unnatural." Actually, it is totally natural. For proof of this, consider the fact that the zodiac (the twelve-part circle of astrological dimensions surrounding the Earth) consists of six positive signs (Aries, Gemini, Leo, Libra, Sagittarius, and Aquarius) and six negative signs (Taurus, Cancer, Virgo, Scorpio, Capricorn, and Pisces). Although an individual's entire chart must be considered, those born under the positive signs generally tend to see the "glass of life" as half-full, while those born under the negative signs generally tend to see it as half-empty.

To illustrate the fact that the sign you are born under, your Sun sign, greatly influences your vision of life, I'll compare one of the positive astrological signs, Sagittarius, with one of the negative ones, Virgo. These signs are both mind-based, but the contrast in their mental approaches to life is so blatant that it makes clear the inherent, or *natural*, distinction between the positive and negative signs.

The typical Sagittarius is optimistic, enthusiastic, and jovial. He has little interest in fault-finding or details. He focuses his attention on the forest, not the trees. But for the Whole to fully express itself on the Earth plane, all twelve "pieces" (or signs) of life's "Great Pie" (or circle) must manifest themselves through humanity. And one piece of the Great Pie is someone who focuses his attention on the trees, or details, of life: Virgo.

Whereas Sagittarius is broadminded, Virgo is narrow-minded. Incessantly analytical, nitpicking, and fault-finding, he is the natural-born critic of the Zodiac. And this "negative," judgmental mindset enables Virgo to excel in fields where details make all the difference. The meticulous measurer of manifest existence, Virgo provides humanity with its craftsmen—its hypercritical perfectionists. And if Tolle had a clue, he'd thank the stars for gracing the Earth with such "negative" people.

Swami Sivananda, one of India's greatest twentieth-century gurus, was a Virgo. If you read his books, you'll find that, like a typical Virgo, he criticizes one thing after another. If you didn't know he was a true guru, you'd swear he was just an unhappy, anal-retentive puritan. But because he was en-Light-ened, rested in the bliss of Being, his negative inborn Virgo astral nature did not obstruct his Self-nature an iota. In other words, once you establish yourself in the divine context of Being, the content of your individual consciousness, whether positive or negative, no longer binds you.

The bottom line concerning negativity is this: If you're an inherently "negative" person, no amount of spiritual practice is going to alter your inborn personal nature. You can practice conscious presence and non-resistance until your eyeballs pop out, and you'll still remain a judgmental, hard-to-please person. And if you resist your "negativity" because you label it "bad," you will just create another layer of dross covering your Soul. Instead of fretting about your negativity, simply reestablish yourself in the divine context of Being, and thereby render *all* your mental modifications—positive as well as negative—transparent (or non-binding) in the Light of Truth.

In order to substantiate his claim that negativity is "totally unnatural," Tolle cites dubious examples from the world of nature. His main example describes how ducks have taught him spiritual lessons about releasing surplus energy and thus avoiding negativity:

> Just watching them is a meditation. How peacefully they float along, at ease with themselves, totally present in the Now, dignified and perfect as only a mindless creature can be. Occasionally, however, two ducks will get into a fight—sometimes for no apparent reason, or because one duck has strayed into another's private space. The fight usually lasts only for a few seconds, and then the ducks separate, swim off in opposite directions, and vigorously

flap their wings a few times. They then continue to swim on peacefully as if the fight had never happened. When I observed that for the first time, I suddenly realized that by flapping their wings they were releasing surplus energy, thus preventing it from becoming trapped in their body and turning into negativity. This is natural wisdom, and it is easy for them because they do not have a mind that keeps the past alive unnecessarily and then builds an identity around it.

When it comes to observing duck behavior, Eckhart Tolle is a rank amateur compared to me. From 2003 to 2009, I owned a house right on the lake in Horseshoe Bay, Texas, and I would spend my days feeding the ducks and watching them interact. The sliding glass doors in my living room were only five feet from the lake, and from my desk I would watch the ducks "socialize" in the water and on my boat slip. Periodically, I would go outside and toss fistfuls of bird feed onto the boat slip and the water, and watch them compete for the food.

Unsurprisingly, my observations about duck behavior differ markedly from Tolle's. First, duck fights are not occasional; they are frequent. Second, after fights, ducks do not always swim off peacefully in opposite directions. Often, one or two ducks will aggressively pursue a fleeing duck, even harassing it in the air when it takes flight. Third, ducks do not vigorously flap their wings just to release surplus energy; they also strenuously flap them to demonstrate bravado. Fourth, ducks are not totally present in the Now; they keep the past alive, just like humans. For example, when certain ducks appear in the presence of others, they are always harassed. Apparently, "forgive and forget" is not the prevalent ethos of the duck community. But rape is. When the mating urge hits these "mindless creatures," they indiscriminately attempt to mount any appealing duck in their immediate area. It doesn't matter if the rape victim is male or female, or if it already has a mate. And if the victim isn't compliant, a second duck often joins in to help subdue him or her. Just imagine how wonderful human society could be if only we humans would live mindlessly in the Now, like Tolle's spiritual idols, the ducks.

In addition to idolizing ducks, Tolle virtually deifies cats. He claims that he has "lived with several Zen masters—all of them cats." He must have better luck with cats than I do. I've had numerous cats as pets, and though I've loved and appreciated all of them, not a single one, in my estimation, qualified as a Zen master. My cats would sadistically toy with mice, batting them around for long periods until mercilessly terminating them. And my cats were all "fraidy cats," skittish creatures ready to run and hide at the slightest unsettling encroachment into their personal space. How about bigger cats, say lions? Do they also qualify as "Zen masters?" I guess if typical lion behavior—a male killing the cubs of a rival male's female and the female then eagerly mating with the new male while "mindlessly" dismissing her dead cubs—qualifies as living in the Now, then lions, according to Tolle's criteria, would also qualify as Zen masters.

Eckhart Tolle's fundamental mistake relative to his apotheosis of sub-human animal behavior is in conflating *pre-rational* existence with *trans-rational* existence. There is a huge evolutionary gap between the ignorantly "mindless" living of pre-rational creatures and the consciously "mindless" living of man, nature's only rational animal. Unless an animal is capable of rational thinking, it lacks the evolved brain, nervous system, and subtle body to reflect or conduct the Spirit. The Bible says as much when it affirms that only man is created in the image of God. Anyone interested in an in-depth consideration of the distinction between pre-rational and trans-rational states of consciousness should consult the writings of the renowned integral thinker Ken Wilber.

Couldn't negative emotions contain important messages? And couldn't these messages be a signal that I need to make changes in my life?

All emotions contain just a single message: how you feel about something. Obviously, a negative emotion means you have negative feelings in relation to something, but the emotion itself is simply a conditioned response to stimuli. If you want to understand the cause of your negative emotion, you will have to examine your value judgments, which, subconsciously, program your feeling-reactions to stimuli.

Tolle says "recurring negative emotions do sometimes contain a message, as do illnesses." But because he despises the mind, Tolle views these negative emotions as no more than "a kind of signal that reminds you to be more present." If you want to live mindlessly, and *stupidly* (like ducks), in the Now, then simply dismiss your emotions and be *thoughtlessly* present in the moment. But if you want to understand your emotions, you will have to employ your rational mind and examine your philosophical and psychological value judgments.

How can we stop negativity from arising, and how can we get rid of it once it takes hold?

Not to experience negative emotions is to be less than human. Only a being devoid of value judgments doesn't experience negative emotions, and such a being has evicted himself from conditional reality. Real spirituality isn't about stopping negative emotions from arising; it is about abiding in the Holy Spirit and allowing its radiance to outshine all your emotions—positive as well as negative. The Holy Spirit is Love-Bliss, and when you can rest in its current, the transcendental, *non-reactive* feeling of Being supersedes and exceeds your personal, *reactive* feelings, rendering them non-binding. Therefore, the radical, non-remedial way to deal with negative emotions, arising or already present, is simply to be wholly present, in Holy Communion, and to allow the power of the Holy Spirit to cleanse you of your negativity by bathing you in its field of blissful Light-energy.

Tolle provides four ways to deal with negativity. He says, you can 1) "stop it [negativity] from arising by being fully present"; 2) "just drop it once you realize that you don't want to have this energy field inside you"; 3) "accept that it is there and take your attention into the feeling";

and 4) "make it disappear by imagining yourself becoming transparent to the external cause of the reaction."

The four ways Tolle recommends are tried-and-true yogic methods to stop negativity, and serious yogis should experiment with all of them in their spiritual practice. But Tolle, negligently, fails to mention the definitive *spiritual* way to arrest negativity: to allow the Holy Spirit, the power of Now, to outshine it with its radiant Light-energy.

Tolle informs us that "There are yet few people on the planet who can sustain a state of continuous presence, although some people are getting close to it. Soon, I believe, there will be many more." The fact is, no one can *willfully* sustain a state of continuous presence. Only by resting in the Spirit-current is it possible to remain in continuous presence, in perpetual *samadhi*. In other words, the en-Light-ened state is beyond your efforts to remain consciously present and your efforts to relinquish resistance or negativity. Only Grace, the Benediction from above, can provide you with the power to abide unbrokenly in the divine Presence.

I've been practicing meditation for years. I've attended numerous workshops, I've read many books on spirituality, and I try to be in a state of nonresistance. But to be honest, I have not found inner peace. What should I do?

Tolle's answer to your question is the predictably simplistic one of "acceptance." He says, "The moment you completely accept your non-peace, your non-peace becomes transmuted into peace."

Mere acceptance will not result in *spiritual* peace. In reality, true spiritual (or Spirit-empowered) peace cannot be found merely by ending the search for peace; it can only be found by the searchless *beholding* of the Spirit Itself. In other words, not only must you relinquish your search for peace, you must also consciously receive the Benediction from above, the down-pouring Holy Spirit. The practice of un-baptized acceptance can, temporarily, transmute your non-peace into peace, but such peace is not *the peace that passeth understanding*. Only the peace resulting from baptized Holy Communion is such peace.

Eckhart Tolle loves to use Zen stories to make a spiritual point, because like most Zen masters, he has little regard for the human mind, particularly its ability to intelligently discriminate or measure reality. Tolle uses the story of Zen master Banzan becoming enlightened in a butcher shop to illustrate the point that spiritual awakening can stem from merely accepting every "cut of meat" (or "every moment of life") as "the best." In other words, if you can somehow convince yourself that everything that exists in a present moment—including rape, murder, genocide, and pollution—is truly hunky-dory, truly for the best, then you too can become an enlightened Zen master. But if you listen to Tolle rail about the human insanity that threatens the very existence of the planet, you can only conclude that he hardly practices what he preaches.

A major problem with the practice of "acceptance," which Tolle fails to address, is that it is essentially mind-based. In order to convince yourself that you shouldn't resist the present moment, you, in effect, have to 'brainwash" yourself to *completely* accept it—because the natural, human tendency is to strongly reject parts of it. Thus, the very attempt not to reject aspects of the present moment breeds conflict. And the more intensely you devote yourself to the practice of unconditional acceptance, the more conflict you will engender.

The Essence of Compassion

In an attempt to describe the enlightened state, Eckhart Tolle restates the classical Hindu mind/lake metaphor:

> Having gone beyond the mind-made opposites, you become like a deep lake. The outer situation of your life and whatever happens there is the surface of the lake. Sometimes calm, sometimes windy and rough, according

to the cycles and seasons. Deep down, however, the lake
is always undisturbed. You are the whole lake, not just
the surface, and you are in touch with your own depth,
which remains absolutely still."

Tolle's restatement is clumsy, at best. In truth, the outer situation of
your life, in and of itself, is never "sometimes calm, sometimes windy
and rough." It simply is, and only your mind's reaction to it makes it
appear one or the other. Thus, the lake's surface is analogous to your
mind—ever fluctuating. But deep down, you are pure, absolutely still
consciousness. But, according to Tolle, you are the whole lake, which
means you are not only pure consciousness, the Self, but also the lake's
surface modifications, the mind. This contradicts what Tolle emphasized
earlier in *The Power of Now*, that you are *not* your mind.

Tolle further describes the enlightened state as "[abidance] in Being—
unchanging, timeless, deathless." This description of the enlightened
state is typical Hindu Advaita Vedanta, meaning bland and lifeless. Being
is radiant Consciousness-Energy (*Siva-Shakti*), not static, eternally stilled
consciousness. But Tolle, ever the exoteric mystic, never ventures into
the energetic dimension of awakened consciousness. For him, "the
power of Now" is simply the cool title of his book, not the literal force-
flow stemming from uncontracted awareness.

If you become detached, doesn't this isolate you from other human beings?

The ascetic-type spiritual practice of passionless non-clinging can isolate
you from other human beings, but truly spiritual, or wholistic, non-
attachment, inherent in oneness with Being, does not cut you off from
others. In fact, oneness with Being stems from the practice of direct
relationship or communion, and such a practice, rather than isolating
you from other human beings, intensifies your connection to them. As
Tolle says, "True relationship becomes possible only when there is
awareness of Being." Put another way, genuine spiritual fellowship
becomes possible only when you practice Holy Communion, which

enables you to be present and in touch with the Whole. But in this context, the practice of non-attachment does not make you remote from others; instead, it serves to remove all barriers to the experience of true spiritual fellowship.

Tolle claims that by staying connected to Being, you can feel another person's Being: "So when confronted with someone else's suffering or unconscious behavior, you stay present and in touch with Being and thus are able to look beyond the form and feel the other person's radiant and pure Being through your own." Contrary to what Tolle says, what you feel isn't the other person's *own* radiant and pure Being, but rather, the *universal* Spirit Itself. The biblical saying, "Wherever two or more are gathered in my name, there I am," makes it clear that spiritual fellowship, or just "witnessing" to another person, awakens you to the all-pervading Lord, not to another person's *individual* Being.

Is compassion seeing beyond a person's form and recognizing their divinity?

Yes, it is. But Tolle's definition of compassion is not a satisfactory description of this Higher Compassion. According to Tolle, "Compassion is the awareness of a deep bond between yourself and all creatures." In reality, true compassion, enlightened *Buddhic* compassion, is the Love-Bliss, or Blessing Power, radiated by a sage. Mind-based compassion can only be felt and practiced sporadically, but *Buddhic* (or Being)-based compassion is eternal, and locking into the current of Being, the Holy Spirit, enables a skillful yogi to be a continuous conduit for this Higher Compassion, or Blessing Power.

Tolle links compassion to the vulnerability and mortality that all humans and living beings share. He says, "A few years from now—it doesn't make much difference—[all of us] will have become rotting corpses, then piles of dust, then nothing at all." Very true, but the Higher Compassion goes beyond this rudimentary recognition of common mortality. The practice of Higher Compassion is you consciously shedding the Grace of God on others by making yourself an open channel for the Divine's power. By becoming such a channel, you see beyond the physical forms of others and recognize the Divinity that is the True Nature of all beings.

Eckhart Tolle informs us that "In compassion the seemingly opposite feelings of sadness and joy merge into one and become transmuted into a deep inner peace. This is the peace of God." Tolle's description of compassion, like his other descriptions of spiritual life, is lifeless and flat (or two-dimensional) rather than Spirit-imbued and full (or three-dimensional). Because he doesn't acknowledge the Holy Spirit as the true power of Now, as the Blessing Energy or Higher Compassion from above, he has no choice but to parrot the stilted and reductive descriptions of compassion found in the East's world-rejecting spiritual traditions. These traditions not only deny the reality of the material world, including the body, they also conflate *Shakti,* the Holy Spirit, with *Maya,* the illusion-creating power of the Divine.

In contradistinction to Tolle, the great tantric traditions of the East— such as Hindu Kashmir Shaivism and Vajrayana Buddhism—properly identify *Shakti*, the *Sambhogakaya,* as the en-Light-ening (rather than illusion-creating) power emanating from the Absolute. This en-Light-ening power, the Holy Spirit, is the vehicle for the Higher Compassion from above. But if a truth seeker's reading of spiritual literature doesn't extend beyond Eckhart Tolle's *The Power of Now*, he would never know this.

A Different Reality

I am convinced the body doesn't have to die. Physical immortality can be achieved if we don't believe in death.

Good luck with your belief. But be advised that every human being who has ever lived has died. If I were a bookmaker, I'd make you a quadrillion to one underdog versus death.

Eckhart Tolle has his own beliefs about the body and death, but, predictably, they fly in the face of reason. First, Tolle says, "The body does not die because you believe in death. The body exists, or seems to, because you believe in death." This is pure poppycock. Severely retarded people and animals have no concept of death, but yet their bodies continue to exist. And the idea that the body merely "seems to [exist]" is ludicrous unless you deny the validity of your senses and mind. Moreover, whether or not you believe in death, the body continues to exist. Yes, you can stop mentally identifying with your physical vehicle and abide, solipsistically, in the exclusive transcendental Self. But the body, despite your vehement rejection of it, will continue to exist until it actually dies.

Second, Tolle says, "The body is an incredible misperception of your true nature. But your true nature is concealed within that illusion, not outside it, so the body is still the only point of access to it." Actually, the body is the correct perception of your true *physical* nature, and in no way is it an illusion. It is true that your true *spiritual* nature must be realized via your physical vehicle, but this does not mean that your form body conceals Being. If your true spiritual nature is indeed concealed within your illusory physical body, as Tolle claims, where exactly within the body can it be found? In the crown *chakra*? In the heart *chakra*? In the pineal gland? Tolle doesn't say. And my guess is that he doesn't say because he doesn't know.

Animals have bodies, but don't have egos or believe in death. And yet they die, or seem to...

Very true. But Tolle, erroneously, attributes this to their particular perceiving consciousness. A staunch advocate of the primacy of consciousness (as opposed to existence), he rejects the reality of an objective universe in which life and death are objective realities. He says, "Remember that your perception of the world is a reflection of your state of consciousness. You are not separate from it, and there is no objective world out there."

The idea that you (as a psycho-physical entity) are not separate from the world is untenable. If there were no separation, you could not perceive discrete objects. And the very fact that you can perceive separate objects is incontrovertible proof that there is an "objective world out there." The only basis for rejecting your perception of an objective world is to reject the validity of your senses and mind. And if you do that, then all your knowledge is fundamentally invalid.

Tolle, like many modern mystics, sees confirmation of the anti-objectivist position in quantum physics, implicitly Heisenberg's Uncertainty Principle, which informs us that the mere observation of subatomic particles alters their behavior and predictability, thereby *seemingly* proving that the observer of phenomena and the observed phenomena cannot be *entirely* separated. If the mere observation of phenomena alters their behavior, then pure objectivity is impossible.

First off, even if your observing consciousness does affect the behavior and predictability of subatomic particles—and this is highly debatable—it does not mean that there is no separation between you and these particles; it only means that there is an *interrelatedness* between you and them. And interrelatedness is far different than non-separation. The term "universe" (etymologically derived from "single turning" or "systematic whole") implies the interrelatedness of all existents—but, again, it is a form of "concept stealing" to conflate this "interrelatedness" with the idea of mystical "non-separation." Second, even if your observing conscious does affect subatomic particles, its effect on the visible physical world is next to nil. You can gaze intensely at a spoon all day, and your focused attention will have no measurable effect on it. James Randi, the renowned scientific skeptic, exposed psychic Uri Geller's mind-power spoon-bending as bogus; and for a number of years, Randi has offered a million dollars to anyone who can demonstrate psychic powers under laboratory conditions. So far, no one has been able to do so.

Tolle's claim that "the observing consciousness cannot be separated from observed phenomena, and a different way of looking causes the observed phenomena to behave differently" has no validity on the physical level. If it did, you could go Las Vegas, adjust your "vision of life," and break the house. I was a professional gambler for ten years in Vegas, and I never saw or heard about anyone being able to predict or control the roll of the dice or the turn of the roulette wheel. If you believe Eckhart Tolle is a spiritual master who can affect phenomena via his enlightened "vision of life," invite him to Vegas and see what he can do at the gaming tables. But my advice to you is: don't bet more than you can afford to lose.

Mystics like Tolle who, explicitly or implicitly, point to Heisenberg's Uncertainly Principle to support their primacy-of-consciousness argument conveniently ignore the negative spiritual implications of doing so. If Heisenberg's Uncertainty Principle is completely true, then (as Heisenberg himself said) causality breaks down, and we are left with a chaotic universe. If you accept the "positive" spiritual implications of the Uncertainty Principle—proof of the primacy of consciousness—you must also accept its "negative" spiritual implications—that God, in effect, plays dice with the universe and that the law of karma is not entirely valid. Albert Einstein, a mystic himself, rejected Heisenberg's Uncertainty Principle because he did not accept the possibility of a chaotic universe.

Eckhart Tolle informs us that "An infinite number of completely different interpretations, completely different worlds, is possible and, in fact, exists, depending on the perceiving consciousness." He is right about the "infinite number of completely different interpretations" but wrong about the "completely different worlds." There is no end to the way consciousness can interpret the world of phenomena, but the universe of existents exists independent of any perceiving consciousness. As Leonard Peikoff, Ayn Rand's foremost interpreter, puts it, "Existence exists, and that is all that exists." The perceiving consciousness cannot create these existents or even tangibly alter their behavior. All it can do is perceive them. And the fact that different beings perceive existence, or aspects of it, differently does not create different worlds; it just creates different interpretations of reality, the universe of existents.

Eckhart Tolle believes that man's collective consciousness creates reality, including social reality. He states, "Our collective human world is largely created through the level of consciousness we call mind." This is a statement right out of the pages of Immanuel Kant (the most evil philosopher in history, according to Ayn Rand, who considered him the archenemy of both the human mind and the idea of objective reality). As Rand puts it, "Kant ushered in the era of *social* subjectivism—the view that it is not the consciousness of individuals, but of *groups* that creates reality. In Kant's system, mankind as a whole is the decisive group; what creates the phenomenal world is not the idiosyncrasies of particular individuals, but the mental structure common to all men." Tolle, clearly a Kantian, believes that "when the majority of humans become free of egoic delusion, this inner change will affect all of creation" and "you will literally inhabit a new world."

What kind of "new world" does Tolle envisage? One that is prophesized in the Bible. Tolle hazily describes it:

> Since all worlds are interconnected, when collective human consciousness becomes transformed, nature and the animal kingdom will reflect that transformation. Hence the statement in the Bible that in the coming age "The lion shall lie down with the lamb." This points to a completely different order of reality.

Isaiah 65:25 in the Bible describes this new order of reality: "The wolf and the lamb"—*not* the "lion and the lamb," as Tolle has it—"shall feed together, and the lion shall eat straw like the bullock: and dust shall be the serpent's meat." And pigs will no doubt fly, I'm sure. But when I informed my cat (regrettably, not a Zen master like Tolle's) that his mice-chomping days were numbered, that his new diet would consist of straw, he hissed at me. However, when I then told him, "And dust shall be the serpent's meat," he began to purr. Straw beats dust, I guess, even in Tolle's Now World Order.

Fogged-out utopians like Tolle love to allude to a new world, a new earth, but when it comes to specifics, a detailed description of the new reality, they are predictably vague. Tolle continues his bleary attempt to describe this New Age:

> What is being born is a new consciousness and, as its inevitable reflection, a new world. This is also foretold in the New Testament Book of Revelation: "Then I saw a new heaven and a new earth, for the first heaven and the first earth had passed away."

Is Eckhart Tolle brainless enough to actually believe in the "new earth" nonsense that he preaches? Or is he simply looking to capitalize on the idealistic gullibility of the New Age masses? Tolle, ever the spiritual idealist (or at least appearing to be so), insists that unless you connect to the transcendental Source, you are incapable of bringing about a better world:

> You are in touch with something infinitely greater than any pleasure, greater than any manifested thing... It is only at this point that you begin to make a real contribution toward bringing about a better world, toward creating a different order of reality. It is only at this point that you are able to feel true compassion and to help others at the level of cause. Only those who have transcended the world can bring about a better world.

History does not support Tolle's assertion that only world-transcenders can make the world better. Untold millions have died and been persecuted by religions stemming from world-transcending saints. Examine the bloody histories of Christianity and Islam and try to make a case that they have brought about a better world. And in India, easily the most spiritual nation in history (if the sheer number of enlightened beings produced is the criterion for "spiritual"), all the great yogis, saints, and sages have been unable to eliminate the terrible poverty and suffering of the masses. Anyone who objectively studies world history would categorically reject Tolle's notion that only world-transcenders can bring about a better world. The Renaissance of the fifteenth and sixteenth centuries, for example, was not championed by world-transcenders, but it led to the birth of science, individualism, and liberty. The U.S. Constitution was not created by mystics living in the Now, but the Founding Fathers who crafted it did more to bring about a better world than all the mystics in history combined. Only a myopic mystic like Tolle could totally ignore the contributions of non-world-transcenders (such as freedom fighters, educators, scientists, and inventors) in bringing about a better world.

It is true that by radiantly *being*, your very presence spreads peace and joy—but it is more than a stretch to assume that this is the only way to make the world better. Tolle says, "You become the 'light of the world,' an emanation of pure consciousness, and so eliminate suffering on the level of cause. You eliminate unconsciousness from the world." The truth is, you can only eliminate your own unconsciousness; you cannot eliminate unconsciousness from the world. And only the rarest beings ever fully eliminate their own unconsciousness. Therefore, if you want to bring about a better world, do not put all your eggs in the single basket of enlightenment; find other positive ways to contribute to humanity

Eckhart Tolle asserts, "But who you are is always a more vital teaching and a more powerful transformer of the world than what you say, and more essential even than what you do." This simply isn't the case. If you objectively examine world history, you'll find that Tolle, again, is wrong. It is the words and actions of men, not their character, or lack thereof, that has essentially determined the course of human history. For example, consider *The Communist Manifesto*, which has powerfully shaped world history irrespective of Karl Marx's state of being. And it is the actions rather than the character of world leaders that has always made the world go round. Jimmy Carter, for example, was a true humanitarian with a big heart, but his disastrous economic policies paved the way for Ronald Reagan and Reaganomics.

According to Tolle, "Your compassion may simultaneously manifest on the level of doing and effect by alleviating suffering whenever you come across it." Therefore, he says, "When a hungry person asks you for bread and you have some, you will give it." Although on the surface it might appear noble to mindlessly and indiscriminately give to the needy, such action is often counterproductive. Instead of benefiting the recipients, it can undermine their strength and independence. In 1960, seventy-eight percent of African American families were two-parent units, but thanks to the gross expansion of the welfare state by liberal Democrats, this figure had shrunk to only twenty-eight percent by the year 2010. By freely giving extra welfare benefits to unwed mothers with children, the well-meaning socialists inadvertently decimated the African American nuclear family.

What Tolle and mystics of his ilk ignore is the role of *productivity*. In order to be able to give, you first have to produce, to create wealth. And the best way to help the needy, and all of society as well, is to teach people how to be productive. Thus, instead of giving a hungry person a piece of fish to eat, teach him how to fish. When a person is productive, he is strong and independent and has self-esteem. But, of course, to world-negating anti-egoists like Tolle, virtues such as self-esteem are antithetical to the enlightenment process.

Tolle says what really matters when you give bread to a hungry person is the "moment of shared Being, of which the bread is only a symbol." "In that moment," he says, "there is no giver, no receiver." Regardless of what Tolle claims, there is still an objective giver and an objective receiver in that moment. You might experience unity in the Spirit with the recipient of your bread, but it is utter nonsense to insist that the giver-receiver dynamic is somehow voided by your act of karma yoga.

Why should there even be hunger and starvation in the world? Why not create a better world by first tackling hunger and violence?

Tolle's prescription for these social ills is no more than a spiritual bromide:

> All evils are the effects of unconsciousness. You can alleviate the effects of unconsciousness, but you cannot eliminate them unless you eliminate their cause. True change happens within, not without.

The real answer to hunger and starvation—as proven by India, China, and other emerging nations—is *not* spiritual consciousness; it is *capitalism*, a dirty word to most primacy-of-consciousness mystics like Tolle. Awakening people to the Now is a wonderful mission, but it has little to do with feeding and clothing the masses. Anyone interested in an intelligent real-world solution to hunger and starvation should read Ayn Rand's book *Capitalism: The Unknown Ideal*.

Capitalism, unbeknownst to most people, is, first and foremost, a social system, not an economic one. And because a capitalist system protects individual rights (including property rights) and encourages free trade among people and nations, it is the real solution not only to world hunger, but to mass violence, too.

Tolle encourages the practice of "passive resistance" as a means to "stop deeply unconscious humans from destroying themselves, each other, and the planet, or from continuing to inflict dreadful suffering on other sentient beings." He says, "Just as you cannot fight the darkness, so you cannot fight unconsciousness." If you try, he claims, you will strengthen the "polar opposites" and "create an 'enemy.'"

Tolle is wrong: you can and need to *aggressively* fight your true enemies, those who threaten your very existence. These enemies are not "created" in your consciousness; they are physical realities. If you don't destroy the Hitlers and Bin Ladens of the world, they will destroy you. "Passive resistance" is a joke of a response to terrorists intent on blowing up you and the free world. If Tolle possessed any real-world insight, he'd identify the two major (evil) forces causing most of the problems on the planet: religious fundamentalism and statism (meaning governments with unlimited power that deny individual rights and political freedom to their citizens). When religious fanatics or statist nations threaten your sovereignty, life, and liberty, then you have no *real* choice but to *violently* fight back.

Eckhart Tolle doesn't emphasize non-spiritual or "effect-level" work to alleviate suffering in the world, which he calls a "bottomless pit." He says, "The causal level needs to remain your remain your primary focus, the teaching of enlightenment your main purpose, and peace your most precious gift to the world."

This raises the question: If you're not *deeply* enlightened, just a student of Tolle's, are you really qualified to teach enlightenment? If you haven't been baptized in the Holy Spirit and can't rest in the Light-energy from above, how can you speak knowingly about the process of spiritual enlightenment? Some great gurus, in fact, strongly warn their students against assuming a teaching role until they are *fully* enlightened. In my face-to-face meetings in the 1980s with Jean Klein (1916–1998), an eminent *Advaita* (nondual) guru, he cautioned me against teaching until I was fully enlightened. But like some of his other students, I ignored his advice. The question of teaching enlightenment prior to your own actual enlightenment is a serious one, and even the gurus don't agree on an answer.

CHAPTER TEN

The Spiritual Meaning of Surrender

True Spiritual Acceptance

The spiritual traditions tell us to "surrender." I don't like that. It seems to imply defeat, fatalistic resignation to life's circumstances. How do you reconcile personal initiative, getting things done, and striving for success with the ideal of "surrender?"

Eckhart Tolle denies that surrender means passively putting up with negative life circumstances, ceasing to make plans, or relinquishing personal initiative; and in a Krishnamurti-like statement, he tells us what it really means:

> Surrender is the simple but profound wisdom of *yielding* to rather than opposing the flow of life. The only place where you can experience the flow of life is the Now, so to surrender is to accept the present moment unconditionally and without reservation. It is to relinquish inner resistance to what *is*. Inner resistance is to say "no" to what *is*, through mental judgment and emotional negativity.

Contrary to what Tolle says, true spiritual surrender is *not* necessarily a matter of yielding to the flow of life, the continuum of conditional existence. Rather, it is a matter of relinquishing resistance to the force-flow of the Spirit-current, the Divine "Will," or Power. The "present [time-space] moment" is not the (timeless, spaceless) Now; it is simply spatial phenomena arising in the current-moment time frame. And as I've repeatedly emphasized, it is not always wise to "accept the present moment unconditionally and without reservation," as Tolle enjoins us to do.

When you relinquish mental judgment, as Tolle recommends, you surrender the uniquely human capacity to measure reality. And if you measure reality, you cannot desist from experiencing "negative" emotions, because such emotions are an automatic, not a volitional, response to your value judgments. From Tolle's "flat" (two-dimensional) spiritual perspective, "Resistance is the mind"; hence you must surrender your mind, your mental judgment. But from a "full" (three-dimensional) spiritual perspective, true surrender is simply relaxing-releasing into the Spirit-current, and within this Spirit-full context, essential, functional mental judgment does not impede your reception of the inpouring divine Power.

Tolle provides us with an example to illustrate his concept of surrender:

> For example, if you were stuck in the mud somewhere, you wouldn't say: "Okay, I resign myself to being stuck in the mud." Resignation is not surrender. You don't need to accept an undesirable or unpleasant life situation. Nor do you need to deceive yourself and say that there is nothing wrong with being stuck in the mud. No. You recognize fully that you want to get out of it. You then narrow your attention down to the present moment without mentally labeling it in any way. This means that there is no judgment of the Now. Therefore, there is no resistance, no emotional negativity. You accept the "isness" of the moment. Then you take action and do all that you can to get out of the mud. Such action I call positive action. It is far more effective than negative action, which arises out of anger, despair, or frustration. Until you achieve the desired result, you continue to practice surrender by refraining from labeling the Now.

Tolle's version of surrender is not true surrender. It is about your *doing* something, about your applying a reductive strategy to negate your reactivity to *select* life situations. As soon as you attempt to implement Tolle's instructions and "narrow your attention" to the present moment, you are creating resistance by contracting consciousness into an exclusive, canalized focus. Further, if you never judged any present moments in your life, you would not have any life values, and thus you would have no desire to act. The reason you got stuck in the mud was because you—based on a life value *judgment*—decided to act, decided to drive. But as soon as you get saddled with a negative life situation, such as being stuck in the mud, then you strategically and *selectively* apply "acceptance" and "non-judgment" in an attempt to negate your emotional reactivity to it.

It is impossible for a human being to consistently—or non-selectively— practice non-judgment, non-labeling. Try it and see. Your efforts will be spasmodic and your results disappointing. Such efforts fly in the face of *human* life, which has no meaning or impetus without value judgments and labels. When your *efforts* to implement Tolle's concept of surrender fail, then, hopefully, you will be ready for the practice of true surrender, true spiritual acceptance.

True surrender is simply letting go of all effort, all seeking, so you can receive *Shaktipat,* the descent of the Holy Spirit. It is the practice of "poverty," or emptiness, which allows you to receive and conduct the Holy Spirit, the true power of Now. But the practice of true surrender is contextual, meaning that it cannot be truly (or consistently and protractedly) practiced exclusive of the discipline of Holy Communion. When, via the practice of Holy Communion, you plug into the divine Presence, the Now, a pressure is felt, the pressure of the Presence wanting to move into and through you. Yielding to this pressure, this force, and allowing it to penetrate you, to flow through you, is true *spiritual* surrender.

Random surrendering—relaxing and letting go—in your everyday life is clearly positive, physically as well psychologically. And when your random surrendering escalates from casual letting go into a serious discipline aimed at relinquishing thoughts from moment to moment, *kundalini* (the dormant, or "sleeping," force of consciousness) can awaken and add a new dimension to your spiritual practice. But the highest and holiest form of surrender is that of effortless reception of the

Holy Spirit. In the context of true Holy Communion, the practice of "poverty," or surrender, transforms you into a Holy Chalice, an empty vessel or great vacuum that literally, not figuratively, sucks down Light-energy from above. By utterly yielding to this Light-energy Plenum, the Holy Spirit, you realize the fruit of holy surrender: the en-Light-enment (or Spirit-irradiation) of your entire bodily being and the realization of your oneness (or identity) with the supreme Being.

Eckhart Tolle believes that "Surrender is perfectly compatible with taking action, initiating change, or achieving goals." He calls this marriage of surrender and action "surrendered action" and explains how it will revolutionize humanity's concept of work:

> Through nonresistance, the quality of your consciousness and therefore the quality of whatever you are doing or creating is enhanced immeasurably. The results will then look after themselves and reflect that quality. We could call this *surrendered action*. It is not work as we have known it for thousands of years. As more humans awaken, the word *work* is going to disappear from our vocabulary, and perhaps a new word will be created to replace it.

Tolle's "surrendered action" is hardly a new concept. In fact, it is simply a synonym for the ancient Indian discipline of *karma yoga,* defined by the late Swami Satchidananda (1914–2002) as "action for the sake of action." The ideal of karma yoga, promoted in the Hindu Bible, *The Bhagavad Gita,* never revolutionized work in India. But Tolle, a New Age visionary, believes that humanity is now ready to awaken en masse and redefine the very meaning of work.

Personally speaking, I can hardly wait for the New Age that Tolle envisions, when nonresistance will make work (the struggle to overcome resistance) obsolete. Then, when I go to the gym to lift weights, I can practice progressive nonresistance instead of progressive resistance to make my muscles grow. All joking aside, Tolle's ideal of surrendered action becoming the new social norm is about as likely as progressive nonresistance becoming the new method for building muscles.

You won't read about it in *The Power of Now*, but spiritual practice is as much about work as it is about surrender. Surrender has no real spiritual significance until you consciously connect to, or attempt to connect to, Being—and connecting to Being involves serious effort. Without this effort, this work, there can be no flow of Grace for you to yield to and rest in. Real spiritual life is a discipline, the discipline of Holy Communion, the practice of direct, immediate relation to the Now, the divine Presence. And unless you become a "born again" disciple baptized in the power of this Presence, the Holy Spirit, you can surrender until Doomsday and still not realize your identity with the supreme Being.

If there isn't any dissatisfaction, if you're totally surrendered and free of resistance, where would the energy or motivation be to take action or bring about change?

Eckhart Tolle defers to nature for the answer to this question:

> In the state of surrender, you see very clearly what needs to be done, and you take action, doing one thing at a time and focusing on one thing at a time. Learn from nature. See how everything gets accomplished and how the miracle of life unfolds without dissatisfaction or unhappiness. That's why Jesus said: "Look at the lilies, how they grow; they neither toil nor spin."

So much for multitasking if you're a Tolle follower. Just one thing at a time and learn from nature is his advice. But not everyone learns the same lesson from nature as Tolle. When I view nature, I see an impersonal machine—Adi Da calls it "Klik-Klak"—with no regard whatsoever for human life, unless you think a tsunami snuffing out a hundred thousand human lives in a single wave is an "accomplishment." And I see plenty of unhappiness. Animals live in fear of other animals and cry out in anguish when they are attacked and mercilessly ripped to shreds. Some unhappy animals, such as apes, even enjoy brutalizing and killing members of their own species. (For details on this phenomenon, read *Demonic Males: Apes and the Origins of Human Violence*, by Dale Peterson and Richard Wrangham.)

What about plants? Do they just grow without toiling and spinning? Hardly. Plants become strong by practicing *resistance* to the elements. When the wind whips, for example, they respond by digging their roots more firmly into the ground. Plants also exercise (negative) resistance to some noise. When subjected to rock music, for instance, they recoil, and their growth is hindered. Conversely, when they are exposed to classical music, their growth is accelerated and they flourish. Unlike Tolle, sad to say, plants are judgmental and full of resistance. But I'm hoping that if I read *The Power of Now* out loud to my favorite plant, Merry Jane, she'll stop shrinking when I jack up the volume on my Deep Purple and Scorpions CDs, and provide me with at least a few decent buds.

Now for the question some of you are doubtless asking: How could Jesus be wrong when he said the lilies "neither toil nor spin?" Simple: he was a *pneumatic* (a master of the Holy Spirit), not a botanist. Jesus also mistakenly believed that the Earth was flat. The message we can learn from this is that even enlightened mystics are not privy to special knowledge relative to manifest existence. And nowhere is this truth more evident than in the writings of Eckhart Tolle.

Eckhart Tolle finally, though indirectly, informs us that non-resistance to what *is* is *not* the same thing as surrender to Being (what IS):

> Any action you take may not bear fruit immediately. Until it does—do not resist what is. If there is no action you can take, and you cannot remove yourself from the situation, either, then use the situation to make you go

more deeply into surrender, more deeply into the Now,
more deeply into Being.

The whole point of real spiritual life is conscious union with the Spirit,
not eliminating your resistance to life situations. Obviously, you don't
want to live your life in an angry, resistant mood, and in general you
should go with the flow and not resist what is. But consciousness is
senior to surrender, and real intelligence (meaning enlightened
discrimination) should dictate when it's appropriate for you to exercise
resistance relative to life situations.

Being fully present to (or not avoiding) a life situation is not the same
thing as surrendering to what is. Being fully present to a situation is a
doorway to the Now, but in the context of your presence, you are free
to either resist or not resist what is. Surrendering to (or not resisting)
what is generally is the preferable choice, but when you are confronted
with an unacceptable or threatening situation, resistance is a natural and
sometimes appropriate response. Again, whether or not you should
resist a particular situation is your call, and only by exercising real
intelligence can you make an enlightened choice.

According to Tolle, "When you enter the timeless dimension of the
present, change often comes about in strange ways without the need of a
great deal of doing on your part. Life becomes helpful and cooperative."
Unfortunately, this isn't always the case. Often, depending on your
karma, the awakened Spirit-energy dredges up all kinds of difficulties,
thereby making your life more, not less, challenging. Read the
biographies and autobiographies of the great yogis, saints, and sages, and
you will realize that life did not always reward their present-moment
communion with help and cooperation.

Transmuting Mind Energy into Spiritual Energy

*Letting go of resistance is not easy. I still don't understand how to let go. If you
say to just surrender, the question is: How?*

Tolle's answer to this question is predictable and predictably lacking:

> Start by acknowledging that there is resistance. *Be* there
> when it happens, when the resistance arises. Observe
> how your mind creates it, how it labels the situation,
> yourself, or others. Look at the thought process
> involved. Feel the energy of the emotion. By witnessing
> the resistance, you will see that it serves no purpose. By
> focusing all your attention on the Now, the unconscious
> resistance is made conscious, and that is the end of it.
> You cannot be conscious *and* unhappy, conscious *and* in
> negativity. Negativity, unhappiness, or suffering in
> whatever form means that there is resistance, and
> resistance is always unconscious.

I have four points to make in response to Tolle's answer. First, it belabors the obvious to say that your mind creates resistance and that this resistance can be felt energetically as an emotion. But does this emotion "serve no purpose," as Tolle asserts? The answer is an emphatic "no." Most (but not all) resistance is an automatic response to an unwelcome demand against your person. It is an essential biological response that, positively, serves to warn your organism of a potential threat to your well-being. The threat may be real or imaginary (as most are), but it is the natural function of your subconscious mind to alert you to any possible hint of danger; and it is the job of your conscious mind, in the form of intelligence, to discern whether resistance to a particular situation is warranted. Second, contrary to what Tolle says, the fact that the resistance is made conscious is not necessarily the end of it. If the resistance is truly warranted, your subconscious mind will again and again bring it to the surface of your consciousness until you conclusively resolve the situation. Third, although mental suffering implies resistance on some level, not all resistance begets suffering. In fact, conscious resistance to threats to your well-being can prevent as well as ameliorate much suffering. Fourth, merely witnessing your resistance or focusing your attention on the Now should not be conflated with the act of surrender, the act of relinquishing resistance. *Letting go* is clearly a different gesture than the *holding on* implicit in witnessing or focusing attention on the Now. In fact, if Tolle were more than a pop guru, he'd elaborate on the fact that the very practices of witnessing and focusing attention on the Now are *willful* conscious exercises that involve *resistance* to one's ordinary (chaotic) state of consciousness.

I am conscious of my unhappy feelings, but my consciousness does not make them disappear.

Eckhart Tolle's response to this observation is to differentiate between the state of ordinary consciousness and the state of "intense present-moment awareness":

> You say that you are conscious of your unhappy feelings, but the truth is that you are identified with them and keep the process alive through compulsive thinking. All *that* is unconscious. If you were conscious, that is to say totally present in the Now, all negativity would dissolve almost instantly. It could not survive in your presence. It can only survive in your absence.

Tolle is correct when he states that your unhappiness stems from identification with negative feelings and that your compulsive thinking keeps the process alive. But this identification is subconscious, not unconscious. It is subconscious because your unhappy feelings stem from identification with your value judgments, which you consciously formed in the past. Compulsive thinking is also a subconscious process because it likewise involves mind-forms stemming from your past self-conditioning. If your feelings and your flow of thoughts were unconscious rather than subconscious, you would not be able to alter their arising patterns by consciously adjusting your premises.

Tolle's claim that total presence in the Now dissolves all negativity almost instantly is pure hyperbole. Your full presence might temporarily obviate your negative thoughts and feelings, but as soon as you relax your "intense present-moment awareness," the same negative emotions that plagued you before will reassert themselves. It is not humanly possible to volitionally sustain the practice of present-moment awareness for protracted periods of time. The only way you can remain plugged in to the Now for an extended duration is through Grace, the descent of the Holy Spirit. And until you are baptized by the Holy Spirit, you cannot receive the Benediction, the Blessing Power from above that *meditates you*! Only by resting in the current of Grace and allowing it to meditate you are you able to attain and enjoy profound *samadhis*—long, deep states of mystical absorption in Being.

Eckhart Tolle truly despises the human mind, identifying it as an agent of planetary pollution and destruction:

> Through surrender, spiritual energy comes into this world. It creates no suffering for yourself, for other humans, or any other life form on the planet. Unlike mind energy, it does not pollute the Earth, and it is not subject to the law of polarities, which dictates nothing can exist without its opposite, that there can be no good without bad. Those who run on mind energy, which is still the vast majority of the Earth's population, remain unaware of the existence of spiritual energy. It belongs to a different order of reality and will create a different world when a sufficient number of humans enter the surrendered state and so become totally free of negativity. If the earth is to survive, this will be the energy of those who inhabit it.

Tolle's message is apocalyptic: Only spiritual energy can rescue the Earth from man's evil mind. Through surrender, humans can bring spiritual energy into this world and save our planet from extinction. Tolle's message is Dark Age nonsense. It is not mind energy that threatens our planet, but rather, anti-mind energy. This anti-mind energy—in the form of secular and religious dogmas that demand unquestioning surrender to their enslaving dictates and authority—views the rational mind as dangerous. But what endangers the world's survival is not the rational mind; it is the anti-reason "mind." For example, consider the case of secular humanists. These well-meaning, peace-loving people, who trust in science and reason rather than in spiritual energy, work hard to make our planet a safer, cleaner, more humane place. Although I am not a secular humanist, their example graphically illustrates the point that rational mind energy can represent the Earth's salvation, not its demise.

Man is the conceptual animal, gifted with reasoning power unavailable to any other creature. But to mystical "thinkers" such as Tolle, the human mind represents a curse, not a blessing. Instead of praising this remarkable God-given faculty, they denigrate it, blaming it for all the problems in the world. This is tantamount to blaming food rather than overeating for obesity. Just as fatness isn't caused by food, man's myriad social problems aren't caused by his mind; they are caused by its *misuse*. But Tolle steadfastly refuses to acknowledge the mind's positive aspects, even denying that it is creative. Instead, true to his colors as a quasi-nihilistic mystic, he throws the baby (the rational mind) out with the bath water (the irrational mind), kicking it soundly before loathingly tossing it down the trash chute.

Jesus Christ was a great mystic, but he was also a man—and as Dirty Harry would say, every man has his limitations. In the case of Jesus, it was his prophetic ability. Two thousand years after his death, the meek have yet to inherit the Earth, and unless scientists can bio-engineer a docile cockroach, I wouldn't advise a wager on the "gentle" inheriting the global turf any time soon. But Tolle, ever the apocalyptic doomsayer, assures us that the Earth can only survive if the "impoverished," meaning the spiritually surrendered, become the prime movers down here. I'm all in favor of spiritual surrender and channeling *Shakti*, but without man's volitional (and creative) mind-energy fully intact, the salvation of the earth is no more than a pipe dream.

Surrender in Interpersonal Relations

Should I surrender to people who want to use, control, or manipulate me? The spiritual texts preach the ideal of unconditional surrender, but that doesn't make sense in everyday life.

Unconditional surrender, in a spiritual context, does not mean letting others use, control, or manipulate you. It means being utterly open to the Holy Spirit and allowing it to bless and enlighten you. Unconditional surrender, or open Being, does not mean relinquishing your ability to intelligently discriminate and make wise decisions in your life. You can be Spirit-full and still tell imposers to get lost.

Eckhart Tolle recommends *consciousness* as the best defense against those who "attempt to get energy and power from you." He says, "It is true that only an unconscious person will try to manipulate others, but it is equally true that only an unconscious person *can* be used and manipulated."

There are two problems with Tolle's recommendation. First, many of the people who attempt to get energy and power from you know exactly what they are doing. To excuse their activity as "unconscious" is to fail to acknowledge the full extent of their evil intentions. Second, Tolle fails to acknowledge that consciousness in this context pertains to consciousness as *mental judgment*, and not to the mindless, pure consciousness he preaches throughout *The Power of Now*. Mental judgment implies volition (will and reasoning), which means *resistance*, the very antithesis of Tolle's concept of surrender.

A discriminating intellect is essential if you are to intelligently decide what is right or wrong for you in a particular situation. But if you don't have mind-acquired knowledge regarding the matter at hand, you cannot make an intelligent decision. Therefore, if you are to avoid being used and manipulated, you must *know* and *think*. In other words, *consciousness* as a defense against an imposition implies the need for both knowledge and judgment. Mere conscious presence won't cut it when you have to make difficult decisions. You will have to use the faculty of reason, which is the faculty of volition. And the use of this faculty contradicts Tolle's call for the "state of complete inner nonresistance" in the face of an imposition.

My situation at work is miserable. I've tried to surrender to it, but I can't. I'm still plagued with resistance. What should I do?

Eckhart Tolle says, "If you cannot surrender, take action immediately." This might not be good advice. It might be better to take some time to carefully consider your options before you act. First, rationally determine what constitutes right action in your situation. If you take action immediately without weighing all the factors involved, you might end up regretting your immediate action.

You have three options in every situation: surrender, action, or resistance. Only real intelligence, which necessarily involves judgment and the mind, can tell you which is appropriate in a given situation. Although surrender and action clearly are the preferable alternatives, sometimes resistance and action are the same. For example, if someone tries to mug you and you react by punching him in the face, your action in this case is equivalent to resistance. And in such a case, immediate action (or reaction) might be the right call.

Does this mean that spiritual nonresistance only concerns the inner life and not the outer?

Yes, and Tolle finally makes this clear when he states, "You only need to be concerned with the inner aspect. That is primary."

But Tolle then contradicts himself, reverting to his original position when he says, "If you can never accept what *is* [which by definition includes the outer], by implication you will not be able to accept anybody the way they are. You will judge, criticize, label, reject, or attempt to change people."

What *is* is not Being; it is life, including the outer life situations that you encounter. Because Tolle, like a broken tape recorder, plays the same trite, grating song—"Accept what *is*"—over and over, I will for the umpteenth time counter his argument by repeating mine: Only a spiritual fool would indiscriminately surrender to what *is* and unconditionally accept people the way they are.

Tolle says, "Observe the attachment to your views and opinions. Feel the mental-emotional energy behind your need to be right and make the other person wrong." But what if your views and opinions are fact and the other person is clearly wrong? For example, if you talk to a fundamentalist Muslim who insists that the Holocaust never happened, do you surrender attachment to your correct view simply to avoid conflict, or do you emphatically tell him that he is wrong? Even if you pretend to relinquish attachment to your mental position in this case, you can't really do so because you know that you are absolutely right and that he is absolutely wrong. And because his position is not only untenable but also potentially dangerous, you no doubt will also judge him harshly, rightly labeling him a brainwashed fanatic.

Tolle summarizes his position on interpersonal communication: "When identification with mental positions is out of the way, true communication begins." Tolle's position is not one that I second. To my mind, true communication begins only when both parties are interested in objective facts. Whether or not an individual identifies with his mental position(s) is of secondary importance; what is of primary importance is his allegiance to objective truth. If two individuals share an allegiance to objective truth, they can always truly communicate on that basis alone. On the other hand, an individual who doesn't identify with his mental positions, but who instead believes that "objective truth" is a myth, cannot truly communicate with anyone. Such an individual believes that each man creates his own "human" truth, which means that objective truth is impossible. If objective truth is impossible, if truth is arbitrarily or subjectively *mind-created* rather than rationally or objectively *mind-identified*, then there can be no basis for true communication between two minds, each of which inhabits its own private universe.

What about nonresistance in the face of a physical confrontation?

In the case of a physical confrontation, Eckhart Tolle recommends nonresistance to counter the opponent's attack. In other words, yin defense sans yang offense:

> Nonresistance doesn't necessarily mean doing nothing. All it means is any "doing" becomes nonreactive. Remember the deep wisdom underlying the Eastern martial arts: Don't resist the opponent's force. Yield to overcome.

I do not second Tolle's nonresistance recommendation. I've been mugged more than a few times (while hanging out in bad neighborhoods late at night), and I can tell you that when you're physically accosted, nonresistance alone just doesn't cut it. In fact, even if you practice Eastern martial arts—and I've practiced judo—after you use leverage to exploit your opponent's force, you need to counter with an aggressive attack of your own. Otherwise, your opponent will come at you again.

Tolle considers "doing nothing" a "very powerful transformer and healer of situations and people." He says that this "actionless activity"—called *wu wei* in Taoism and *shikantaza* in Soto Zen—"implies inner nonresistance and intense alertness." But intense alertness is the very antithesis of nonresistance. The very effort to remain constantly alert, in open awareness, implies energy or work, the very opposite of the nonresistance that Tolle preaches. In fact, Wikipedia describes *shikantaza* as "a very demanding practice, requiring diligence as well as perseverance." But Tolle never explains how the dialectical interplay between intense alertness (conscious presence) and nonresistance (effortless absence) is resolved. Tolle presents us with the thesis (intense alertness) and the antithesis (nonresistance), but not with the *synthesis.*

The *synthesis,* of course, is the Holy Spirit, the true power of Now. In an electrical circuit, voltage (electromotive pressure) is the thesis, ohms (resistance reduction) the antithesis, and amperage (current flow) the synthesis. In the spiritual "circuit," intense alertness (conscious pressure) is the thesis, nonresistance (letting go) the antithesis, and the Holy Spirit (Blessing flow) the synthesis. But Tolle, true to his "flat" brand of mysticism, never mentions the Holy Spirit as the integrating or synthesizing factor in his mystical exegesis. Grace is not a subject he wants to broach, perhaps because he knows that much of his New Age audience includes self-help junkies allergic to the idea of Divine descent.

Like many mystics, Tolle conflates the ego with resistance. For example, he says, "The ego believes that in your resistance lies your strength," and that "Resistance is weakness and fear masquerading as strength." In actuality, the ego is often what helps an individual overcome fear and resistance. For instance, if a boy is afraid to jump off a high diving board, it is his ego, his need to display personal courage, that enables him to conquer his fear and make the leap. Tolle and mystics of his ilk love to paint only a one-sided, pejorative picture of the ego. Yet when you carefully study these mystics' lives and even meet many of them (as I have), you discover a startling fact: most of them have bigger egos than you do! In other words, if you want to be a great sage, a spiritual hero, don't waste your time trying to get rid of your ego. Instead, simply contemplate the Divine and awaken to your Self-nature, which, in fact, is pure or perfect Ego, or *I Am*-ness.

Transmuting Illness into Enlightenment

If someone has an illness and surrenders to it, wouldn't that compromise his ability to fight and overcome his condition?

Real surrender is not a matter of surrendering to a particular condition, good or bad; it is a matter of surrendering to the Unconditioned, the

Divine. Regarding illness, surrender to the Divine does not preclude measures to combat the condition. Do what is appropriate to fight the illness, but do so in the context of opening to and receiving Divine Help, the Holy Spirit.

Tolle's spiritual prescription for dealing with physical or psychic pain is the correct one:

> If you have a major illness, use it for enlightenment. Anything "bad" that happens in your life—use it for enlightenment. Withdraw time from your illness. Do not give it any past or future. Let it force you into intense present-moment awareness—and see what happens... Become an alchemist. Transmute base metal into gold, suffering into consciousness, disaster into enlightenment.

Everything that exists is energy, including consciousness. When physical or psychic pain causes your consciousness to contract into a state of constricted energy, you can free that energy simply by "expanding" your consciousness. And you "expand" your consciousness by plugging it into the divine Source. Plugged-in present-moment awareness, Holy Communion, connects you to the divine Source (or Force Field), enabling you to directly (and immediately) receive Grace—consciousness-expanding Energy, or Help, from above.

Dealing with Disaster

Is Grace a miracle that redeems those who surrender in the face of disaster or limit-situations (moments in which the mind confronts its own restrictions and is able to release itself from them)? It is, according to Eckhart Tolle:

> Limit-situations have produced many miracles. There have been murderers on death row waiting for execution who, in the last hours of their lives, experienced the egoless state and the deep joy and peace that come with

it... Of course, it is not really the limit-situation that
makes room for the miracle of grace and redemption, but
the act of surrender.

First, it is hardly a miracle that a death-row convict facing imminent
execution would surrender. What real alternative does he have? Second,
the descent of Grace is *not* a miracle; it is a natural, lawful response of
the impersonal Divine to anyone who truly opens to It.

Miracles *cannot* occur in a karmically lawful universe. If you believe in
the law of karma, the law of cause and effect, then you must deny the
possibility of miracles. To do otherwise is to be guilty of a contradiction,
and there can be no contradictions in reality. (In other words, if you
hold contradictions in your consciousness, then you have, in effect,
evicted yourself from reality.) If the Deity, the Uncreated, periodically
flouts the law of karma by Intervening in creation via "miracles," then
the order of the Cosmos is disrupted and the universe is reduced to
unpredictable chaos. If you believe in miracles, then welcome to the
New (or Now) World *Disorder*.

Tolle touts surrender as the one step, the single key, to redemption. He
says, "you are just one step away from something incredible: a complete
alchemical transmutation of the base metal of pain and suffering into
gold. That one step is called surrender."

Tolle is wrong: alchemical transformation of a human being cannot be
reduced to the single gesture of surrender. The complete formula for
spiritual transformation can be found in the great Indian yoga equation:
Sat = *Cit* (or *Siva*)-*Ananda* (or *Shakti*). In other words, for you to awaken
to Truth or Being (*Sat*), you must unite your consciousness, contracted
(*Cit*, or *Siva*), with divine Energy (*Ananda*, or *Shakti*). Thus, if you seek
true redemption in the Spirit (*Ananda*, or *Shakti*), you must not only
surrender, but must do so *within the context* of consciously connecting to
and channeling the Spirit (the Redeemer Itself).

Suffering, Surrender, and Peace

If a stoic matter-of-factly accepts pain and suffering, is that true surrender?

No, that is just clinical or objective *mental* acceptance of one's internal state. True *spiritual* surrender goes beyond mentally accepting internal pain; it is about *consciously allowing* the Holy Spirit to invade and possess you. The Holy Spirit crashes down on its true devotees, and to yield to *Its* invasion is true *spiritual* surrender.

Tolle's remedy for internal pain is to "accept what is *inside*." This, in his words, means:

> Do not resist the pain. Allow it to be there. Surrender to the grief, despair, fear, loneliness, or whatever form the suffering takes. Witness it without labeling it mentally. Embrace it. Then see how the miracle of surrender transmutes deep suffering into deep peace. This is your crucifixion. Let it be your resurrection and ascension.

As I have pointed out, surrender involves no miracle; it simply a matter of recognizing and releasing your internal "garbage." And your internal garbage, your suffering, is best disposed of by allowing the Baptist Fire, the flaming Holy Spirit, to incinerate it.

Tolle, predictably, fails to mention the esoteric, or Spirit-energetic, dimension of crucifixion. For the baptized disciple, crucifixion is the pain he must endure in the face of Spirit's passage into and through his gross psycho-physical vehicle. This passage of Spirit-energy through his bodymind "divinizes" him, purifying every dimension of his being. But the agonizing psychic and physical pain that he must endure in the divinization, or "deification," process as the Baptist Fire rages through him is analogous to what Jesus experienced as he carried his cross to Calvary.

Crucifixion for the disciple culminates in his awakening as a Christ, an enlightened Son of God. This occurs when the descending *Shakti*, or

Spirit-power, severs the knot in his Sacred Heart-center (located just to the right of the center of his chest, and distinct from the *anahata,* or heart, chakra). Once his Heart-knot is severed, the disciple's ego (or separate-self sense) is terminated, and he is spontaneously "resurrected," rising from the ashes of his ego-death as the radiant Christ, or Self. Upon the cutting of his Heart-knot, the Spirit-current reverses direction, and the disciple—now an "ascended" spiritual master—rises out of the Heart-center in the "form" of Heart-*Shakti,* the radiant Force-current of the Self.

Eckhart Tolle, the king of pop mysticism, has nothing penetrating or profound to say about "resurrection" or "ascension." He loosely uses the terms and fails to elaborate on what they really mean. But given Tolle's penchant for "surface" mysticism, what more could we realistically expect from him regarding an esoteric matter such as spiritual transfiguration?

How is it possible to surrender to suffering when suffering is non-surrender? In other words, how can you surrender to non-surrender?

Eckhart Tolle doesn't directly answer this question. Instead, he tells you to put talk of surrender aside when your pain is deep:

> When your pain is deep, all talk of surrender will probably seem futile and meaningless anyway. When your pain is deep, you will likely have a strong urge to escape from it rather than surrender to it. But there is no escape, no way out.

Because direct surrender is not a realistic option when your pain is deep, there seems to be no way out from your suffering. But Tolle has the solution to your problem:

> When there is no way out, there is still always a way *through.* So don't turn away from the pain. Face it. Feel it

fully. *Feel* it—don't think about it!... Stay alert, stay present—present with your whole Being, with every cell of your body. As you do so, you are bringing a light into this darkness. This is the flame of your consciousness.

But Tolle not only substitutes the practice of staying alert and present for that of surrender, he actually conflates the two practices:

> At this stage, you don't need to be concerned with surrender anymore. It has happened already. How? Full attention is full acceptance, is surrender. By giving full attention, you use the power of Now, which is the power of your presence. No hidden pocket of resistance can survive in it. Presence removes time. Without time, no suffering, no negativity, can survive.

Does full attention equal full acceptance equal true surrender, as Tolle asserts? No! The practice of full attention, full presence, involves work (willful effort), the antipode of surrender. The practice of presence is a discipline that implies resistance (non-surrender) to your ordinary unconscious condition. By attempting to remain fully present, you are volitionally countering your conditioned tendency to retract from integral connectedness into self-contraction (the formation of consciousness that is suffering).

The power of your full presence (*siva*) generates a pressure, a conscious force; but if you do not yield to this pressure and allow it to translate into an energy flow (*shakti*) that you can channel, you will create palpable tension, resistance that can be felt viscerally. This *descending* energy flow is the power of Now. But until you've been baptized, your plugged-in presence will not "produce" this pulled-down power from above. Tolle talks about "the flame of your consciousness," but until the Holy Spirit, the Baptist Fire, intersects your consciousness, igniting it, *divinizing* it, your presence will lack the "Fire-Power" necessary to fully consume your internal "garbage."

Full attention (integral presence) is the thesis; surrender (non-resistance) is the antithesis; and the power of Now (the Holy Spirit) is the synthesis. Contrary to what Tolle says, the power of Now is *not* the power of your presence; it is the Power of the Divine's Presence, and until you plug into that Presence and receive *Its* Grace, *Its* Blessing Power, you cannot transcend time, suffering, or negativity for protracted periods.

The Horizontal/Vertical Way of the Cross

Does the Christian expression "the way of the cross" signify that deep suffering is the way to salvation?

Exoterically speaking, yes. Esoterically speaking, it means that in order to achieve God-union, you must integrate the "horizontal" practice (or dimension) of plugged-in presence with the "vertical" practice (or dimension) of pulled-down power. Plugged-in presence (or present-moment awareness) allows you to transcend time and live in eternity; pulled-down power (Light-energy from the Highest), allows you to transcend space and live in infinity. Integrating the horizontal practice of plugged-in presence with the vertical practice of pulled-down power is a severe ordeal, and thus a cross to bear.

Tolle tells us that people who find God "did not find God through their suffering, because suffering implies resistance. They found God through surrender." But the fact is that without intense suffering, very few people are moved to unconditionally surrender. Pain, not pleasure, is the great motivator in the spiritual battlefield.

Can surrender be equated with finding God?

According to Tolle, it can, but because enlightenment is a nondualistic state, he prefers to equate it with the realization of Being:

I don't call it finding God, because how can you find that which was never lost, the very life that you are? The word God is limiting not only because of thousands of years of misperception and misuse, but also because it implies an entity other than you. God is Being itself, not a being. There can be no subject-object relationship here, no duality, no you and God. God-realization is the most natural thing there is. The amazing and incomprehensible fact is not that you can become conscious of God but that you are not conscious of God.

If God-realization is the most natural thing there is, as Tolle claims, then why is it so difficult to realize God? Because contrary to what Tolle says, God-realization, unlike, say, the ability to walk or talk, is *not* a natural thing, is *not* a human birthright. Buddhist monks and Hindu yogis devote their lives to seeking permanent oneness with Being, yet only a fraction of them manage to achieve it. The Buddha himself, an extraordinarily gifted yogi, spent six years doing constant *sadhana* (spiritual practice) before he achieved *Nirvana* (union with Being, the end of becoming). But Tolle, ever glib, ever superficial, cavalierly asserts that consciousness of God, the Unborn, is a natural, or inborn, ability.

The realization of Being, as Tolle correctly points out, involves no subject-object relationship. But what Tolle fails to point out is that in order for this radical nondual realization to happen, the yogi must unite *Siva* (Consciousness) and *Shakti* (Spirit-energy) in his Heart-center. And before *Shakti* can permanently embrace *Siva* in the Heart-center, she must, like a serpentine, wind her way through the yogi's network of *nadis* (subtle-body nerve channels), opening *chakras* (centers, or "knots," of intensely rotating vortices, or "wheels," of *pranic* energy) on her way to the Divine union in the Heart.

This process of Spirit-energy (or *Kundalini*) opening, or purification, of the yogi's *nadis*, is an evolutionary process that takes *time*. Consequently, even if the yogi is gifted and able to intensely commune with the divine Presence, before he can permanently live in the Now (and realize his identity with the divine Being), he must allow *Shakti*, the "Goddess of divine Power," to gradually purify his subtle-body infrastructure by "roto-rootering" his *nadi* network, particularly his central channel, the *Sushumna*, which runs from the base of the spine to the crown of the head and which contains the seven major *chakras*. Until his *nadi* network is cleansed and his major *chakras* opened through the Grace-full descent and *spontaneous* circulation of *Shakti*, it is not possible for the yogi to permanently rest in, and as, divine Being.

The hierarchical continuum of the mystico-spiritual enlightenment process is: *communion* (Holy Communion), *union* (Divine Union), and *identity* (nondual Beingness). But many contemporary *Advaita* (nondual) spiritual teachers, like Tolle, ignore this hierarchical continuum and emphasize direct and immediate awakening to nondual Being. After all, their reasoning goes, if your True Nature is Being, then it takes *no effort*, just surrender, to realize your identity with Being. The problem with this reasoning is that although effortlessness does indeed yield a temporary feeling of free existence, or *being-ness*, it does not, in and by itself, directly translate into the realization of divine *Being-ness* (Consciousness-Energy, or *Siva-Shakti*). You can let go until the universe collapses, but unless you are able to yogically integrate the gesture of self-emptying with the practices of conscious *communion* with the Spirit and conscious *reception and conductivity* of the Spirit's Light-energy, your surrendering alone will not propel you through the hierarchical continuum of enlightenment into the realization of nondual, divine Being.

True to his apocalyptic vision of the future, Eckhart Tolle reminds us yet again that he foresees massive upheavals, as even the Earth itself rebels against man's destructive insanity:

> At this time, as far as the unconscious majority of humans is concerned, the way of the cross is still the only way. They will only awaken through further suffering, and enlightenment as a collective phenomenon will be predictably preceded by vast upheavals. This process

reflects the workings of certain universal laws that govern the growth of consciousness and thus was foreseen by some seers. It is described, among other places, in the Book of Revelation or Apocalypse, though cloaked in obscure and sometimes impenetrable symbology. This suffering is inflicted not by god but by humans on themselves and on each other, as well as by certain defensive measures that the Earth, which is a living, intelligent organism, is going to take to protect herself from the onslaught of human madness.

Tolle's reverence for the Book of Revelation and what it forebodes is not shared by all spiritual gurus. Dr. David R. Hawkins, for instance, in the April/May 2007 issue of *Four Corners Magazine*, had this to say about the Book of Revelation:

Even in the New Testament, which calibrates in the 800s, you have the Book of Revelation that calibrates at 70. In every religion, negative or evil has managed to sneak in the door and contaminate it. I have bulwarked everything I have said. Experientially, I have been the witness, testified to [the authenticity of my teachings], and calibrated them. I have cited the references in history that confirm them and have tried to show students how to confirm a statement. All of my books are extensively referenced. So I feel that my work is more safeguarded than any teaching I know of in history.

Thus, we have two big-name gurus with two diametrically opposing points of view regarding the Book of Revelation. If I'm a betting man— and I am—my money is on Dr. Hawkins, not Eckhart Tolle.

Consciousness and Choice

What about people who, seemingly, want to suffer? For example, a woman who remains with a physically abusive partner. Why do these people choose pain?

Eckhart Tolle believes that people who are not spiritually conscious lack the power to choose, that their pain stems from the conditioned patterns of their minds. In other words, free will does not truly exist for these "unconscious" individuals; they have no choice about the pain in their life. Tolle explains:

> Choice implies consciousness—a high degree of consciousness. Without it, you have no choice. Choice begins the moment you disidentify from the mind and its conditioned patterns, the moment you become present. Until you reach that point, you are unconscious, spiritually speaking. This means that you are compelled to think, feel, and act in certain way according to the conditioning of your mind.

Choice, as Tolle says, implies consciousness; but contrary to what he says, choice does not begin when you disidentify from the mind. In fact, the mind, the faculty of reason, is itself the faculty of volition, the faculty of choice. That the mind is free to choose between alternatives in every moment is *self-evident*. For instance, in this very moment, you can choose to either put this book down or continue reading it. Because you clearly have free will, you are not compelled to think or act according to the dictates of your mental conditioning. Yes, your mental conditioning *impels* you to think and behave in certain ways, but it does not *compel* you to do so.

Does choice really involve a "high degree of consciousness," as Tolle claims? I don't think so. For example, consider the case of a woman on a strict diet who is confronted with yummy-looking chocolate cake and Haagen-Dazs ice cream at a friend's birthday party. The woman can either stick to her diet or indulge herself. If she employs her *rational mind* and exercises *will-power*, she will politely refuse the mega-calorie treat. But if she is irrational and weak-willed, she will give in to temptation and stuff herself on the super-fattening food. Choice is available to everyone in every moment, and the more rationally and *will-fully* you think and act, the less you will be subject to your conditioned patterns.

But to Tolle, who sees the world in black and white, if you're not spiritually present, then you're no more than a Pavlovian dog, a Skinnerian automaton.

In Tolle's Skinnerian world of human automatons, if a woman is stuck in an abusive relationship, it is simply because she has "no choice." "The mind," Tolle informs us, "always adheres to the known," which means the woman is no more than a glorified robot, compelled to follow the instructions of her mental programming. In reality, there are many different reasons why women stay in abusive relationships—such as low self-esteem, economic considerations, and good times that counter the bad. And anyone who Googles the subject will quickly realize that Tolle doesn't know what he is talking about regarding this complex matter.

Eckhart Tolle is Immanuel Kant on 'roids, escalating Kant's attack on man's rational faculty to a whole new level. Whereas Kant sought merely to exempt consciousness from the law of identity (A=A), thereby rendering reason impotent as a tool of cognition, Tolle seeks to annihilate man's mind, reducing it to a completely programmed mechanism that is not only dysfunctional, but even insane:

> It always *looks* as if people had a choice, but that is an illusion. As long as the mind with its conditioned patterns runs your life, as long as you *are* your mind, what choice do you have? None. You are not even there. The mind-identified state is severely dysfunctional. It is a form of insanity.

If choice is an illusion and you really have none, as Tolle insists, how is it that you could decide to read this book or *The Power of Now*? Moreover, how could you make the choice to open to the Now, the State to which, according to Tolle, you need to awaken in order to attain the power of choice? Unsurprisingly, Tolle never answers these questions.

◇ ◇ ◇

If people don't have a choice, does that mean that nobody is responsible for what they do?

That's exactly what it means. But Tolle, predictably, fails to acknowledge this. His complete answer (below) to the question is an exercise in avoidance, a non-answer:

> If you are run by your mind, although you have no choice, you will still suffer the consequences of your unconsciousness, and you will create further suffering. You will bear the burden of fear, conflict, problems, and pain. The suffering thus created will eventually force you out of your unconscious state.

Think of the ramifications if people were no longer held accountable for their actions. But Tolle, not wanting to consider this, conveniently sidesteps the question.

If choice is not possible until we are conscious and surrender, then neither is forgiveness.

True forgiveness, according to Eckhart Tolle, is not possible for those who don't live in the Now. He says, "You cannot truly forgive yourself or others as long as you derive your sense of self from the past." In other words, as Tolle argues throughout *The Power of Now*, the mind cannot forgive. But clearly it can—when it has good reason to do so. For example, you might not be able to forgive your neighbor for poisoning your cat, but if your daughter irresponsibly wrecks your car, you almost assuredly will forgive her if she sincerely apologizes and immediately gets a job to pay for the damage.

Tolle insists that "Only through accessing the power of Now, which is your own power, can there be true forgiveness." And this is so because the Now "renders the past powerless," which means that "The whole concept of forgiveness then becomes unnecessary." In other words, according to Tolle, forgiveness is impossible if you're not living in the Now, and unnecessary if you are. If Tolle is correct, then there is no point in even concerning yourself with the concept of forgiveness.

How do I realize this Truth beyond time?

Tolle's answer is: "When you surrender to what *is* and so become fully present, the past ceases to have any power. You do not need it anymore. Presence is the key. The Now is the key."

My answer is: When you connect to the Presence of Being (the true Now), and allow Its Power (the true power of Now) to en-Light-en you, then you spontaneously realize the Truth (or Being) that is prior to and beyond time. When the Power (or Spirit-energy) emanating from the Presence of Being unites with your consciousness (or soul), the resulting union Spirit-ually awakens you as Consciousness-Power (*Siva-Shakti*), the divine Being Itself. Connectedness is the key. Reception is the key. Union is the key.

How can I tell if I've surrendered?

Tolle says, "When you no longer need to ask the question." I say, when all seeking comes to an end and you effortlessly behold the divine Being as your Self-nature.

Spiritual Reading List

The selections on this reading list are culled from the more than one thousand spiritual books I've read over the past forty years. For seekers interested in "cutting to the chase," getting to the heart of real spiritual practice right away, I suggest *The Knee of Listening*, *The Cycle of Day and Night*, *First and Last Freedom*, *Mysticism*, *Meditations on the Tarot*, *The Philosophy of Sadhana*, *Hridaya Rosary*, *Talks with Sri Ramana Maharshi*, and *Teachings of Tibetan Yoga*. For those interested in or needing basic introductory meditation texts, I recommend *How to Know God; Open Heart, Open Mind;* and *Mindfulness in Plain English*. And for thinkers interested in the function of the human mind or the subject of egoism, I suggest *Objectivism: The Philosophy of Ayn Rand*.

Advaita Vedanta

Highly Recommended

Ashtavakra Gita, trans. Hari Prasad Shastri. (Timeless Advaita Vedanta text. Available at www.shantisadan.org. Other translations also available.)

Be As You Are: The Teachings of Ramana Maharshi, David Godman. (Best introductory book on the teachings of Ramana Maharshi.)

Sat-Darshana Bhashya and Talks with Maharshi, Sri Ramanasramam. (A learned devotee's in-depth consideration of Ramana Maharshi's teachings within the framework of Indian-yogic philosophy.)

Sri Ramana Gita, Ramana Maharshi. (An utterly unique, ultra-profound text that details the function of the Amrita Nadi in the Self-realization process.)

Talks with Sri Ramana Maharshi, Ramana Maharshi. ("Must" reading. A truly great and inspiring book. Avoid the dumbed-down version published by Inner Directions.)

(Note: *Sat-Darshana Bhashya*, *Sri Ramana Gita*, and *Talks With Sri Ramana Maharshi* are available at www.arunachala.org.)

Recommended

I Am That: Talks with Sri Nisargadatta Maharaj, Maurice Frydman. (Classic, überpopular text.)

Vivekachudamani (Crest Jewel of Discrimination), Swami Prabhavananda and Christopher Isherwood. (Other translations of Shankara's teachings also available.)

(Note: Anyone interested in Advaita Vedanta might also benefit from books by Adyashanti, Jean Klein, and Papaji/H.W.L. Poonja.)

Buddhism (Original)

Highly Recommended

Some Sayings of the Buddha, F.L. Woodward. (Easily the finest presentation of the Buddha's teachings on meditation and contemplation.)

Recommended

Buddhism: An Outline of its Teachings and Schools, Hans Wolfgang Schuman. (Solid academic book.)

Mindfulness in Plain English, Venerable Henepola Gunaratana. (Best introductory text on insight meditation.)

The Heart of Buddhist Meditation, Nyaponika Thera. (Classic text on insight meditation.)

The Living Thoughts of Gotama the Buddha, Ananda Coomaraswamy and I.B. Horner. (Classic text. Excellent introduction to Buddhism.)

The Way of Non-Attachment, Dhiravamsa. (Unique Krishnamurti-influenced book on Insight meditation. Out of print.)

Buddhism (Tibetan)

Highly Recommended

Teachings of Tibetan Yoga, Gharma C.C. Chang. (Superb Mahamudra presentation. "Must" reading for serious meditators.)

The Cycle of Day and Night, Namkhai Norbu. (Outstanding Dzogchen meditation manual. "Must" reading for serious meditators.)

The Golden Letters, John Myrdhin Reynolds. (Scholarly exposition of the history and practice of Dzogchen in relation to the Garab Dorje, the first teacher of Dzogchen.)

The Precious Treasury of the Way of Abiding, Longchen Rabjam. (Marvelous ultra-mystical text by a revered Vajrayana master. If you appreciate this book, get *A Treasure Trove of Scriptural Transmission: A Commentary on The Precious Treasury of the Basic Space of Phenomena*, by the same author. Note: Other translations/annotations of Rabjam's texts are available.)

The Supreme Source, Namkhai Norbu. (The fundamental tantric text of Dzogchen.)

The Tibetan Book of the Great Liberation, W.Y. Evans-Wentz. (Mystical, mind-expanding translation of/commentary on Padmasambhava's *Yoga of Knowing the Mind and Seeing Reality*. Compare this translation and commentary to John Myrdhin Reynolds's in *Self-Liberation Through Seeing With Naked Awareness*. Skip Carl Jung's ridiculous "Psychological Commentary.")

Recommended

Cutting Through Spiritual Materialism, Chogyam Trungpa. (Enlightening text by a modern "crazy wisdom" master.)

Naked Awareness, Karma Chagme. (Excellent material on Dzogchen and Mahamudra.)

Self-Liberation Though Seeing With Naked Awareness, John Myrdhin Reynolds. (Compare this translation of/commentary on Padmasambhava's *Yoga of Knowing the Mind and Seeing Reality* to the inimitable W.Y. Evans-Wentz's in *The Tibetan Book of the Great Liberation.*)

Tibetan Yoga and Secret Doctrines, W.Y. Evans-Wentz. (Classic, ultra-mystical text.)

Wonders of the Natural Mind, Tenzin Wangyal. (The essence of Dzogchen in the Native Bon Tradition of Tibet.)

Buddhism (Zen)

<u>Highly Recommended</u>

The Diamond Sutra and the Sutra of Hui Neng, trans. A.F. Price. (Other translations of these timeless sutras also available.)

The Zen Teaching of Huang Po, John Blofeld. (Easily the best book on Zen.)

<u>Recommended</u>

Kensho, The Heart of Zen, Thomas Cleary. (My favorite Cleary text on Zen.)

The Practice of Zen, Gharma C.C. Chang. (Great autobiographical accounts of enlightenment. Out of print.)

The Way of Zen, Alan Watts. (Classic introductory text by the godfather of American Zen.)

The Three Pillars of Zen, Philip Kapleau. (Classic, popular Rinzai Zen text that emphasizes the *satori* experience.)

Tracing Back the Radiance: Chinul's Korean Way of Zen, Robert Buswell, Jr. (Outstanding account of a great Zen master's spiritual evolution.)

Zen Mind, Beginner's Mind, Shunryu Suzuki. (Classic, ultra-popular Soto Zen text.)

Zen Teaching of Instantaneous Awakening, Ch'an Master Hui Hai; trans. John Blofeld. (Fine Dharma instructions by a great Chinese Ch'an master.)

(Note: Scholarly types will enjoy Heinrich Dumoulin's *Zen Buddhism: A History (India and China)* and *Zen Buddhism: A History (Japan)*, Vol. 2. Serious students of Buddhist philosophy will appreciate Gharma C.C. Chang's *The Buddhist Teaching of Totality*, which expounds Hwa Yen Buddhism's wonderful, all-embracing philosophy in relation to Zen. If you enjoy reading Zen, check out Thomas Cleary's numerous books at Amazon.com.)

Christianity, Judaism, and Gnosticism

<u>Highly Recommended</u>

Meditations on the Tarot, Valentin Tomberg. (An astonishing journey into Christian Hermeticism. "Must" reading for anyone interested in Christian mysticism.)

Meister Eckhart. (*The Complete Mystical Works of Meister Eckhart* is the book I recommend—but it costs $98. *Meister Eckhart*, trans. Raymond B. Blakney, is a fine compilation of Eckhart's sermons, and goes for about $15. Scholarly types will want to supplement either of the aforementioned books with *The Mystical Thought of Meister Eckhart*, by Bernard McGinn.)

Mysticism, Evelyn Underwood. (Wonderful, classic, early twentieth-century text by the first lady of Christian mysticism.)

Recommended

Inner Christianity, Richard Smoley. (Clear and thoughtful guide to the esoteric Christian tradition.)

Jewish Meditation, Aryeh Kaplan.

Open Mind, Open Heart, Thomas Keating. (Classic, best-selling text on the Gospel's contemplative dimension.)

The Big Book of Christian Mysticism: The Essential Guide to Contemplative Spirituality, Carl McColman. (Good introductory text and resource guide for those interested in Christian mysticism.)

The Mystic Christ, Ethan Walker. (Excellent book for Christians.)

The Practice of the Presence of God, Brother Lawrence, Robert Edmondson, and Jonathon Wilson-Hartgrove. (Classic text on the practice of establishing a conscious relationship with the Divine.)

The Secret Book of John, trans. Steven Davies.

The Sermon on the Mount According to Vedanta, Swami Prabhavananda.

The Work of the Kabbalist, Ze'ev Shimon Halevi.

(Note: Scholarly types who are into Western Christian mysticism will love the fine texts by Prof. Bernard McGinn. Check out McGinn's *The Presence of God: A History of Western Mysticism* series. This four-volume series includes *The Foundations of Mysticism*, *The Growth of Mysticism*, *The Flowering of Mysticism*, and *The Crisis of Mysticism*. Beyond this series, McGinn has also graced us with *The Essential Writings of Christian Mysticism*, an immensely rich anthology of the greatest Christian mystical literature. Selections in this volume include writings from such great mystics as Origen, Augustine, Pseudo-Dionysius the Areopagite, St.

John of the Cross, Bernard of Clairvaux, Meister Eckhart, John
Ruusbroec, and many more. Relative to a scholarly consideration of
Jewish mysticism, I also recommend Gershom Scholem's *Major Trends in
Jewish Mysticism*. Not only is this text the canonical modern work on the
nature and history of Jewish mysticism, but it is also a thoughtful and
incisive academic consideration of mysticism in general.)

Daism

Highly Recommended

Hridaya Rosary (Four Thorns of Heart-Instruction), Adi Da Samraj.
(Excellent technical devotional-meditation book.)

The Knee of Listening, Adi Da Samraj. (Best spiritual autobiography ever
written. "Must" reading for mystics.) Get a copy of the latest edition,
but also get a copy of an earlier edition written under either the names
of Franklin Jones or Bubba Free John. These earlier editions, unlike later
and current editions, contain Da's outstanding "Meditation of
Understanding," instructions on the practice of "real meditation," or
"radical understanding.")

*The Liberator: The "Radical" Reality-Teachings of The Great Avataric Sage, Adi
Da Samraj*, Adi Da Samraj.

The Method of the Siddhas, Adi Da Samraj. (A truly great spiritual book.
Out of print and only available used. Try to get a copy written under the
names of either Franklin Jones or Bubba Free John. The current revised
edition of the book, entitled *My "Bright" Word*, lacks the direct visceral
impact of the original text.)

*The Way of Perfect Knowledge: The "Radical" Practice of Transcendental
Spirituality in the Way of Adidam*, Adi Da Samraj.

Recommended

He-And-She Is Me: The Indivisibility of Consciousness and Light In the Divine Body of the Ruchira Avatar, Adi Da Samraj.

Ruchira Avatara Hridaya-Siddha Yoga: The Divine (and Not Merely Cosmic) Spiritual Baptism in the Way of Adidam, Adi Da Samraj.

Santosha Adidam: The Essential Summary of the Divine Way of Adidam, Adi Da Samraj.

The All-Completing and Final Divine Revelation To Mankind: A Summary Description Of The Supreme Yoga Of The Seventh Stage Of Life In The Divine Way Of Adidam, Adi Da Samraj.

(Note: The four books on the Recommended List contain a number of the same essays. Nonetheless, each book includes enough unique material to merit its reading.)

Hinduism (Yoga)

<u>Highly Recommended</u>

The Bhagavad Gita, translations by Eknath Easwaran, Swami Prabahvananda and Christopher Isherwood, S. Radakrishnan. (Many other fine translations/annotations also available.)

The Yoga of Spiritual Devotion: A Modern Translation of the Narada Bhakti Sutras, Prem Prakesh. (A simple, inspiring text on the spiritual path of love and devotion.)

Yoga Philosophy of Patanjali, Swami Hariharananda Aranya. (The best account of classical yoga I've encountered. Many other fine translations/annotations also available.)

<u>Recommended</u>

Be Here Now, Baba Ram Dass. (Classic introductory book on Eastern philosophy. An easy and entertaining read.)

How to Know God, Prabhavananda and Isherwood. (Best introduction to the yoga philosophy of Patanjali.)

The Essential Swami Ramdas, Swami Ramdas. (Inspiring writings of a great twentieth-century *bhakti* yogi.)

The Gospel of Sri Ramakrishna, Swami Nikhilananda. (A revered *bhakti* classic.)

The Synthesis of Yoga, Sri Aurobindo. (Profound essays on yoga by Sri Aurobindo, the renowned twentieth-century Indian guru-philosopher. If you appreciate this book and crave more Aurobindo, get a copy of *The Life Divine*.)

The Upanishads, translations by Mascara; Prabhavananda and Isherwood. (Other fine translations also available.)

The Yoga Tradition, Georg Feuerstein. (Outstanding reference book on the history, literature, philosophy, and practice of yoga.)

Kashmir Shaivism

Highly Recommended

Pratyabhijnahrdayam: The Secret of Self-Recognition, Jaideva Singh. (The basic introductory handbook to the abstruse philosophical system of recognition. Not for the intellectually challenged.)

Siva Sutras: The Yoga of Supreme Identity, Jaideva Singh. (The foundational text of Kashmir Shaivism.)

The Doctrine of Vibration, Mark S.G. Dyczkowski. (A scholarly analysis of the doctrines and practices of Kashmir Shaivism.)

The Philosophy of Sadhana, Deba Brata SenSharma. (Outstanding text that deals clearly and extensively with the ultra-important topic of Shaktipat, the Descent of Divine Power, or Grace. "Must" reading for serious mystics.)

The Triadic Heart of Siva, Paul Eduardo Muller-Ortega. (An ultra-esoteric text about the Heart (Hridaya) as Ultimate Reality, Emissional Power, and Embodied Cosmos.)

Recommended

Kundalini, The Energy of the Depths, Lilian Silburn. (As an Amazon.com reviewer puts it, "The foremost modern exposition of Kundalini.")

Spanda Karikas: The Divine Creative Pulsation, Jaideva Singh. (An elaboration of the dynamic aspect of Transcendental Consciousness.)

Miscellaneous

Highly Recommended

The First and Last Freedom, J. Krishnamurti. ("Must" reading for all mystics. If you appreciate this book and want to read more Krishnamurti, get his multivolume *Commentaries on Living*.)

Introduction to Objectivist Epistemology, Ayn Rand. ("Must" reading for all mystics.)

Objectivism: The Philosophy of Ayn Rand, Leonard Peikoff. ("Must" reading for all mystics.)

The Way of Chuang Tzu, Thomas Merton. (Other translations also available.)

Recommended

A Brief History of Everything, Ken Wilber. (If you're interested in "integral thinking," you'll love this book. If you appreciate it, get *Sex, Ecology, Spirituality: The Spirit of Evolution*.)

Alan Oken's Complete Astrology, Alan Oken. (Best overall book on astrology.)

Ayurveda: The Science of Self-Healing, Vasant Lad. (Fascinating and enlightening exposition of the principles and practical applications of Indian Ayurveda, the oldest healing system in the world.)

Awaken Healing Energy Through the Tao, Mantak Chia. (Classic introductory handbook to the practice and principles of Taoist energy-yoga.)

Return to the One: Plotinus's Guide to God-Realization, Brian Hines. (Accessible modern exposition of an ancient classic, the *Enneads*. Also check out the Armstrong and Mackenna translations at Amazon.com.)

The Mystique of Enlightenment: The Radical Ideas of U.G. Krishnamurti, U.G. Krishnamurti. (U.G. was the ultimate spiritual iconoclast. Jean Klein called him "pathological." I call him a"great read.")

The Perennial Philosophy, Aldous Huxley. (Classic text by a great writer.)

The Tao Te Ching. (Numerous translations available.)

ز

CPSIA information can be obtained
at www.ICGtesting.com
Printed in the USA
BVHW01s1406171217
503008BV00001B/119/P